D0913917

HOT BLOOD

HOT BLOOD

The Money, the Brach Heiress,
the Horse Murders

KEN ENGLADE

ST. MARTIN'S PRESS
NEW YORK

Design by Ellen R. Sasahara

Library of Congress Cataloging-in-Publication Data

Englade, Ken.
    Hot blood : the money, the Brach heiress, the horse murders / by Ken Englade.—1st ed.
        p.   cm.
    ISBN 0–312–14358–3
    1. Insurance crimes—United States—Case studies.   2. Race horses—Wounds and injuries—United States—Case studies.   3. Horsemen and horsewomen—United States—Case studies.   4. Fortune hunters—United States—Case studies.   5. Missing persons—United States—Case studies.   6. Brach, Helen Marie Vorhees.   I. Title.
    HV6769.E54   1996   96–1105
    364.1—dc20   CIP

First Edition: July 1996

10   9   8   7   6   5   4   3   2   1

For Dennis and Sheila

Contents

Acknowledgments

FOR THEIR assistance in helping me in various phases of my research, I am especially indebted to the following people: John Menk, Susan Cox, Marilyn Abbey, Jesse Andrews, Heidi Hizel, Dr. Bebe Poor, Melanie McMillion, and Jinny Schreckinger. This is inadequate to express my appreciation, but I hope it helps.

Author's Note

Tom Burns legally changed his name to Tim Ray in 1988 in an attempt to escape prosecution in Florida on theft charges not related to his horse-killing activities. Despite the change, he continues to be known as Tom Burns and was addressed this way during the Lindemann/Hulick trial. Except in some specific cases where I note that he is known by both names, I refer to him throughout as Tom Burns or Tommy Burns or Burns.

Alan Levinson is referred to in official documents both as Alan and Allen. I use the latter spelling.

Some of the dialogue represented in this book was constructed from available documents, some was drawn from courtroom testimony, and some was reconstructed from the memory of the participants. Some of the scenes depicted were invented for dramatic impact based on testimony and interviews.

In order to protect their privacy, a few of the characters have been given fictitious names. Such names have been put in italics the first time they appear.

A glossary of some of the more common horse-world terms and a list of the most prominent characters can be found at the end of the book, along with a chronology and several appendices.

Introduction

Because of the complicated series of events described in this narrative, I have had to depart somewhat from the usual style. Some characters have been introduced out of chronological context, and the story skips back and forth in time and place.

Unlike most chronicles in this genre that deal with a relatively small number of participants, this story is populated not only by numerous people but by a considerable number of horses as well. There are a lot of names to keep track of.

To be candid, I had more trouble organizing this book than any I have ever written. When I first sat down to write and considered the breadth and depth of the subject, I almost panicked. Then I recalled that Steve Miller and his three-man crew of investigators spent four and a half years trying to put all the pieces together. The realization that I was going to have to accomplish roughly the same thing in only a few months left me shaken. But in the end what I have done is to follow Miller's trail, relating developments more or less as they unfolded to him and his team.

Miller began his journey by deciding to reopen the investigation into the disappearance of Helen Brach, the heiress to the Brach Candy Company fortune, who, when she turned up missing in February 1977, became the richest American woman ever to vanish without a trace.

From there, he and his men followed their noses down long, winding trails that sometimes deviated remarkably from where they thought they were going to go. This book does that, too, though ultimately the path becomes clear. Although the main roads never converge, connecting routes open up unexpectedly and help to bring other events into focus.

In actuality, this book relates two stories. One examines the unscrupulous practices of a handful of dishonest horsemen in Chicago; the other scrutinizes the widespread but highly illegal agenda followed by prominent horse owners and trainers far from the Windy City, specifically from New England to Florida and back.

I have tried to show in the prologue that this tale deals with more than the Helen Brach investigation, yet the Brach case is the foundation upon which the whole structure rests. It was the impetus of the investigation and it is the thread that connects all the pieces.

I have sought to remain focused on these two points, although it was tempting to wander down other avenues. For example, while investigating the Brach murder, federal authorities stumbled upon leads to the man who killed three boys in Chicago in 1955. Although that crime is mentioned here, the saga of Kenneth Hansen is a story unto itself and is not developed in depth in these pages. By the same token, references are made to the notorious Silas Jayne and his family's enterprises. But the odysseys of individual members of the clan are followed only insofar as they relate to the main themes of the book.

Basically, this is a story about greed and how it consumed all manner of people, from a low-life con man like Richard Bailey, to a merciless horse killer like Tom Burns, to respected veterinarians like Ross Hugi and Dana Tripp, to someone near the very top of this country's socioeconomic structure, George Lindemann, Jr., a would-be Olympic equestrian and the son of a business tycoon worth between $600 million and $800 million.

It is not a pretty story, but hopefully it is an instructive one.

Q: Now, am I correct that a thoroughbred is known as a hot horse? It's a hotblood, right? When we talk about a thoroughbred, we talk about a hot horse, a tense horse, a fresh horse, an excitable horse. Is that right?

A: Yes.

—Defense attorney Jay Goldberg during cross-examination of Molly Ash Hasbrouck, a young horse trainer testifying in the trial of George Lindemann, Jr., and Marilyn Hulick

HOT BLOOD

Death of a Thoroughbred
December 15, 1990

T OM BURNS paused, peering intently into the night. Not a soul was in sight, although that didn't mean a lot, considering the fog was so thick that he couldn't see more than a few feet. The fact was, he didn't *want* to see anyone, or, especially, have anyone see him. Not when he was on a job.

He could hear dogs barking in the distance, but that didn't concern him. He had been promised they would be locked up, just as he had been assured that Cellular Farms would be deserted except for a security guard at the main gate. And that was a long way off.

Puffing like a jumper that had just been put through its paces, the out-of-shape, corpulent Burns, using a tiny penlight to illuminate his path, zigzagged through the trees at a respectable clip, angling toward the barn. Like everything else at the extravagant horse-training facility that sprawled over fifty very valuable acres on the New York–Connecticut line near Greenwich, the stable was posh almost beyond belief: roomy stalls, engraved nameplates, brass poles everywhere with built-in electrical outlets. It was a long way from what Burns was used to.

He slowed to catch his breath. Even though there was no sign of anyone about, Burns, gulping in the cold, damp air, commanded himself to be cautious. While he was eager to get the job done, he didn't want to take a chance that he might be spotted, not after the way he had paraded himself around the main compound earlier in the day. At the time, he couldn't help but gawk: Cellular Farms, owned by the superrich Lindemann family, was unlike any other horse farm he had ever seen. Covering the ground were old-world cobblestones, rounded, well-worn, and ancient-looking. The buildings themselves had undeniable European lines, not surprising, since they had been imported and painstakingly reassembled piece by piece. With shrubbery, a lush lawn, and seasonally flowering plants, the main courtyard resembled a garden, right down to its memorable centerpiece. Burns had done a double take when he saw that; it was a three-foot-tall statue of Buddha.

His main fear was that while he had been acting like a tourist, he might have been recognized by any of the ten or so workers who were scampering around making preparations to transport the Cellular Farms horses to Florida for the beginning of the 1991 show-horse competition. The fact that there were so many people around worried Burns. In the eight years he had been working as a horse hit man, he had always been careful about avoiding being tied directly to a crime. He *did* have a reputation, of course. He wasn't called "the Sandman" for nothing. It was true that when he showed up at a facility, otherwise-healthy horses mysteriously "went to sleep," but, because he always had been prudent, there was nothing more than gossip to connect him to the deaths.

But he felt that this night he was pushing his luck. Even though it was nigh onto ten o'clock and the weather was in his favor, he knew he was taking a chance. If he'd had his druthers, he would have waited a few days. In fact, he had argued vigorously with Marilyn Hulick about the wisdom of carrying out the execution on the very day of his visit. It didn't make sense, he had contended. All it would take was some nosy and observant groom to tie the sudden death of a very expensive horse to Burns's unexpected appearance. But the tough-looking bottle blonde who managed Cellular Farms with an iron fist had been adamant. Her words still rang in Burns's ears: "I want it done *tonight*."

"Why?" Burns had asked, perplexed. "What's the hurry?"

"Because George is out of the country," Hulick had replied, referring to George Lindemann, Jr., the diminutive Olympic equestrian hopeful entrusted with running the elaborate facility. Still in his mid-twenties, Lindemann had been given the keys to the facility by his parents, George senior and his wife, Frayda, soon after he had graduated from Brown University. "Make it go," said his father, who had amassed a fortune estimated at from $600 million to $800 million by manufacturing contact lenses and mobile telephones and who was then involved in natural gas.

Up to then, however, the younger Lindemann had not been able to bring the operation out of the red; Cellular Farms was losing up to a million dollars a year. Lindemann's driving ambition was to be a member of the U.S. equestrian team in the Olympics and Cellular Farms was his vehicle. As the man who called the shots, one of his decisions had been to spend $250,000 for a promising horse named Charisma, a handsome bay hunter with championship potential. But there was a problem: In the year that Lindemann had been riding Charisma, the horse had been a shockingly inconsistent performer. Instead of helping to anchor Lindemann's Olympic dreams, Charisma had proved a tremendous disappointment. That was why Burns had been called in; the horse was to be murdered and the insurance money would keep the investment from being a total loss.

Hulick had locked her brown eyes on Burns and set her jaw. "It has to be tonight," she repeated. "George is gone and tomorrow we're moving the horses to Florida. It *has* to be done before then."

Burns had reluctantly agreed. After all, Hulick was offering a lot of money. He would get his usual fee of 10 percent of the horse's insured value, in this case $25,000—plus expenses, naturally, another $10,000. If Hulick wanted him to drop everything back in Libertyville, Illinois, and fly east on a moment's notice, she would have to pay for the prompt service.

Sweating despite the cold, partly because of the unaccustomed exercise and partly because he was starting to feel the effects of the half a dozen drinks he had bolted down on the way to Cellular Farms, Burns quietly let himself in through the unlocked barn door. As unerringly as if he had been there a hundred times instead of just once, he went straight to the horse that Hulick had led him to earlier, ignoring the other twenty or so animals.

Outside, it had been deathly still; the only noise had been the faraway barking of the dogs. Inside the barn, though, it was considerably noisier. Horses shifted restlessly in their stalls, banging loudly against the boards and emitting explosive snorts that sounded vaguely like the barks of seals in West Coast rookeries. Burns inhaled deeply. The feral-like horse smell and the pungent odor of equine urine relaxed him, bringing back memories of happy hours spent around his aunt's stable when he had been a child, soon after his parents had been divorced and before he ran away in search of adventure and money.

Cocking his head, Burns listened intently, trying to filter out the background noise to see if he could detect sounds indicating the presence of another two-legged creature. Hearing none, he slowly approached the stall marked by a brass plate engraved with the name Montash, the previous occupant.

Burns moved slowly so as not to spook Charisma, a strategy more cautionary than necessary. Show horses are accustomed to strangers being about: Stable hands, grooms, veterinarians, trainers, riders, and even visitors move through barns in a steady stream at all kinds of weird hours. After a few months of that, horses learn to accept an alien presence with equanimity. This was especially true of Charisma, who was remarkably good-natured and gregarious, openly welcoming anyone who approached him.

Still, Burns moved slowly and deliberately, carefully uncoiling his "rig," a specially adapted heavy-duty electrical extension cord with alligator clips at the end where the female plug normally would have been. Holding the penlight in his teeth so his hands would be free, Burns gently stroked Charisma's forehead, whispering softly. Charisma bobbed his head and rolled a large, friendly brown eye in Burns's direction, seemingly happy with the unexpected attention. Still talking quietly to the gelding, Burns attached one of the clips from his rig to Charisma's ear.

Backing slowly away, he moved to the horse's hindquarters and delicately lifted his tail. Inured by countless veterinary examinations, Charisma stood patiently when Burns attached the other clip to the flesh around his anus.

Giving Charisma a final pat, Burns hustled out of the stall and made his way quickly to a nearby brass pole, where he knew from his afternoon visit there was an electrical outlet. Without hesitation, he rammed the male end of the cord into the receptacle. As he had come to learn through vast prior experience, the result was immediate; Charisma dropped as if struck by lightning. Except for the heavy thump when the high-priced animal hit the floor, there was no sound at all, not even a grunt.

One of the major advantages of electrocution, which was Burns's favorite method of execution, one he had deviated from only once—and that had been six years before when he used a drug to incite a heart attack in a horse named Town Gossip—was that it was almost always undetectable. Unless the killer was careless and misattached the alligator clips so they left burn marks, electrocution was undiscernible even with the most thorough autopsy. The only way to tell for sure if a horse had been deliberately killed by electrocution was for the killer or the person who hired him to confess.

Shrugging in his heavy jacket, Burns reentered the stall, carefully stepping over the steaming pile of manure that Charisma had evacuated in death, and collected his rig. Another thing he liked about electrocution was that he was convinced it was painless. He had heard of other horse hit men who used different methods. Fire was popular with some killers; Ping-Pong balls shoved up the nostrils or a plastic bag secured around the head were methods favored by others. But to Burns, electrocution seemed the most humane, and that was important to his self-image. Burns thought of himself as a compassionate killer.

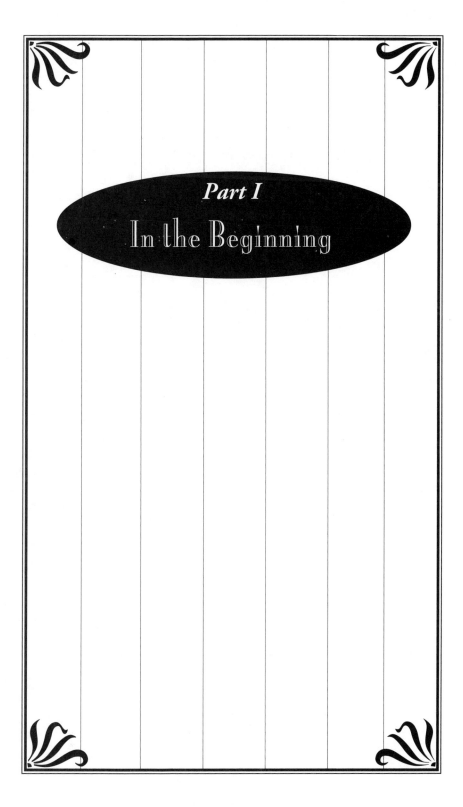

Part I

In the Beginning

1

"Murder by Mail Fraud"
Early December 1989

GINGERLY GRIPPING the bag from Berghoff's, the popular German restaurant adjacent to the Dirksen Federal Building in Chicago's South Loop, in his left hand, Steve Miller set about the tedious task of clearing a space in the center of his cluttered desk.

He made a start by transferring a stack of yellow legal pads that contained his trial notes to a corner already occupied by interoffice memos and a pile of pink "return this call" reminders from his secretary, then enlarged the opening by balancing a speakerphone on top of a three-inch-tall stack of investigators' reports. Finally, he had his makeshift table.

"All *right*," he said, eagerly opening the sack. Hungrily unwrapping the still-warm grilled halibut sandwich, he looked around to make sure the others had found a place to sit amid the mounds of paper stacked haphazardly around his cramped fourth-floor office.

Jimmy Delorto, the wiry, grizzled investigator from the federal Bureau of Alcohol, Tobacco and Firearms (ATF), juggled his turkey sandwich in one hand while shifting a heap of "dailies," the quickly typed transcripts from the current trial, from the seat of a straight-backed wooden chair to the floor. David Hamm, a beefy Illinois State Police sleuth, had cleared a spot on the sagging couch and was already digging into his corned beef, ignoring the fact that it wouldn't hurt him to trim some of the flab that bulged over his belt.

"Everybody comfortable?" the host asked companionably, popping the tab on a diet root beer. Without waiting for confirmation, he bit the end off his pickle slice.

Miller's dark eyes were rimmed in black, a seemingly perpetual condition for the hard-charging thirty-four-year-old government lawyer who needed long hours and a fresh challenge like caffeine addicts need coffee.

It had been a long, twisting road for Miller since he finished high school in Evanston, a well-to-do northern suburb of Chicago. Shunning the local college—Northwestern—he had enrolled at Washington University, in St. Louis, and quickly fell into the counterculture lifestyle, letting his hair grow long and stringy, growing a scraggly beard, demonstrating against the lingering war in Vietnam, and espousing every liberal cause that came along. Then, after graduating from WU's law school, he did an abrupt about-face, starting work immediately after graduation as a financial specialist in the civil-law division of the U.S. attorney's office in Chicago. Tossing out his grungy jeans and clipping his receding dark hair, he took up three-piece suits, polished wing tips, and more conservative views.

That had been in the late seventies. Now, in the late eighties, he had accomplished another, although slightly less radical, transformation. Some ten years after receiving his first paycheck as a government lawyer, he decided he was bored with the civil process and asked to be transferred to the criminal-law division. Almost immediately, he wondered if the choice had been a wise one; his first case was a real lulu.

Essentially, it was an unsolved murder involving a former policeman named Thomas York. In 1978, York's wife had been murdered. No one was ever charged and York collected on her insurance policy. Three years later, York's partner in a suburban bar, an unfortunate woman named Gail Maher, was killed in an explosion that demolished the establishment. It looked as if York was going to collect on the insurance and walk away, since investigators had found no direct evidence tying the onetime cop to the murder.

Faced with a puzzle that local investigators had been unable to solve, Miller went at it from a different angle. Since murder, except in very special circumstances, was not a crime in the federal system, Miller donned his financial-expert hat and approached the case as if it was an economic crime. Zeroing in on the insurance claim, which Miller was certain had been falsified, the prosecutor convinced a grand jury to issue an indictment against York for swindling. Because the former cop had used the postal service to file the claim, the charge was mail fraud. But since the issue at York's trial would actually be the murder of Gail Maher, Miller dubbed his strategy his "murder by mail fraud" plan. It was an imaginative and innovative approach. And it paid off. York was convicted and sentenced to forty years in prison.

Even while the York case was wending its way through the system, another similar case landed on Miller's desk. This time, the murder victim had been a man, a multimillionaire German immigrant named Werner Hartmann, who had been blasted with an automatic weapon when he stepped out of the shower in his home on June 9, 1982. Police suspected his widow, a sexy former stripper, had been involved in his death, but she had a good alibi: She had been out partying with her husband's daughter by a previous marriage when the incident occurred. The two of them found the body when they returned home at dawn.

Operating on the assumption that the motive was three-quarters of a million dollars in insurance money, Miller discovered that Hartmann's signature had been forged on the policy in which his widow was named beneficiary. Harking back to his strategy in the York case, Miller won indictments against the widow, Debra, a former lover, and one of his friends for lying to the insurance company, again the "murder by mail fraud" strategy. On the day he sat down to lunch in his office with Delorto and Hamm, the Hartmann trial had been going on for about a week.

"How do you think it's going?" Hamm asked around a mouthful of corned beef.

Miller nodded his head and swallowed. "We got 'em," he said confidently. "No question in my mind."

"That's good to hear," interjected Delorto, who also had been involved in the York investigation. "We're on a roll."

"Damn right," Miller agreed enthusiastically. "Let's get 'em while the going's good." Flinging the empty bag into the wastebasket, Miller leaned back, put his feet on the desk, and glanced from one man to the other. "Anybody have any ideas on what we're going to do next?" he asked, quickly adding, "Since this one's all but over, that is."

Hamm grinned broadly, his florid face breaking into a hundred small wrinkles.

"I'd like to see you prosecute Richard Bailey," Hamm said, reaching for his soda.

Both Miller and Delorto looked curiously at the state police officer.

"Who's Richard Bailey?" Delorto asked.

"And what did he do?" added Miller.

"He scammed a woman out of fifty thousand dollars," Hamm replied, settling back on the couch.

Both men waited for him to continue. When he did not, Miller looked at him sharply. "That's it?" he asked. "He cheated a woman? Fifty thousand isn't really big-time," the prosecutor pointed out. "This is a major crime unit and I don't really think it's worth our time. But," he added solicitously, "if you want to get this guy, I can help you find the right prosecutor."

"Just a second," said Hamm, obviously enjoying himself. "I haven't finished."

"Well, go ahead," said Miller, sipping his root beer.

"Bailey's a con man. He's cheated a number of women. Maybe even Helen Brach."

Miller's feet came off his desk. "Helen Brach, huh?" he asked, his interest rising.

He had still been in law school when Helen Brach disappeared, but, like everyone in Chicago over thirty, he knew the bare essentials. The heiress to the Brach candy fortune had mysteriously vanished in 1977. Despite thousands of man-hours invested in the investigation, no one had ever been charged in connection with the incident, which obviously, after almost thirteen years, had to be viewed as a kidnapping and murder. Some of the best investigators and prosecutors in the country had worked the case, but no one had ever gotten enough solid information to take to a grand jury. Miller knew that if he could break the Brach case open, his future would be assured: He could write his own ticket just about wherever he wanted to go in Chicago, whether it was in law or politics.

"But why this guy—what's his name? Bailey? What's his background?" Miller asked.

"Basically," replied Hamm, "he's a con man. He used to run a driving school—you know, one of those places where they teach you how to drive a car—in St. Louis, until his license got revoked."

"What did he do?" asked Delorto.

"He had a lot of women clients," Hamm explained. "A lot of women who spent a lot of money, except they never learned how to drive."

"Is that it?" Delorto wanted to know.

"No," said Hamm. "He also was involved in the horse business in Chicago, reportedly cheating a lot of ladies who ended up buying expensive animals whether they wanted them or not."

Miller had been listening carefully. Hamm's phrase "a lot of women" had rung his bell; he could hardly contain his excitement. In a flash, like being struck by the proverbial lightning bolt, the idea had come to him. "That's it!" he said loudly, jumping to his feet.

Hamm and Delorto stared at him. "What's it?" Delorto asked.

"Yeah," Hamm echoed. "What in hell are you talking about?"

"A possible way to prosecute Bailey," Miller said. "Forget the fifty-thousand-dollar fraud. If we can put a case together, we may be able to use RICO."

Hamm and Delorto looked at him blankly.

Drawing boxes and little circles with connecting lines and arrows, Miller explained how they might get at Bailey. RICO was an acronym for the Racketeer Influenced and Corrupt Organizations Act, a comprehensive law that allows federal attorneys to get beyond the mechanics of a single incident of illegal activity. Passed by Congress in the 1970s to help prosecutors win convictions against organized crime figures, RICO permits a prosecutor to bring before a jury evidence of a number of crimes under a single charge if it can be shown that the crimes constitute a demonstrable pattern of criminal behavior.

"Sounds pretty good to me," Delorto said.

"Wait," said Miller. "Let me finish. It isn't that simple. A number of criteria needs to be met before RICO can apply."

"Like what?" asked Hamm.

"First," said Miller, "there have to be several people involved, like a gang. And they can't just commit one crime; they have to commit a series of crimes that are more or less related. That's the pattern. And it has to continue for an extended period of time."

"Like when Bailey was running the stable?" Delorto asked. "But that was a long time ago, wasn't it? Surely the statute of limitations has run out on that?"

"Yeah," said Miller, "but if we can find a recent incident that helps form the pattern, we can go back and bring out the others, even if they are too old to be tried on their own. We have to know if Bailey is involved in what's called 'an ongoing fraud.' If we can show that Bailey *and others*," he said, "are perpetrating an ongoing fraud and have done the same thing before, then we can go back and bring in other things."

As Miller outlined the particulars of RICO, Hamm also grew more excited. "I think," he said slowly, "that you need to know about Barbara Morris."

Miller put down his pen and folded his hands on the desktop. "Who?" he asked carefully.

Hamm flashed a Cheshire cat–like grin, then launched into a fascinating tale.

2

An Elaborate Con

Barbara Morris studied the front page of the *Pioneer Press,* searching for something to catch her attention. Yawning, she flipped quickly through the sports section and landed on the features page. That took two minutes. Offhandedly, she turned to the classifieds and her eyes lit on the "Personals" column. Figuring *that* might be interesting, she scanned the small type. When she got to the one that began "I have a beautiful farm with horses . . ." she stopped and read it closely.

The carefully crafted piece of self-promotion described the writer as "a handsome, fun-loving Leo" who lived in an exurban Eden complete with "horses, llamas, ducks, geese, peacocks & a German Shepherd dog." Among his favorite things, the writer said, were sports, the theater, cooking, and fine restaurants. What was missing from his life was someone with whom he could establish a long-term relationship. "If you are young, slim, trim, classy and a smart lady," he concluded, "please call."

Morris smiled wryly to herself. A striking-looking woman with angular features and a fashion model's figure, Morris figured if her husband were still alive, he would have considered the ad hilarious. What woman, he would have joked, would possibly be gullible enough to fall for a line like that? A Leo he would have said, chuckling. Singles bars. "What's your sign? Do you come here often?" But that was earlier. Now she was a widow with an empty seat across the table and an otherwise-empty bed every night, and she looked at things from a different perspective. What the hell, she figured, reaching for the phone. What did she have to lose?

Morris had been in her mid-forties when her husband died of cancer almost two years before, in 1987. A pilot for United Airlines and a commodities broker on the side, he had been wise about money and made sure that she was left financially secure—not filthy rich, but with enough to keep her more than comfortable.

She lived in an expensively furnished, well-maintained home in Inverness, a wealthy suburb northwest of Chicago. She drove a nice car and her closets were filled with designer clothes. There was enough in her bank account to allow her to indulge—within reason—her every whim. She also had women friends, her health, and all the time in the world to enjoy herself. What she did not have was male companionship.

When she picked up the *Pioneer Press,* a Wilmette-based newspaper that circulates throughout the wealthy North Shore area of Chicago, she was lonely to the point of desperation.

To her surprise, the writer of the ad, a man whose name she soon learned was Richard Bailey, was every bit as charming as he claimed.

Sixtyish, with dark curly hair that was turning sexily gray, he possessed an engaging grin that she found particularly attractive. He drove a late-model red Mercedes-Benz convertible and, true to his declaration, he knew all the area's better eateries. While he could more than hold up his end of a conversation, he proved to possess an even rarer trait: He was a good listener. He hung on her every word, only occasionally interjecting innocuous comments.

It was not that he did not have his quirks, however. Although he dressed in expensive, well-tailored clothing, his style was flashy by the standards of Chicago's conservative Gold Coast Establishment. But that, Morris reckoned, along with his occasional rough speech and an ostentatious pinky ring, added rather than subtracted from his appeal.

Bailey pursued Morris with a diligence men of his apparent class and position usually devote to the stock market. He flattered her almost to the point of embarrassment, continuously telling her how beautiful she was and how much he admired her style. Hardly a day went by when he did not send along a little gift: a card, a bouquet, sometimes just a single rose. Within a few weeks, Bailey was professing his love for her and pleading with her to marry him. The result was predictable: She was overwhelmed.

While she felt more than a moderate attraction for this man who had suddenly appeared in her life—he *was* dashing and exciting, she told herself—she hesitated. Her instincts told her not to move too quickly. When he suggested marriage, she told him she wanted to think about it, wanted to wait awhile so they could get to know each other a little better.

One Sunday afternoon in October, Bailey asked her if she would go with him to help him select some statuary for his garden.

She replied eagerly that she would.

Bailey picked her up in his convertible, but instead of going to a landscaping outlet, he asked her if she objected to making a small detour. Wheeling his little red sports car through the gently rolling hills of the Illinois lake country, he turned down a side road and through the gates of a picture-perfect horse farm. A sign at the gate read INDIAN CREEK STABLES.

Braking to a stop in front of a row of neatly kept horse stalls, Bailey turned off the ignition and agilely hopped out.

She was impressed with the layout and wanted to know whose farm it was.

Bailey replied that it belonged to a business associate and friend of his, a veterinarian named Ross Hugi.

Bailey got out of the car, explaining that there were some matters he needed to discuss with Hugi. Leaving her to stroll around the paddock area, he walked briskly into the main house.

When he returned a few minutes later, he was wearing an uncharacteristically long face. Immediately, she asked what was the matter.

Fate had struck him a cruel blow, Bailey replied. With seeming reluctance, he explained that several weeks before his friend Hugi had offered him the opportunity to turn a quick profit in a horse deal. His entrance fee was sixty thousand dollars, but all Hugi needed at the time was ten thousand down. But now, Bailey said, the veterinarian was telling him that he had to come up with the balance immediately or he would lose his original investment. The difficulty, he added with apparent embarrassment, was that his checking account was temporarily deficient. Under the circumstances, he moaned, he had no choice but to risk losing his down payment.

Suddenly, he brightened. Unless, of course, he added, Morris would agree to loan him the money so he could consummate the deal and protect his original investment. It was all perfectly legal, he said, waving a paper he claimed was a contract substantiating what he had already told her. If she was worried about the loan, he would sign over the deeds to the four broodmares that he planned to buy and she could use the animals as collateral.

Morris smiled at what she took to be his shyness. Pulling out her checkbook and a pen, she filled in the blanks for fifty thousand dollars, wondering what it was going to be like to be a horsewoman.

It did not take her long to find out. Almost immediately, the boarding bills began arriving. The horses, which she belatedly discovered did not seem to be nearly as good an investment as she had been told, were costing her forty dollars a day, day in and day out, Sundays and holidays included, for food and shelter. And so far, Bailey was giving no indication he was going to repay the loan.

The bills continued to pile up and Bailey continued to dally. It was then that Morris began to get suspicious.

She became even more leery when Bailey suggested yet another investment. What he proposed she do was go into partnership with him toward the purchase of a stallion named Victory Morn. He described the horse as a magnificent animal that could command a stud fee of up to five thousand dollars per contract. At that rate, they could earn their investment back rapidly and start making money.

How much was he talking about? she asked.

He would put up fifty thousand dollars of his own money, he said, and she could finance the remaining hundred thousand.

There was no need to take just his word on Victory Morn's worth, however. To assure her that the horse was worth the price, he arranged an expert to call her. When he called, the man repeated essentially what Bailey had already told her: The stallion was an excellent bargain.

By now, though, Morris's antennae were definitely up. Telling Bailey she needed time to think about an expenditure of that magnitude, she postponed a decision.

Then, out of the blue, another man called. Identifying himself as a local horseman, he said he had heard on the stable grapevine about the four broodmares she owned.

When she tried to tell him they weren't really hers, at least not by intent, he suggested that she hire him as her agent to sell the horses for her—for a fee, of course.

Feeling she was being set upon from all sides, Morris was not sure what to do. Then, taking a woman friend into her confidence, she blurted out what had happened.

When the friend heard the name Richard Bailey, her jaw dropped. A Richard Bailey, she remembered reading in the newspapers, had been linked with Helen Brach.

At first, Morris did not know whom she was talking about and the friend had to explain who Helen Brach was and what had happened to her.

Troubled by what her friend had to say, Morris became convinced that Bailey had cheated her and that the other two were in on the scam.

Eventually, Morris found her way to Hamm, but the state policeman had been unable to convince prosecutors in the state's attorney's office that the case was worth pursuing.

"Not worth pursuing?" Miller asked in amazement. "If we can find out more about Bailey's background and define if those other two men were involved in previous scams with Bailey, that might be our ticket. The Barbara Morris incident is our ongoing fraud, and if we can establish a pattern we may have our predicate for opening up the Helen Brach investigation."

Glancing from Hamm to Delorto, Miller issued a succinct order: "Get me some more on Richard Bailey."

3

A Natural-Born Con Man

E VER SINCE he was a little kid, Richard Bailey had been a talker. At first, when he was *really* young, he tried to fight his way out of situations. Balling up his fists, he'd lower his head and charge, swinging his arms like the duck's wings on one of those backyard windmills. But it didn't take him long to realize that he was always getting whipped, mainly because he wasn't very big. It figured. With a brother who was destined to be a successful jockey, there probably wasn't a genetic disposition to big men in the Bailey family pool.

Bailey's problem stemmed from his eyes—not his vision, but his eyelids. Because his mother had German measles while she was pregnant with Richard, the baby was born with paralyzed lids. They were permanently droopy. The other kids teased him unmercifully because he had to walk around with his nose in the air. When he figured out that it didn't do him any good to fight, he learned to negotiate, to try to sweet-talk his adversaries. He learned to live with rejection and became a master at making himself likable and appealing.

Maybe it was because he was always an outcast among the other kids that he dropped out of school in the ninth grade and concentrated on working around the family farm in Kentucky. It was the time of the Great Depression and his father must have been happy with the help, especially when there were eleven other children at home; that was a lot of mouths to feed, even in good times.

Manual labor apparently did not agree with Richard, since as soon as he was old enough, he joined the Air Force and didn't show up again at the family dinner table for more than four years. When he did return to the family homesite, he brought along a young bride, a fourth-grade schoolteacher named Eunice, to whom he would remain married, at least technically, until 1990.

At some point not long after he left home, he had surgery on his eyes and his early problem was corrected to a degree. Although his eyelids still appeared droopy, they no longer looked particularly abnormal. But there was one side effect to the operation. Since the paralysis could not be cured, the surgeon attached his eyelids to the cornea so he could close the lids by looking quickly down, then back up. To moisten his eyes, he had to blink. This made it look as if he suffered from a mild tic. Other than the problem with his eyes and being rather short at five four or five five, Bailey looked like an average guy. He kept his body trim and his wavy dark hair was always in place.

At about age twenty-one, he left Kentucky for the second time. It must have been a difficult decision, because he had no marketable skills and no education. As a result, he had to take whatever job he could find.

For at least part of the time, he and Eunice lived in California, although that period of his life remains rather mysterious. After that, they moved to St. Louis, where Bailey worked as a dance instructor at Arthur Murray's, which may have been the first time he came into steady contact with fairly well-to-do older women. Even at that stage of his life, Bailey exhibited a marked proclivity for ingratiating himself with females.

After he left the dance studio, he took a job as a driving-school instructor, again dealing in large part with older women. Once he learned how driving schools operated, he quit his job and opened his own facility, specializing in giving instruction to middle-aged females, many of them financially well-off.

Contrary to most driving instructors, Bailey made his money by *not* teaching his customers how to drive, preferring to keep them on the hook by convincing them they needed a never-ending series of expensive lessons. Just how effective this could be was exemplified by an anecdote he later related to a would-be protégé in an attempt to explain how to run a successful scam. He had one elderly female customer, he recounted, who he bled so dry that she had no money left to pay her utility bills and was reduced to eating dog food. When the woman's son found out about it, he sued Bailey for a sizable amount of money. The moral, Bailey said, was "never take a pigeon's last dollar. Take as much as you can, but don't leave them destitute."

Eventually, investigators for the state of Missouri tipped to his tactics. In 1970, his license to run the driving school was revoked after an industry regulatory board found that he had been taking thousands of dollars from students without ever letting them finish the course.

From St. Louis, Bailey moved to Chicago. He apparently intended to open another driving school, but instead he fell into a new, potentially much more lucrative industry that would provide his ill-gotten bread and butter for the next twenty years: the world of stables and show horses.

It began when Bailey signed up for riding lessons and then bought a horse. As a result, he spent a lot of time around the stables and was exposed for the first time in his life to people of real substance, people who had enough disposable income to be able to afford to spend thousands of dollars on horses and horseback riding.

Soon he began hanging around an establishment called Northwestern Stables, which was owned by a man named Frank Jayne, Jr. There, he resumed capitalizing on his ability to charm women. When one would come in for riding lessons, Bailey would chat her up and tell her how much she could benefit from having a horse of her own.

After he peddled a few animals, with most of the money going to Jayne, he went into business for himself. He would buy an animal from Jayne and sell it at an inflated price to one of the women who happened by. One of the first lessons he learned during his early days in the equestrian milieu, right up there with how to board a horse, was how ignorant most people, especially middle-aged women, were about how things worked in the equine industry.

It took Delorto and Hamm several days to come up with the information on Bailey. In the meantime, the Hartmann case went to the jury and, as Miller had predicted, the panel quickly voted to convict the widow and the two men.

Miller exchanged glances with Hamm and Delorto when the verdict came in. "This calls for a little celebration," he said, smiling broadly. "Let's grab some lunch."

Miller picked nervously at his Wiener schnitzel, trying to calm himself enough to revitalize his appetite. He was excited about the Hartmann verdict, but he was more thrilled by the information the two men had brought him about Bailey.

"It looks good," he said enthusiastically, speaking about Bailey. "Real good." Idly, he tore off a chunk of brown bread and popped it into his mouth. "Here's to us," he added, raising his stein of beer and clinking it against those of Delorto and Hamm. "We did a good job."

"Debra Hartmann probably wouldn't say that," Delorto said, grinning.

"That's for sure," agreed Hamm, delicately setting his glass of beer down on the spotless white tablecloth.

"Hartmann's over with," Miller said decisively. "It's ancient history. Now we need to look to the future."

"Meaning Richard Bailey and Helen Brach," Delorto said.

Miller nodded. "Exactly. You guys have made a start with digging up that information about Bailey; now we need to carry it to the next step. If we want to make a case under RICO, we need to get a better handle on Bailey's scams, especially if they involved others. Then we can see how Helen Brach ties in—if she does."

"I hope the hell she does," said Hamm, who had participated in the early Brach investigation when he was a young trooper. As had almost everyone who had been involved in the case, he had come away extremely frustrated and angry that no one had ever been able to solve it. "People just don't disappear," he said, "especially not women who were as rich as Helen Brach."

"All the more reason," said Miller, "that we need to find out what we can. Maybe over the years some tongues have loosened or there's some new information out there that no one is even aware of. I want you," he said, pointing at Delorto, "and you," he said, pointing at Hamm, "to scour the courthouses in all the suburban counties."

"What are we looking for?" asked Delorto.

"I wish I knew exactly," Miller said. "But to begin with, we have to assume that Barbara Morris is not the only woman Richard Bailey ever cheated. And she's probably not the first who was angry enough to try to do something about it. Begin by looking for civil suits that may have been filed against Bailey. Chances are one or more of the women he scammed tried to get some of their money back. If they did, those cases would have gone straight into civil court and criminal investigators probably wouldn't even know they existed. Let's see if we can find anything."

"Good idea," said Delorto, pushing away his empty plate. "Why don't we come here more often?" he asked rhetorically. "I could eat a ton of that creamed spinach. It has to be the best in the world."

Miller smiled and looked at Hamm. "Anyone for dessert?"

4

Carole Karstenson—Phase One

STEVE MILLER gazed in amazement at the foot-high stack of papers that had accumulated on his desk in just a few short days. Thumbing through them, he saw with a mixture of glee and trepidation that the whole pile consisted of civil suits filed against Richard Bailey in half a dozen counties surrounding Chicago. It was more than he'd hoped for, more than he'd planned for.

Shuffling through the stack, he became engrossed. He had expected maybe three or four complaints stretching back a few years. Instead, Hamm and Delorto had come back with papers documenting that Bailey's career as a professional con man stretched back to the early seventies.

Checking the names, Miller saw that 99 percent of his victims were women and that there was a central theme that ran through the papers: All of the activities about which the victims were complaining had to do with horses.

The prosecutor sighed. If his knowledge of horses and the horse industry was reduced to words and printed on paper, it wouldn't fill half a page. Still, he reckoned, this was as good a time as any to start learning.

Spreading the papers out on his desk, Miller began organizing them chronologically so he could see exactly what he had to work with. As he began putting them in order, he was struck by one thing: None of the suits had been filed on behalf of Helen Brach.

He stopped, considering that fact. The whole idea from the beginning had been to see if Bailey was connected to Brach. Yet the preliminary indications were that he was not. He felt a twinge of disappointment, then moved quickly to squash it. It was too early to tell, he reasoned. Way too early. Don't jump to any conclusions, he told himself, until the documents at least have been examined.

Once he had them in reverse order, the oldest first, he started to read. Skimming at first, he slowed his pace the deeper he got into the top document. Cutting through the legalese, he found himself spellbound by the story that was unraveling. Flipping back to the front page, he saw that the suit had been filed by a woman named Carole Karstenson, who, according to the suit, had first met Bailey in 1972, eighteen years before.

It began, Miller read, when Karstenson, then a forty-nine-year-old widow, drove to a commercial training/riding facility called Northwestern Stables to pick up one of her two daughters, Mindy, who had a horse, Gray Ghost, stabled there.

After parking her car, she was walking toward the barn area to look for her daughter when she was greeted by the owner, a man named Frank Jayne, Jr., a name that at the time meant absolutely nothing to the prosecutor.

Jayne welcomed her effusively and invited her inside, telling her there was a friend of his in the office whom he wanted her to meet.

When Karstenson entered, she saw that the man—a flashily dressed dark-haired fellow wearing a pleasant grin—was waiting for them.

"Carole," Jayne said ardently, "I'd like you to meet Richard Bailey. He's a wonderful man, one of the nicest guys I've ever met."

Pulling her aside, Jayne also confided that Bailey was independently wealthy, divorced, and had two children, whom he adored.

From Karstenson's point of view, this was interesting but hardly vital information. Barely a year before, her husband, an executive for Sears, had died on the operating table while undergoing bypass surgery. He had left her well provided for and since then she had been able to adjust to his absence at her own pace without worrying about how to pay the mortgage or put food on the table. While she thought she was recovering well from his death and managing to get her life back on a somewhat even keel, his passing was still fresh enough to kill any interest she might have had in developing a relationship with another man. However, as determined as she was, she neglected to account for Bailey's single-minded perseverance. Therefore, it came as somewhat of a surprise several weeks later when Bailey called and asked her to dinner.

Smiling to herself, Karstenson told him that she appreciated his call but felt unable to accept the invitation. She was still grieving over her husband, she explained.

Bailey thanked her politely, said he understood, and hung up. Then, a few days later, he called her back. Again she refused. And again he called her back. He kept after her until she finally accepted his invitation.

Much to Karstenson's surprise, her first date with Bailey turned into an extremely pleasant evening. He took her to one of the city's trendier restaurants, ordered an extremely expensive bottle of wine, and regaled her with tales of his youth. Halfway through dinner, like any proud father, Bailey whipped out his wallet and flipped it open. "These are my kids," he said happily. "They're living with my ex-wife."

Although Karstenson had no way of knowing it, Bailey had just uttered one of his more common lies. The children were real enough, but the "ex-wife" was a pure fabrication. At the time, Bailey was married.

After that, lie piled upon lie, all slipping easily and fluently from Bailey's lips. He told her that he owned a stable in the nearby community of Dundee. A lie. He told her he thought she was beautiful. A lie. He told her he had been looking for a woman like her all his life. Another lie. In fact, just about everything Bailey told Karstenson after that was at best partly untrue.

After that first evening, Karstenson saw Bailey frequently. "We were together from about midmorning until after dinner practically every day," she recalled in her statements to her lawyers. He poured on the flattery, telling her she was gorgeous and sexy. He sent her white roses with notes that read: "To a classy lady." And when she talked, he hung on her every word. Lonely and naïve, Karstenson fell for him completely. "Within a very short time," she said bitterly, "I was in love with him." Which is exactly what Bailey had planned on.

Part of the reason Karstenson was so vulnerable was because of her physical condition. Just before she met Bailey, she had been diagnosed as suffering from ulcers, but in reality it turned out to be much more serious. Within weeks, Karstenson dropped from her normal weight of about 140 pounds to 125 and was still going downhill.

Bailey, in response, was very solicitous, urging her to adhere strictly to the diet prescribed by her physician, and he took her on long drives in the country in an attempt to cheer her up.

One day while they were on one of their frequent morale-boosting drives, Bailey steered his Mercedes into Northwestern Stables, explaining that he needed to see Jayne about a horse he was buying. Jayne greeted them by telling Bailey that his horse had arrived, an announcement that seemed to catch Bailey by surprise. "Already!" he exclaimed. "I wasn't expecting him yet."

Turning to Karstenson, in Jayne's presence, Bailey told her that he was "a little short of cash" and didn't have the money to pay Jayne the balance that was due on the horse's delivery. He asked her if she could loan him fifteen thousand dollars. "I'll give it right back to you," he promised.

Embarrassed for him because he had to ask her for money, especially in front of someone else, Karstenson readily agreed, feeling she couldn't say no because she was in love with him.

In the meantime, Karstenson's health continued to deteriorate. Her weight sank below one hundred pounds and she had difficulty keeping food down. Her health problems, however, did not keep her from seeing Bailey on almost a daily basis.

One weekend, while on a visit to the country home of one of Karstenson's children, they were walking through the wooded countryside when Bailey paused on the shore of a small lake, seemingly enraptured by the scenery.

"Oh, what a beautiful place to get married," Bailey exclaimed unexpectedly.

"Huh?" Karstenson replied, caught by surprise.

"I said," Bailey replied, " 'Oh, what a beautiful place to get married.' Will you marry me?"

"I have no intention of marrying you or anyone else," Karstenson replied. However, the rejection seemed to have no effect on Bailey, since his courtship continued just as fervently as before.

In October 1973, about nine months after her first date with Bailey, he took her to see an addition that Frank Jayne was making to his stables, a brand-new barn. Pointing to the new building, Bailey suggested that they go into partnership, leasing the facility from Jayne and starting their own horse-breeding enterprise. The suggestion delighted Karstenson. "It was something I could do with someone I loved and it gave me something to do with my life," she said later.

Bailey told her they would need $150,000 in seed money to get the enterprise going. Karstenson would put up $100,000 and he would add the remaining $50,000, providing his self-vaunted horse expertise in place of cash. Most of the money, he revealed, would be used to buy a string of twenty horses that they would need to get the business going. Three weeks later, on November 5, Karstenson gave Bailey a check for the full $100,000.

All the while, Karstenson's health continued to deteriorate. Claiming it was for her own good, Bailey took her to Florida, but they had been there only a short time when Bailey told her he needed to return to Chicago to check on their business.

"There's a problem," he said ominously when he returned. He said something unexpected had come up in relation to his stable in Dundee and he had needed to sell ten of their twenty horses to raise fifty thousand dollars to take care of it. Plus, he added, Jayne was reneging on the barn-lease agreement, so he had moved their ten remaining horses to his own stable.

All the while, Karstenson was getting sicker. Upon her return to Chicago, her physician was alarmed at her condition and ordered her immediately into the hospital.

Bailey, still professing concern about her health, suggested she check herself into the famed Mayo Clinic, since its doctors were internationally known. "I've been there myself," he told her. He helped her pack a suitcase, then bundled her into his car and drove her to Rochester.

As soon as Karstenson was settled in her room, Bailey pulled out a sheet of paper and asked her to sign it.

"What is it?" she asked.

"A power of attorney," Bailey replied.

When she read the document, she saw that it gave Bailey the authority to trade and buy new horses in her name.

Unwilling to commit to additional expenditures, Karstenson refused to sign, offering instead to draw up a substitute agreement, which limited Bailey's authority to selling rather than buying horses.

Bailey was infuriated. "This isn't worth the paper it's written on," he said, tossing it on the floor. "You won't hear from me for a while," he said, spinning on his heel and making for the door. "I'm going on a trip to South America."

Karstenson was shocked. The man she had believed to be kind and gentle—the attentive lover, the sensitive suitor who wanted her to marry him in a ceremony on the shore of a sylvan lake—had walked out on her in her darkest hour because she would not give him carte blanche use of her bank account. Burying her face in her pillow, she began to sob.

5

Carole Karstenson—Phase Two

K ARSTENSON HAD little time to recover from her heartbreak. A few days after Bailey unceremoniously dumped her, she was lying in her hospital bed, staring at the ceiling, when a heavyset man in his sixties, who was wearing a bad toupee, walked in and greeted her like an old friend.

Struggling to place his face, she recalled only that it was someone she had seen around Jayne's stable but had never formally met. Behind him, waiting in the corridor, were a woman and a young girl.

"How're you feeling?" the man asked jovially. "I hope they're treating you right."

Seeing the look of nonrecognition on her face, the man hurriedly introduced himself. "I'm Robert Lee Brown," he said. "You've probably seen me around Northwestern Stables." Gesturing to the woman and the girl to come into the room, he added, "And this is my wife and daughter."

Pulling up a chair, Brown told Karstenson that he had heard the talk around the stable about the problems she was having with her horses and he had a proposition that might benefit both of them.

The ten horses that were left from the original twenty she had bought with Bailey were badly in need of training. "But I can take care of that." His fee would be fifteen thousand dollars.

Karstenson's expression turned gloomy.

"But," Brown added quickly, "I promise you that once I'm through with them, I'll be able to sell them for a hundred and fifty thousand."

Karstenson smiled. If he could do that, it would mean a $35,000 profit for her.

A few weeks later, toward the end of January, her hopes for a speedy resolution to her horse problem were dashed. Brown had returned to her hospital room and brought her bad news. The horses, he said, were in worse shape than he had figured. There was, he added, only one good horse in the bunch: Bull Lea's Whirl.

How good is he? Karstenson asked.

"Oh," Brown said, shrugging, "I'd say he's worth way over fifty thousand dollars."

When she didn't respond immediately, Brown suggested that she trade the nine other horses, inferior animals all, for two good broodmares. Then he could mate them with Bull Lea's Whirl.

Karstenson pondered the proposal. "That would mean I'd have only three horses instead of ten," she pointed out, "and I could save in boarding costs."

Brown vigorously nodded his assent.

"Okay," she said, "go ahead."

To her surprise, Brown was back again in less than two weeks. If she *really* wanted to make money on her new enterprise, he said, she needed more broodmares. Specifically, he recommended she buy a string of thirteen already-pregnant mares to go with the two that she had recently acquired in trade. Once that was done, he could take the whole group and sell it to a man who had already committed to buy the lot for $300,000. The catch was, the new horses would cost her an additional $113,000. It would be worth it in the long run, Brown added hastily, since the sale would leave her $57,000 in the black even when her long-ago $15,000 loan to Bailey was figured in.

At that point, not counting the loan, Karstenson already had put up $100,000 toward the partnership and $15,000 in fees to Brown. Buying the new mares would bring Karstenson's total investment, including the loan, to $243,000.

"There's a problem," she told Brown. "Your idea makes sense, but I don't have a hundred and thirteen thousand dollars."

Brown smiled broadly. "Don't worry about that," he said. "Give me as much as you can and I'll take your note for the balance."

Reaching for her checkbook, Karstenson wrote out a check for $78,000 and signed a note Brown hastily drew up for the remaining $35,000.

That night, for the first time in months, she rested easy. For one thing, her health problem seemed to have straightened out. After her original doctor warned her that she probably was going to die, her case was taken over by another physician, who diagnosed her as suffering from a rare blood disease. Although it was serious, the disease was treatable. Brown's news had been icing on the cake.

Once she started feeling well again, Karstenson took more of an interest in her horse enterprise. One of the first things she decided to do was ask to *see* the horses she had bought. A few days later, she hurried to the stable for her first look at the stallion that served as the linchpin of the whole operation, Bull Lea's Whirl.

While she had built up a mental image of a huge, magnificent horse that was going to sire a lot of equally magnificent foals, the animal she finally saw on a visit to the Dundee stables was anything but grand.

"My God," she said in amazement, "he's all lathered up. He looks ill. Are you sure he's okay?"

"Sure," Brown said, "he's fine."

"Well, why is he all sweaty?" she asked.

"He's just been ridden and the groom hasn't had time to wipe him down," Brown answered easily.

Karstenson looked carefully at Brown. "I don't think so," she said.

Brown shrugged and changed the subject.

The next day, she was at a horse show when Brown came bustling up to her.

"I have bad news for you," he said. "We found Bull Lea's Whirl dead in his stall this morning."

In addition, Brown had more bad news. "Because Bull Lea's Whirl is dead, the man who wanted to buy the string says he's no longer interested. He says without the stallion, the string certainly isn't worth three hundred thousand."

Karstenson went into an emotional tailspin. Her prize stallion, Bull Lea's Whirl, was dead and the pregnant mares she had purchased were foaling, increasing the size of her string far beyond what she had planned on. Anxious only to get out of the horse business, she told Brown she wanted to sell the lot.

"Don't do that," Brown said in alarm. "What you really need is a new stud."

"Let me think about it," Karstenson replied.

The only good news for Karstenson in that period was that she and Bailey had effected a reconciliation. For Valentine's Day, he sent her flowers and gave her a pearl necklace. But his generosity had a price. A few days later, he asked if he could borrow three hundred dollars. Flustered, she handed him the money.

A few days later, he called and told her things were looking up. "I've got such a surprise for you, baby."

"What's that?" she asked.

"I'm not going to tell you over the phone," he said. "Meet me at the Dundee stables."

When she arrived, Bailey was already there, wearing a huge grin.

"What's the surprise?" she asked excitedly.

"Come on, we'll show you," he said.

He and Brown took her to a stall that contained a large chestnut stallion.

"Here's your new stud," Bailey said proudly. "Bob and I drove down south just to find him."

Impressed by the animal's size and apparent robust health, Karstenson was delighted.

"What's his name?" she asked.

"Elmadge," Bailey replied.

"How much did he cost?"

Bailey grinned. "Only twenty-five thousand."

Up to that point, Karstenson had coughed up $208,300 in cash and had signed a note for $35,000. With Elmadge, her total obligation soared to $268,300.

But if the purchase of Elmadge was good news, there was bad news as well. Soon afterward, a veterinarian who had been recommended to her by Brown and Bailey, Ross Hugi, called and told her he was not satisfied with the conditions under which her broodmares and their new foals were being kept at Jayne's stables. To improve the situation, he suggested moving them all to his stable.

By this time, Karstenson was beginning to get suspicious. To help allay her doubts, she arranged for an independent appraiser to examine the animals, beginning with the new stallion, Elmadge. Telephoning Hugi, she explained what she had done and told him to expect the appraiser. But when the expert showed up to examine the new stallion, he discovered that Elmadge, like Bull Lea's Whirl, had mysteriously died.

Elmadge's death was the final straw for Karstenson. Convinced she had been swindled, she hired a lawyer and told him to begin preparing a civil suit. Soon afterward, however, she began receiving threatening phone calls.

Phoning late at night, an anonymous male would tell her, "You're rocking the boat. Do you know what happens to people who rock the boat? They drown. And their kids drown, too." Another call informed her that "her life was on the line." Still another warned that a barn she owned was going to be burned.

Trying to take her mind off her problems, Karstenson went for a horseback ride. When she got to the point where the trail crossed a busy road, she waited as usual for a break in the traffic. But one car aimed straight at her with its horn blaring, rather than passing by. Her horse spooked, reared, and threw her off, badly injuring her back.

While she was recuperating, her barn burned to the ground. Thoroughly frightened, Karstenson decided to wash her hands of the whole matter. Though she had once been financially comfortable, her experience with Bailey and Brown had left her almost penniless. Later, when her civil suit was being argued in court, she discovered how badly Bailey and his friends had gulled her. The broodmares that Brown had sold Karstenson for $113,000 had cost him $25,000, and the stallion Elmadge, which she had paid $25,000 for, had cost Brown and Bailey a mere $900.

6

Widening the Scam
1975-1990

Jean Robinson peeked out the front window of her residence along chic Lake Shore Drive and did a double take. She could hardly believe her eyes, but there it was for the whole world to see. Richard Bailey, the charming fellow who owned the stable she had visited the day before, had arrived to pick her up for their dinner date, and he was driving an honest-to-God Rolls-Royce.

That fact had barely had time to sink in when the doorbell rang and the suave horseman was asking her if she was ready to go.

Feeling not a little self-conscious, she slid into the passenger seat, sitting stunned and mute while Bailey drove to the Drake Hotel, where he had reserved a table for two.

"Would you like some wine?" he asked her graciously as soon as they were seated. Barely waiting for her to reply, he signaled the sommelier. While they put their heads together, conferring over a suitable bottle, Robinson glanced shyly around the room. This, she decided, was definitely new territory for her. She could barely contain her shock when she saw that the wine that Bailey had decided upon cost two hundred dollars a bottle.

An unpretentious, typical housewife, Robinson had been married to the same man for twenty-six years and would be married to him still if he had not died in 1974, a little more than a year previously. She took his passing hard, going into a blue funk from which she thought she would never emerge. It was only just recently that she started to break out of her self-imposed exile. One of her first ventures into the outside world was to meet a friend at the stable where she kept a horse. The first person she met there was Richard Bailey.

She had no sooner driven into the lot than Bailey had appeared, smiling broadly and offering profuse greetings. After Robinson left, Bailey got her phone number from her friend. She had barely walked in the door when he called, telling her how happy he was to have met her.

While she thought it was a bit odd, she put the incident aside—at least until the next morning, when Bailey called again and asked her to dinner.

It was Bailey, she remembered, who did most of the talking that evening, and it was largely in the form of extravagant compliments on her hair, her eyes, her wit, her conversational ability, and her charm. "I don't know," he said at one point, leaning across the table and whispering in her ear, "if you're aware of how much I'm attracted to you."

It was too much for the flustered Robinson. She was overwhelmed.

The next day, he called and asked her to dinner again. This time, before he arrived, a messenger delivered a bouquet of red roses. The card read, "Love, Richard." When Bailey showed up in the Rolls, he spirited her off to yet another of the city's fancier restaurants. During the meal, he again complimented her extravagantly and told her what a wonderful, classy woman he thought she was. But she almost dropped her fork when he softly told her that he would like to marry her.

"Just a minute," she said, her cheeks flaming. "This is going too fast. I'd need a lot of time to think about that."

Bailey laughed off her comment and called her again the next morning, inviting her to dinner for the third night in a row. That night, Bailey began talking about how grand it would be for the two of them to fly to Las Vegas and be wed in one of the city's numerous chapels. "And by the way," he added, "could you loan me fifty thousand dollars?"

Robinson looked at him sharply, not sure if he was joking.

"I wouldn't ask you," Bailey said, confirming that it was not a prank, "but I'm a little short of cash right now and I need the money to close a horse deal." He would pay her back in just a few days, he promised, complete with interest.

Robinson begged off, saying she did not have fifty thousand dollars to spare but that she might be able to lend him ten thousand.

"That would help," Bailey replied unsmilingly.

The next morning, when Robinson was on her second cup of coffee, the doorbell rang. It was a man she had never seen before. "My name is Frank Jayne," he said, introducing himself. "I'm here to pick up the check for Richard Bailey."

Over dinner that night—the fourth in a row—Bailey made no mention of Robinson's ten-thousand-dollar check, although he did ask her again for more money.

"The best I can do," she said firmly, "is another three thousand dollars."

Bailey looked at her solemnly. "I really need more than that," he said, but he did not refuse the offer.

Although she tried a number of times in the next few weeks to get in touch with Bailey to ask him when he planned to repay the money, he never returned her calls. Eventually, her lawyer contacted his lawyer and they worked out a settlement, but it was barely enough to pay her legal bills. As for Bailey, after she gave him the second check, she did not see him or hear from him again for twenty years, and that was in a courtroom where she appeared to testify against him.

By the time Linda Holmwood met Richard Bailey in 1976, she was already suffering from severe emotional problems, which were augmented by alcoholism. That, however, only gave Bailey a weakness to work on.

Their paths crossed when she showed up at Bailey's stable one day to help her daughter, Gail, shop for a horse. A few months before, Holmwood had been divorced after twenty years of marriage, and her teenage daughter was depressed about the situation. Holmwood figured it would cheer her daughter up if she bought her a horse, since Gail had been taking riding lessons.

It was only a matter of days before Bailey began inviting Holmwood into his office and plying her with champagne while Gail ran through her paces with the trainer.

Since Holmwood had died long before Miller began to investigate Richard Bailey, it was impossible for the prosecutor's investigators to question her directly. But by talking to Gail, her brother, Ed, and by delving through Holmwood's financial records, it was possible to put together a picture of her experiences with Bailey.

Taking advantage of her need for drink, Bailey pressed Holmwood to buy not just one horse but several. All told, within an incredibly short ten-day period, she gave Bailey ninety thousand dollars for horses of dubious heritage and questionable ability, including one animal that was represented to her by Bailey and one of his cohorts, a trainer named Jerry Farmer, as being the famous Mai Tai. In reality, it was a much inferior horse that resembled the well-known animal. Holmwood was drunk at the time.

Since she had quickly run through the funds she had been awarded in her divorce settlement, Holmwood, at Bailey's urging, borrowed from a local bank to pay for more horses. Finally, apparently believing that Bailey intended to marry her, Holmwood sold her house to settle the loans and moved into a tiny apartment decorated with plastic furniture.

The marriage never took place. As soon as Bailey realized that Holmwood had no more money, he quit seeing her and told his security people not to let her onto the stable grounds. She died of liver failure in 1982. By then, she was totally without funds and survived partly by shoplifting food from various supermarkets.

Vivian Bravos, owner of a small bank in a northern suburb, had been a widow for several years when Bailey called her out of the blue one afternoon late in 1975. He said he had seen her at the stables, had been attracted to her, and had gotten her number from a friend. Would she have dinner with him? he asked.

As with Jean Robinson, Bailey showed up for their first date behind the wheel of his Rolls-Royce, then spirited her off to an expensive dinner at the Drake.

The next day, Bailey sent her white roses and asked her to go out with him again. And again. And again.

After several dates, Bailey brought up the subject of horses. "Why didn't you invest in a racehorse?" Bailey asked, bragging that with his expertise and connections he could easily find her a winner.

When Bravos told him that was out of the question, Bailey begged fifty thousand dollars from her as a loan so he could purchase a string of ten horses he had been eyeing. He had been studying them for some time, he told her, and they were prime horseflesh. But if he didn't act quickly, he would lose the opportunity to make a killing. He promised to pay her back within a few days, plus interest. Bravos weakened. "Okay," she said, writing him a check for fifty thousand dollars on May 9, 1975.

To show his good faith, Bailey gave Bravos the titles to the horses.

After that, Bravos did not hear from Bailey for weeks. When she tried to reach him, she was unable to get through. But she knew she was in trouble when she received a boarding bill of $1,440 for the animals from a stable owner named Jerry Farmer. Despite repeated attempts, she still was unable to reach Bailey, but she refused to pay the boarding bills.

Then, almost two months after making the loan, which Bailey still had not repaid, Bravos was contacted by another man, Robert Lee Brown.

Claiming he was a friend of Bailey's, Brown said he would like to be her agent in an attempt to sell her horses, the ones that she had never wanted to own. If she signed a contract with him for ninety days, Brown promised, he would not let the horses go for less than $55,000, which would give her a $5,000 return on her loan. Of course, he added, he would have to charge her a fee: three thousand dollars in advance. She paid him.

Some sixty days into the contract, Brown wrote Bravos and told her he could not continue to be her sales agent unless she paid the boarding bills, which were accumulating at the rate of $150 per month per horse. Alternatively, Brown said, he would buy the horses himself, provided Bravos would loan him the money from her bank. It was a sly offer, since she would be out still more money if Brown did not pay off the loan and she would still be stuck with the horses.

Realizing then that she had been taken, Bravos refused. Her only recourse was to sell the horses at public auction. The string brought in a total of seven hundred dollars. She had lost $52,300 because of Richard Bailey.

Miller shuffled through the other documents. What they showed were eight other cases in which Bailey had defrauded his victims in scams related in some way to the equestrian industry. In most of the cases, Bailey had used the same con, with only minor variations. In each case, though, the results were predictable: Bailey's targets always ended up losing.

Two of his victims had pooled their resources and put up thirty thousand dollars for a horse, but once Bailey had the money in his pocket, he claimed the animal was no longer available at that price and if they still wanted the horse they would have to give him another fifteen thousand. When they balked at that suggestion, Bailey recommended a second animal which could be purchased for only an additional $7,500.

In fact, the $37,500 horse turned out to be both lame and seriously ill. When one of the buyers refused to pay boarding bills, Bailey allegedly threatened her with physical harm.

In another case, also a pooled arrangement, three people lost thirty thousand dollars that they put up to purchase and board a horse that Bailey represented as an animal in excellent health. In actuality, the horse suffered from a chronic respiratory ailment and required daily medication.

7

A Whole New World

S TEVE MILLER looked up from the stack of documents and grinned. "Great stuff!" he said excitedly to Delorto. "These show us the pattern and they show us that others were involved. Those are the essential elements for RICO. I think we're ready to go."

Delorto smiled back. "Guess it goes to show how little we know about a lot of things."

"Ain't that the truth," replied Miller. "Up to now, I knew virtually nothing about the equine industry. And I still have a hell of a lot to learn."

To the uninitiated, it all looks so effortless. Sleek, beautifully groomed horses with cookie-cutter riders in immaculately pressed jodhpurs, well-fitting dark jackets, and bulletlike black helmets gracefully going through their paces, vaulting effortlessly over low fences—a magnificent melding of man and mammal working together as a flawless team: That's the image. The reality is a little more gritty.

Ever since the early days of this country, and in England before that, the ownership of horses has occupied a special position in the social pecking order. Over the years, horses have come to represent a currency, virtually the *only* currency, that distinguishes the truly wealthy and cultured from the nouveau riche and the wanna-be cosmopolitan. Horses are not just hay eaters or draft animals; they are part of a tapestry that represents the country's real upper class, the thread that weaves through the loftier levels of society from one coast to the other, from the Canadian border on the north to the Mexican on the south.

Smart, hard-driving, ambitious businessmen can make fortunes in boardrooms and manufacturing plants; their wives can throw unimaginably lavish parties and work themselves into exhaustion for the most deserving charities. Their children can graduate with honors from Ivy

League universities. But none of the things can guarantee *arrival* at a certain social stratum. The quickest and surest road to that brand of success is through horses. And the cost of membership into this group is enormous. Owning a show horse and participating in one or more of the seven thousand or so events that are held around the country each year is not for the marginally well-off or the fiscally timid. Unlike buying cars, airplanes, or yachts, it takes a *lot* of money to swim in those waters.

The admission ticket is the horse, and horses are expensive.

Thoroughbred racehorses, for example, can sell for hundreds of thousands of dollars. But only a relative few horse owners dabble in racehorses. Someone thinking along those lines may as well play the lottery. Statistics show that only 15 percent of all the two-year-olds who race every year ever get to the winner's circle. Almost 60 percent earn less than five thousand dollars throughout their racing careers, and a remarkable 12 percent never win any money at all.

On the other hand, most persons interested in owning horses turn to hunters or jumpers. The distinctions lie in objectives. Although both types specialize in vaulting over obstacles, the goal is different.

With hunters, the emphasis is on style and the courses over which they compete are designed to simulate British hunting fields. What a hunter event amounts to is a ninety-second fox hunt without the fox. Each horse is rated individually and does not directly rival another participating in the same event. The aim is to complete the course as smoothly and artfully as possible.

Jumpers, however, are competitive. Jumper events consist of two rounds. In the first, the horse tries to get over the obstacles without knocking them down. The second time around the course, the emphasis is on time.

In their events, hunters earn points and the goal is to work their way toward three invitation-only shows held every autumn, one in Pennsylvania, one in Washington, D.C., and one in New Jersey. Together, they are often referred to as the "indoor season" or the Super Bowl for horses.

For jumpers, there is no Super Bowl. They compete for cash.

Hunters and jumpers, while expensive by non-horse-world standards, are not as expensive as racehorses. However, it is not rare for a buyer to pay a quarter of a million dollars or more for a prime animal.

The horses found at stables that are open to the public—the kind that Bailey dealt with—generally are those suitable for inexperienced or intermediate riders, the kinds that parents are seeking for their children.

It does not, however, mean that the animals or their upkeep is inexpensive.

The cost of a run-of-the-mill two-year-old suitable to be trained as a hunter/jumper is typically in the five figures, depending on age, heritage, training, and previous performance. And then it goes up, not infrequently reaching tens of thousands of dollars. But the cost of the horse is only the beginning.

A horse needs to be stabled, tended to by an attendant who will groom, feed, water, and exercise the animal. The horse needs to be shoed about every six to eight weeks, at a cost of sixty dollars per shoe. It must be examined regularly by a veterinarian, who will scrutinize the animal's teeth and gums, analyze its fecal matter, test the urine, and make sure inoculations for a variety of potential ailments ranging from tetanus and encephalitis to flu and anthrax are current. These services can cost as much as the rent on a small apartment and do *not* include fees for training sessions for both animal and rider, fees that commonly run about a hundred dollars a pop.

Nor does it include the cost of equipment. Tack—saddles and all the accessories (bits, bridles, reins, martingales, halters, nosebands, lead shanks, crown pieces, throatlatches, cavessons, and all their variations)—also comes dear. A saddle alone, if it's a designer brand such as a Beval or an Hermès, retails for about twenty-five hundred dollars.

And those who ride the horses don't jump aboard in the show ring in jeans and sneakers. Custom-made high-topped boots; mutton-legged breeches; bespoke split-tail, tight-waisted jackets with bone buttons; velvet bowlers or derbies; collarless "equestrian" shirts from Savile Row haberdashers, complete with choker and gem-decorated stickpin; and soft tailored gloves are de rigueur. These items easily add another one thousand to fifteen hundred dollars to the tab. Some parents start their children in the ring as young as three, so they can look forward to more than a dozen years of clothing expenses.

If the horse is going to be entered in a show—and what's the sense of having an expensive, magnificent animal if it isn't going to be flaunted?—some type of transportation will be needed to get the animal from stable to fairgrounds. That means a truck and trailer, or at least fees for paying someone to transport the horse. It means an entry fee of about four hundred dollars per show. It means that the owner who does not travel with the animal flies to the city where the show is being held. It means staying in a top-rated hotel and dining at the four-star restaurants that are frequented by other wealthy horse owners, places where lunch can cost more than a week's worth of groceries for a family of four. It means entertaining lavishly and tipping generously.

Also, as might be expected, the competition on the circuit is horrendous. The number of devotees runs in the hundreds of thousands and only a few win the coveted prizes or points. The pressure is always on: Owners need better and more expensive horses, more up-to-date equipment, bigger and better trucks, and exclusive veterinary treatment. Riders have to project a certain image, which means more expensive clothing and tack. They constantly need to improve, which means more lessons. They need to keep their skills sharp even during the slow months of winter, which means flying to equestrian training camps in Florida or California.

What it *really* means is one hell of a lot of money. Ostensibly, the reward is points, a ribbon, or a cash prize. The true reward, though, is peer recognition; the ultimate goal is winning the admiration and respect of others who travel in the same circles.

While the owner of the horse may profit from peer acceptance and personal satisfaction, the benefit to the seller is from the sale of the horse and the postpurchase services, such as training. In some respects, this parallels the operation of an auto dealership. A person comes in looking for a new car, which the salesman is happy to show him. If the would-be buyer ends up driving the vehicle home, the salesman leaves for the day with cash in his pocket and the dealership owner gets a cut of the sales price, plus more profit later if the new owner brings the vehicle in for servicing in the dealer's shop.

It is much the same in the horse-sale business, with one extremely important difference. A potential car buyer has a good idea of what the vehicle is going to cost him; a potential horse buyer has no idea how much he's going to have to spend. When Richard Bailey learned this, a whole new world opened up to him. The price of a horse, he gleefully realized, was determined by whatever the traffic would bear. The adage "There's no blue book on horses" became one of his favorite lines.

Bailey and his friends quickly perceived that by finding an unsuspecting buyer with a deficit of knowledge about horseflesh, they could make a very tidy profit by charging grossly exaggerated prices.

But overpricing horses has been a practice that has existed ever since the first person sold or traded an animal. While it was extremely significant to Bailey's moneymaking scheme, his group truly excelled in devising ways to carry this a step or two further. Selling one horse could bring a tidy profit. Selling two horses would be better. Selling a whole string of them would be a master achievement. Once the sale was made, the buyer could then be charged for additional services: stabling, boarding, training, shoeing, and veterinary treatment, either real or invented. These fees could easily run as much as three thousand dollars a month. Furthermore, the group refused to let the situation rest with the sale of a horse. There always was pressure for the owner to upgrade to a more expensive animal; to schedule more training sessions; to add a broodmare or stallion.

It had not taken Bailey and his friends long, Miller realized, to determine the potential and work out a master plan. Grabbing a pen and a fresh legal pad, Miller diagrammed what he perceived as the basics of the scheme, writing names in little boxes and drawing lines to show how it all interconnected.

One of the boxes represented Bailey. While he himself had little knowledge about horses, he knew a number of people who did.

Miller drew another box and inserted the name Robert Lee Brown. A veteran stable owner and trainer, Brown was the one who initiated Bailey into the horse world.

Another box. Northwestern Stables. At the time Bailey was being initiated into the industry, the owner of Northwestern Stables was Frank Jayne. Later—after Jayne was convicted of selling cocaine—Bailey would buy Jayne's stable and run it as his own.

Another box: Jerry Farmer, a man recognized throughout the industry as a top-notch trainer. Uncommonly handsome, with a trim athletic build and a strong resemblance to Robert Redford, Farmer was soft-spoken, articulate, and always impeccably groomed. To Miller, he looked more like a bank president than a con man.

Still another box: Dr. Ross Hugi. Shorter than average, five five or five six, wiry, with a cowboy's rolling, bowlegged walk, Hugi was a successful forty-six-year-old veterinarian with his own apparently prosperous stable. He added legitimacy and he also was the source for a wide range of drugs that were administered to the horses while sales were being conducted: drugs to make a lame or sick horse look healthy, or to mask temperament problems, such as making an aggressive horse appear docile. What had prompted him to get mixed up with the others?

Miller wondered. Greed? A search for adventure? The prosecutor shrugged. Who knows? he thought to himself.

Clicking his pen, Miller connected the Brown and Farmer boxes and made a notation. Both were middle-aged men who had spent their lives around horses and were virtual walking encyclopedias on the subject.

Next to the Northwestern box, he scribbled a reminder that Jayne was an important figure for Bailey to have in his corner, because of his family connections.

Other characters, not worth boxes, were represented only by notes. One was a suburban Chicago policeman who provided access to records the group found useful in perpetuating the scheme, including valuable Social Security numbers. Another was a corrupt banker who could supply credit ratings on demand.

Underneath the Northwestern box, he sketched a series of lines radiating downward. At the bottom were generic entries: grooms, riders, stable hands.

Since the main members of the group were ever on the alert for potential victims, they were anxious to make sure no one got by them. To accomplish that, they enlisted a small army of stable minions to act as worker ants. Having been promised cash bonuses, these low-paid employees were urged to scoop up whatever scraps of information they could find about anyone who might be a future buyer.

When a stranger appeared at Northwestern Stables, surreptitious note was taken of the arrival. The make of car was observed—the more expensive the model, the better. Someone also jotted down the license number, which could then be fed to the friendly cop and cross-referenced through the law-enforcement computer system for name, address, and other interesting information stored in the electronic filing system.

If the visitor looked promising, someone drove by his or her home to check out the neighborhood and see if the house itself looked expensive. Simultaneously, the name was given to the banker, who ran a credit check or perused other available records to determine the person's financial worth.

If the victim was a middle-aged or older woman, Bailey was utilized to lay the groundwork, approaching her as a possible suitor. Other members of the group might be summoned later to corroborate whatever Bailey said or effect subsidiary scams in the good guy/bad guy mold.

Miller was impressed with the organization and foresight that went into the operation. It had proved to be both highly efficient and remarkably cynical. A victim was never released until every possible dollar had been culled. Bailey and his team members, Miller realized, had it down to a science. Like unfeeling, hungry spiders, they lurked at the edges of their web, waiting for gullible quarry to venture in. Once he recognized the scope of the overall plan, Miller understood why the equine industry proved such fertile ground for the schemers. However, he did not yet comprehend why Chicago—the city itself—was so ripe. In the next few weeks, that would become clearer. Once he learned about Silas Jayne, a lot of his questions were answered.

8

Flashback: Silas Jayne
January 19, 1969

H E STOOD spraddle-legged in his foyer, his hands thrust deep into the pockets of a robe, his right fist clenched around the butt of a .38-caliber pistol. Trim, muscular, dark-haired, with a distinctive gravelly voice, he glared at the closed door with eyes as pale and hard as steel ball bearings. "Who's there?" he rasped.

For a heartbeat, there was only the sound of the wind blowing new snow across the wintry landscape. Then there were two quick thuds, coming close together. As Silas Jayne stood fixed in place, muscles tense and jaw clenched, two bullets ripped through the oak, showering him with small splinters. One of the slugs tore through the robe and creased his side.

"Son of a bitch!" he ejaculated, drawing his pistol. Raising his arm, he fired three quick shots without opening the door, then spun on his heel and dashed upstairs. Sprinting into his bedroom, he grabbed a second pistol from the drawer of a nightstand and hurried to the window, which had a view overlooking the front of the house. Staring into the floodlit yard, he could see a dark form retreating across the winter-ravaged lawn, heading toward the trees that bordered the property. With another curse, he emptied both pistols. Hurrying to the closet, he grabbed a World War II carbine, one of more than two dozen firearms he kept around the house. Chambering a round, he ran downstairs and out the door.

The snow on the stoop was flecked with a dark, wet substance that Silas knew immediately was blood. With a grunt of satisfaction, he darted across the yard, following the trail. Within minutes, he caught up to his quarry, a young man who was trying to scale the fence while clutching at his bleeding wound. Silas grinned and slowly lifted the rifle. Firing at point-blank range, he punched off round after round, watching with gratification as the bullets hit home, sending the man spinning and twitching. He quit firing only when the clip was empty.

Turning his back on the twisted form that lay in a bloody heap at his feet, Silas returned to the house, picked up the telephone, and called the police. It was shortly before midnight on January 19, 1969.

When detectives arrived a few minutes later and flipped the body, they were taken aback by the amount of damage done by the high-powered bullets. The dead man's face was no more than a bloody pulp, an unrecognizable mass of tissue and broken bone. After searching the pockets, they found a wallet identifying the dead man as Frank H. Michelle, Jr., age twenty-eight, occupation, private investigator. They also found a crudely drawn map showing the way to Silas's house, along with another name—George Jayne—and a telephone number.

When the investigators asked Silas who George Jayne was, he shook his head. "That's my brother," he said coldly. "We've been feuding for years."

Indeed they had. The Jayne brothers' feud was bitter, long-running, and shockingly violent. Frank Michelle's death was not the first in the battle between the siblings, and neither would it be the last. Before it was over, George Jayne would be dead and Silas would go to prison for plotting his murder. Unfortunately, the bloodletting between the brothers extended beyond the family and sucked in uncounted others in strange and mysterious ways.

Born on July 3, 1907, in upstate Illinois, into a family that had been in this country for nine generations, Silas was the eldest son in a progeny that included eight girls and four boys. His father, Arthur, was a truck driver with reputed underworld connections. Arthur and Silas's mother, Katherine, separated when the children were young and she went to work managing a nearby resort. Left without a guiding hand, Silas's natural tendency toward violence grew without apparent restraint. One family legend has it that when he was little more than kindergarten age, Silas was bitten by one of the geese that roamed the family farm, an act that so infuriated the youngster that he slaughtered the entire flock.

He dropped out of school in the third grade. At age seventeen, he was convicted of rape and served a year in a reformatory. Several years later he and his two younger brothers, DeForest and Frank (George, sixteen years younger than Silas, was too young to participate), took their first tentative step into the industry that would sustain them for the rest of their lives: They set up a facility devoted to the import and sale of horses.

Operating out of the town of Woodstock in northern Illinois, the brothers brought in mustangs captured on western rangelands and prepared them for market. This was in the 1930s and the western influence was still visible as far east as the hills along the Wisconsin-Illinois border. When a new shipment of horses arrived by train, Silas, Frank, and DeForest were there to meet it. Grouping the animals into a herd, they would drive them down Woodstock's main street to their ranch. Like the Western cowboys they seemed eager to emulate, Silas and DeForest often would ride into town for a wild night of drinking, whoring, and brawling. It was not long before they became known, and feared, as "the Jayne Gang."

If the horses were trainable, the brothers broke them and either sold them or kept them as part of the stock for their equestrian school, an operation that catered to daughters of rich area residents. If a horse proved too wild to be broken, it was sold to a slaughterhouse to be converted into dog food. In the short run, the business proved highly profitable and the Jaynes seemed to prosper.

Then, in 1938, DeForest, then twenty-eight, committed suicide. Two years later, Silas and Frank moved to River Grove, a town northwest of Chicago, not far from O'Hare International Airport, where Silas opened the Green Tree Stable. George, the youngest brother, followed several years later, settling in the town of Morton Grove, near Skokie, and also opening a stable. This occupational decision set the stage for twenty years of turmoil that eventually ended in George's violent death.

Unfortunately for George, he found himself in competition with Frank and Silas, and Silas was unhappy. In 1952, when he was twenty-nine, George was vacationing in Florida with his wife and three children. While they were sunning themselves on a bright white beach, fire ravaged their home, destroying everything. The cause of the fire was never determined. George suspected Silas but was never able to prove it.

From all accounts, George and Silas could hardly have been more different. George was known as personable, trustworthy, and honest, while Silas was regarded as a shady character who wasn't afraid to break the law. By the time of the 1969 shooting, he had already been linked to a number of crimes.

On October 16, 1955, three young boys—Robert Peterson, fourteen, John Schuessler, thirteen, and his brother, Anton, eleven—disappeared on their way home from a movie. Their naked bodies were found two days later in a ditch in a Chicago-area forest preserve. Their eyes and mouths had been taped closed and at least one of them had been sexually assaulted.

At the time, investigators made a loose connection between the murders and Silas. In the wake of the publicity that attended the discovery of the bodies, two people went to the police and reported hearing screams coming from a Silas-owned stable on the night the boys disappeared. This gave credence to another clue uncovered by investigators: A close examination of the boys' bodies had turned up traces of feed or fertilizer of the type used around stables. When questioned about possible knowledge of the event, Silas kept silent.

In 1961, both Silas and his brother George had horses entered in a show called Oak Brook Hounds, a locally prestigious event. George's horse was ridden in the competition by his daughter Linda, then fourteen. When George's horse beat Silas's, Silas was enraged. "I'll never talk to you again, you bastard!" he screamed. Then, when another of George's horses beat Silas's at a show two years later, Silas was so angry that he promised to kill his brother.

A few weeks later, a gunman fired twenty-eight rounds into George's office, but George, sensing trouble, had left the building and driven off in a borrowed car minutes earlier, having left his desk light on and his own vehicle parked outside.

That was only the beginning of the *real* trouble. Not long afterward, someone tried to run George off the road. Then someone left a bundle of dynamite at his back door. A fuse running to the explosive had been lit, but it sputtered out before reaching the explosives. Finally, on June 14, 1965, a dynamite bomb actually went off, killing one of George's riding instructors, a twenty-two-year-old model and horse trainer named Cheryl Lynn Rude.

Cherie Rude had been having lunch with Linda Jayne at George's house when George handed her the keys to his Cadillac and asked her to drive it back to his office so he could finish some chores at home. When she turned the ignition, it tripped a switch that set off three sticks of dynamite affixed to the steering column.

George blamed Silas and claimed the bomb was meant for him.

Investigators tracked down two suspects. When they were grilled, they admitted they had been offered fifteen thousand dollars by Silas to kill George. However, the offer was made three days *after* the bomb killed Rude. One of the men said he and a friend had been offered three hundred dollars by Silas to kill George in 1962, three years previously. It was they, he said, who had fired the bullets into George's office. Despite the fact that both men gave statements, officers were unable to gather enough evidence to charge Silas with murder in connection with the bombing, but they did charge him with conspiracy.

Silas went on trial in March 1966. Out for his hide was an up-and-coming prosecutor named Patrick Tuite. Although Tuite thought he had a good case, the prosecution collapsed when the man who had promised to testify against Silas took the stand and claimed a sudden memory loss. The judge found the witness with the faulty memory in contempt, fined him one thousand dollars, and sentenced him to thirty days in jail. Silas went free.

Three years later, in 1969, George hired a retired police officer, Frank H. Michelle, Sr., as a security man. Michelle's son, Frank junior, was brought on as a private detective to try to find out what Silas was up to. One thing the younger Michelle did was plant a tracking device on Silas's Cadillac.

Twelve days later, when he believed the bug had stopped working, the younger Michelle crept onto the grounds of Silas's ranch, apparently intending to find the malfunctioning device and replace it. That was the night he was killed by Silas, who was never charged in connection with the death, which was officially rated a justifiable homicide.

After Michelle's killing, however, the feud between the brothers intensified. It reached a bloody climax two years later, on October 28, 1970. On that night, George Jayne was at home, celebrating his son's sixteenth birthday. After dinner, George sat down to play a few rubbers of bridge with his wife, daughter, and son-in-law. As he gathered and shuffled the cards, there was a loud crash and a nearby window shattered. George sprang to his feet, his eyes wide. Blood spurted from a hole in his chest like water from a drinking fountain. Without a word, he collapsed, dead by the time he hit the floor.

On May 22, 1971, seven months after George's murder, Silas and three other men were indicted on charges stemming from the killing. One pleaded guilty to a reduced charge of conspiracy and was sentenced to three years in prison. Another confessed. Apparently worried about the strength of the prosecution's case against him, Silas hired the best lawyer he could think of, the famous F. Lee Bailey, reportedly paying him a $250,000 retainer.

With Bailey pushing the buttons to slow the process down, it was almost two years before Silas and the fourth man finally went on trial. As was the case with the main witness in the 1966 trial that followed the bombing death of Cherie Rude, the main witness retracted his confession. Taking the stand in his own defense, Silas denied under oath that he had had anything to do with his brother's death.

The jury chose not to believe him: All three men were convicted, but Silas was found guilty on a lesser charge: conspiracy to commit murder. At age sixty-six, Silas was sent to the Vienna Correctional Center in southern Illinois to serve his time. He was paroled six years and one month later, on May 23, 1979. But even while behind bars, his influence continued to be felt.

In 1976, when Silas, then age sixty-nine, was roughly halfway through his sentence, there was a fire at a stable in Wisconsin that killed some three dozen horses valued at $750,000. Many months after the fire, a man named Charles Johnson was arrested and accused of starting the blaze. Although he admitted committing the crime, he said Silas put him up to it. It turned out that Johnson was a former cell mate of Silas's at Vienna.

In late 1979, seven months after he was paroled on the conspiracy conviction in connection with his brother George's death, Silas was indicted by a federal grand jury in East St. Louis on charges of masterminding the Wisconsin stable fire, but he was acquitted.

That trial marked Silas's last trip into a courtroom as a defendant. On July 14, 1987, Silas died "either of leukemia or an infectious disease" in a hospital in Elgin. He was eighty years old.

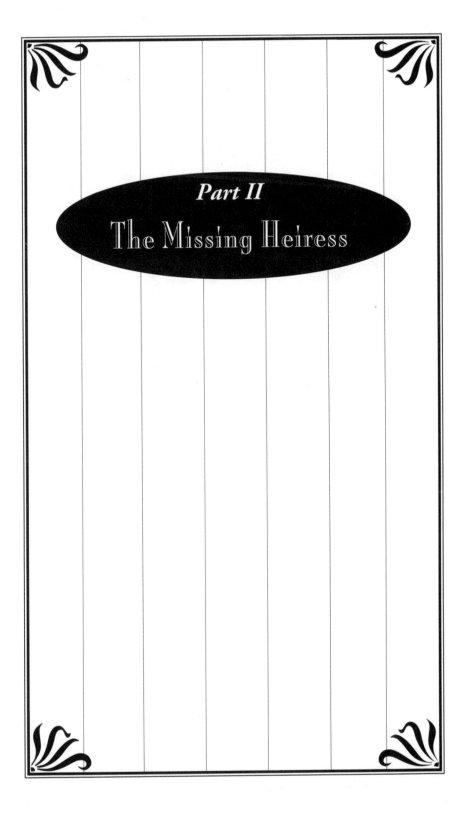

Part II
The Missing Heiress

9

The Road to Riches
Miami Beach, Florida 1951

I F THAT'S the way you're going to be, you can just take me home," the woman screamed, stamping her foot.

"Gladly," replied the man, obviously her husband, loudly enough to make it plain that he had no interest in keeping his voice down either.

A few feet away, Helen Vorhees turned politely away, her cheeks as bright as the bougainvillea that grew on the lush lawn outside. She knew it was not ladylike to eavesdrop on someone else's conversation, especially when the talk was pregnant with acrimony and mutual accusation. But it was hard to follow the precepts of etiquette when an argument was taking place only a few feet away and the two people were yelling loudly enough to be heard out by the swimming pool.

Ordinarily in her job as receptionist, she was not witness to such public displays. But in this instance, there was really nothing she could do about it, especially when the man and his wife were valued and long-time members of Indian Creek Country Club. Helen knew them by sight, knew that they came from Chicago but nevertheless were in Florida quite often.

Despite the voice of conscience that was whispering in her ear, Helen found herself listening with interest to the spirited argument. It had been going on for several minutes and Helen was not at all surprised to see them storm out the door. What did surprise her, however, was the fact that the man returned alone a few minutes later, seemingly quite calm. Smiling broadly, he walked up to her and apologized for the ruckus. "I'm Frank Brach," he said quietly, bowing slightly like a European count. "Would you care to join me for a drink in the lounge?"

Under most circumstances, Helen would have said no. Although she liked men, she had kept a wary distance from most members of the opposite sex since the divorce from her husband, a handsome but unfaithful bon vivant. The divorce, in fact, had been one of the reasons she had come to Florida, leaving her parents and a younger brother behind in Unionport, Ohio, an area that had been populated by members of her family for nine generations. The other reason was that she was tired of the dead-end jobs that had fallen her way back in Ohio. Taking tickets for a bus company and keeping the books at a pottery factory were not very exciting ways to make a living. She thought she could do a lot better in the Sunshine State, even if she did have to start out in a position that she probably got only because of her looks.

Helen had never had any problem attracting men. As a svelte auburn-haired beauty with large brown eyes and a dazzling smile—a Rita Hayward look-alike, some said—she was aware that men were physically drawn to her, and they were constantly asking her for dates. But she was picky. Although she went out fairly regularly, she had no room in her life for a steady suitor. But that was before she met Frank Brach, a dignified, serious-looking man of sixty who exuded wealth and respect. Although she was a little more than twenty years younger, there was a certain chemistry that brought them together and made the years disappear.

As she learned more about him, the attraction became even greater. And over drinks that night, Frank told her a lot about himself.

He said that June, the woman with whom he had been arguing, was his second wife. His first wife was named Eunice and they had been divorced for twenty years. He had married her when he was only twenty-four and almost immediately they had two children, a son, Frank junior, and a daughter, Joyce. As the children grew older, he and Eunice drifted further apart. Finally, after sixteen years, they had called it quits. About four years after that, he met and married June. They, too, had been married for sixteen years but, he added with a sigh, it looked as if the relationship was not going to continue much longer.

His business, he told her, was candy. Although he had made quite a bit of money in his later years, he had not been born into a wealthy family. His father, Emil, owned a neighborhood sweetshop in Chicago.

When he was fourteen, Frank joined his father and his brother, Edwin, older by two years, working in the store. What made the Palace of Sweets different from the scores of other candy stores scattered around the city was Emil's caramel. It was his secret weapon. While all the other tiny candy makers in Chicago were boiling their caramel, Emil was baking his. That made his product distinctive and extremely popular.

After Frank graduated from high school, he joined Edwin and his father at the office full-time. Since Frank had exhibited something of a flair for dealing with the public, he became the company's marketing expert. Together, the father and the two sons made a formidable team. The business flourished; sales soared. Within a few years, the Brachs had become the city's largest candy manufacturer, and it wasn't long before the company began shipping its product across the country. Only by then, it was no longer called the Palace of Sweets. Emil was so grateful for his sons' presence that he made them partners and renamed the business the E. J. Brach & Sons Candy Company.

Helen was impressed with Frank's story about his early days; it made her happy to know that he had grown up poor, because that was true of her upbringing as well. Her father, Walter, had been an engineer in the coal fields, just one step above a day laborer. She was the older child and she had only one sibling, a brother named Charles, who worked as a car inspector for the railroad. He and her parents—her mother's name was Daisy—still lived in Ohio and probably always would.

After that first night, she and Frank continued to see each other. Several months later, Frank and June were divorced and Frank asked her to marry him.

The separation from June had not been a pleasant one. In a document filed in a court in Ohio, June referred to Helen as a man-stealer who had trapped Frank by arranging illicit tête-à-tête's in hotels in Miami and Pittsburgh. When the divorce decree was granted, June was awarded $100,000 in cash and $300,000 in alimony. Frank could afford it.

After the wedding, Helen moved into Frank's rambling eighteen-room house in Glenview, a northern Chicago suburb. As far as houses go, it wasn't grand in the style of the typical millionaire's home. By many standards, it was quite plain. A boxy two-story structure with a clapboard exterior, its most outstanding exterior feature was the seven-acre tree-covered parklike plot on which it was located. Inside, though, it was plush, especially after Helen redecorated from top to bottom with tasteful antiques.

By all accounts, Frank never complained about Helen's spending. In fact, he was more than generous, buying her jewelry, furs, expensive clothes, and cars.

At Helen's urging, he built a house for her along the Tappan Reservoir in Ohio and he voiced no objections when she spent four or five months a year there. He also built houses nearby for her parents and her brother.

It wasn't as if they needed another residence. In addition to the house in Glenview, they kept a penthouse apartment in Fort Lauderdale that overlooked the Intracoastal Waterway and boasted its own doorman and private elevator. Each January, Frank wrote a check for the entire year's rent, deciding to pay for twelve months simply so they could have the freedom to come and go whenever they pleased.

After Frank's father, Emil, died, Frank and his brother inherited the company. Then, within six months, Edwin died, too, leaving everything to Frank. Not long after that, Frank began losing interest in the business. His only children, Frank junior and Joyce, both from his first marriage, were not involved in the business, so he had no reason to keep it going. Since he was well into retirement age by then, he decided to get rid of the company, selling it to a conglomerate called American Home Products for a handsome price that ensured that Helen would be comfortable after he died. He remained for a while in an advisory capacity, but then his health began to fail.

When he entered semiretirement, Frank remained loyal to two men who had been with him for years. One was Everett Moore, a CPA who had started with him as a part-time tax man and gradually expanded his role to full-time financial consultant. The other was Jack Matlick, who had begun working for Frank in the late fifties as a handyman when he wasn't working his regular job as a truck driver for a dry-cleaning company. Within a couple of years, though, Matlick joined Frank full-time. His duty was to take care of whatever needed to be done around the Glenview house, whether it was fixing a leaky pipe or driving Frank to the doctor.

After Frank died in 1970 at age seventy-nine, Helen kept Moore on because she needed someone to take care of the books and taxes. As the heiress to an estate worth $30 million, give or take a few million, Helen had a definite need for financial advice. But Matlick's role was not so well defined. He had been useful to Frank, but Helen felt that she did not need a majordomo. If the plumbing broke down, she could find someone in the Yellow Pages to take care of it. So she gave Matlick a bonus, told him how much she appreciated how helpful he had been to Frank, and wished him good luck, never expecting to see him again. But six months later, he knocked on her door. He had been unable to find a job, he said, and he desperately needed a paycheck. Helen hired him back and soon he began performing more duties for Helen than he ever had for Frank.

He not only was chauffeur and handyman; under Helen, he became the sole caretaker of the Glenview estate. When Helen was in residence, Matlick lived with his wife in a cottage on a farm in nearby Schaumburg—property that Frank had bought in the early thirties—and commuted to Glenview on a daily basis to mow the lawn, trim the shrubs, or weed the garden. He also ran errands and drove Helen wherever she wanted to go when she did not feel like driving herself.

After Frank's death, Helen's latent car fetish surfaced and she began amassing vehicles like golfers collect putters. At one time, the Glenview garage housed five expensive automobiles: a late-model salmon-colored Cadillac sedan, a lavender Rolls-Royce, matching pink and red Cadillac convertibles, and a pink Lincoln Town Car. Helen *loved* pink. She was so fond of it that before Frank sold the candy company, she talked him into making it the official color of Brach & Sons.

Matlick's duties were relatively simple. If something broke, he either fixed it himself or saw that it was repaired. When Helen was in Florida or visiting her brother in Ohio—in fact, when she was away for any reason—Matlick moved into a guest room at the Glenview house and stayed there until she returned. He also drove her to the airport when she was going on a trip and picked her up when she returned, which was no simple task, considering Helen's traveling requirements. Her idea of packing light was a dozen suitcases; on occasion, she carried three times that many.

In time, Matlick became indispensable, earning for himself an actual title. Helen called him her "houseman."

With Moore and Matlick managing her everyday affairs, Helen had little to do except indulge herself. In addition to her fixation for cars, Helen also had a well-developed sweet tooth. Not long after Frank died, she converted one of the little-used rooms in the Glenview house into a twenties-style soda fountain, complete with marble-topped counter and tiny tables.

Far from locking herself away, Helen led an active but well-circumscribed social life. She had a passion for ballroom dancing, which she tried to gratify every chance she got. She also maintained a rather small but close circle of friends with whom she kept in close contact. When she could not see them in person, she kept in touch by telephone, spending hours every day making or receiving calls. She also had three pet projects to which she devoted considerable time and, in at least one case, money.

One was animal rights. She shared the Glenview house with a handful of dogs, all of which she treated like children. Once when one of them, a mutt named Candy, became ill while she was on vacation in the Bahamas, she chartered a plane to rush home to help tend the stricken animal. Despite her attentions, the dog died. So she bought a fancy, expensive casket, held a proper wake, and then arranged to have the mongrel buried in the family mausoleum, along with Frank, her parents, and another of her mutts, Sugar.

Like Frank, she had no one she felt she really needed to leave her money to. Her parents were dead, and while her brother, Charles, would inherit some of her fortune, she planned to leave the bulk of it to a foundation she created to help support her favorite charities, one of which was a California-based group called the Animal Protective Institute. Each year, she mailed a hundred-thousand-dollar check to its director, Belton Mouras. Although that seemed like an excessive donation, it was not particularly large for a person of Helen's means. She made three times that much each year just in interest on a trust that Frank had set up for her.

Another of her favorite diversions was keeping a journal. Helen was a dedicated diarist, religiously recording her thoughts and observations into bound ledgers specifically designed for the purpose: pads with padded covers secured by tiny locks. When she filled a volume, she filed it away in her dresser.

A third favorite pastime—one which others later pointed to as proof that she was nothing more than a rich kook—was a strong belief in automatic writing, a device she believed helped her communicate with the dead. She accomplished this—or thought she did—by taking a standard yellow legal pad and a pen or pencil and secreting herself inside a quiet, darkened room, usually late at night. Then she would relax her body, letting her mind go blank. As she waited for contact to be made with the netherworld, she loosely held a pen poised over a blank sheet of paper, confident that the spirits would guide her hand. When she awoke from her trancelike state minutes or hours later, she often discovered that she had filled sheet upon sheet with words she was convinced were messages from beyond the pale. Needless to say, the writing was not always legible; much of it looked a kindergartner's scribblings. But readable or not, it boosted her conviction that she had been on a journey into a world where most are denied entrance. She put enough credence in this regimen to save her sheets of paper, filing them away in a bottom drawer of her dresser, along with the diaries.

As an offshoot of her interest in the afterworld, she found a spiritualist she could trust and kept in contact with her almost every day.

When investigators tried to put her life together later, they were amazed by the diversity of her interests and how she had managed to keep them all balanced without being labeled a hopeless crackpot.

In spite of her money and her sociability, there was one ingredient missing from Helen's life: a man. Before she met Frank, she had been relatively monastic as far as males were concerned, and after he died, she reverted to that mode—at least for a few years. The situation abruptly changed in 1973.

Ironically, the impetus for the change was not Helen Brach, but a friend of hers named Helen Hirschman.

10

Enter Richard Bailey

O N A BRIGHT, sunny afternoon early in the fall, Helen Hirschman stopped at a car wash in Morton Grove to have her vehicle cleaned. While she was waiting, another patron, a well-dressed man driving a Cadillac Eldorado, began chatting her up.

"You have a wonderful tan," he said, smiling broadly. "Where did you get it?"

Innocently, Hirschman explained that she commuted regularly to Florida.

"That's funny," he replied, "I go to Florida a lot myself." Like a faucet that had just been opened, the man continued to talk, drawing Hirschman ever deeper into conversation. Before she left, he had wrangled her name and telephone number.

The next day, he called and invited her to lunch. She turned him down. The next day, he called again. Once more, she said no. So he called again. Finally, she explained to him that she was a happily married woman and had no interest in going out with him. *However,* she added, she had a friend who might like to meet him. Together, they hatched a simple plan to arrange the introduction.

The following Friday, Helen Brach and the Hirschmans, who were Brach's landlords in Florida, were having dinner at a popular Morton Grove steak house. They were on dessert when a man Helen Brach had never seen before walked by their table. Helen Hirschman waved and called him over.

"Helen," she said, speaking to Helen Brach, "I want you to meet someone. This," she said, waving grandly at the man she had met at the car wash, "is Richard Bailey."

Acting as if he had known them all for years, Bailey joined the party and was soon laughing and joking with the two Helens, discussing animals, automobiles, and a love of dancing.

Several times after that, Bailey called Helen Brach and asked her out, but each time she refused. Finally, she agreed to have lunch with him a few weeks later when she was visiting Fort Lauderdale. How much he knew about Helen's financial situation at that point is unclear, but he undoubtedly knew she had money—lots and lots of it. And for Bailey, that was enough.

Many of the men with whom Richard Bailey came in contact were awed by his seemingly magic touch with women. Early on, Frank Jayne hung the nickname "Golden Tongue" on him and it stuck for years. To males, Bailey came across as arrogant, obsequious, and crude, a man given to insulting remarks and bantam rooster–like bravado. One employee at Jayne's stable once asked him what Helen Brach was *really* like, and Bailey bluntly replied: "She's a bad biff." Another asked him, since he was almost always seen with older women, how he could stand sleeping with grandmothers. "It's easy," Bailey shot back. "I just close my eyes and think of the money."

One day he was driving down Glenview Road with one of the men with whom he later went into partnership and they passed an elderly woman who was trying to navigate down the sidewalk on a walker. "See that woman!" Bailey said excitedly, turning to point. "That's *exactly* the type of woman I'm looking for."

While men tended to regard him as smarmy and too much taken with himself, women, particularly emotionally confused middle-aged women, seemed to find him irresistible. Years later, when his female victims finally began to talk about their relationships with him, they used almost identical words to describe his appeal: "He made me feel like I was the only woman in the world. . . . I've never been treated like that by any other man. . . . I simply fell in love with him."

Whether Bailey had this effect on Helen Brach is unknown. Bailey has consistently denied that he had a romantic relationship with the heiress and there is no documented evidence to show otherwise.

When Steve Miller's investigators began trying to nail down this rumor some fifteen years later, they had little luck. In addition to the Bailey friend who quoted the con man as saying Helen was "a bad biff," the investigators tracked down a man named Lance Williamson, whom Bailey apparently was grooming as a protégé at one time. Williamson related how one day as he was driving down Wagner Road with Bailey and they sped past the Brach residence, Bailey tapped him on the shoulder and pointed toward Helen's house. "There's my baby," Williamson quoted him as saying. "My honey lives there." Then, Williamson said, he waved and gave a fake little smile.

Helen's friends—those who were still alive by the time the Miller investigation got cranked up (Helen would have been eighty years old in 1991 and her friends were her contemporaries)—said Helen claimed she did not harbor any romantic feelings toward Bailey.

One woman who knew Helen well, Bertha DeVito, told ATF agent Daniel Ivancich, who had joined Miller's team as a permanent member, that Helen had shrugged off a suggestion that she and Bailey might get married. "She said she would not even consider marrying him until he could prove that he had more money than she did."

On the other hand, Bailey's sister, Faye Hanley, who also claimed to be a close friend of Helen's ("We were like sisters," she said in sworn testimony) asserted there was a deep emotional bond between the two. "The relationship could not have been lovelier; it was kind . . . it was nice," said Hanley. "Helen thought Richard was the nicest man she had ever met."

Reason would argue against a romance between Brach and Bailey. Before she met Frank, Helen, for all intents and purposes, had been celibate for years. From what her friends said as well, Helen was not completely fooled by Bailey, recognizing his ability and reputation as a gigolo but electing to remain on good terms with him because she enjoyed his company. There also was an age factor: In 1973, when they met, Helen was sixty-two and Bailey was only forty-four. Helen probably would have thought twice about becoming romantically involved with a man eighteen years her junior.

However, if the relationship was not romantic, it at least was close.

Helen often gave Bailey gifts of clothing and jewelry, and on New Year's Eve 1976, Helen paid Bailey's way to New York and arranged a room for him at the swank Waldorf-Astoria Hotel so they could welcome in 1977 by dancing the night away to the music of Guy Lombardo and his Royal Canadians. That night, according to Bailey, Helen also gave him an expensive sweater to show her appreciation for his company.

The fact that Helen subsidized Bailey's New York trip simply for an evening of partying would not have been out of character for either of them, considering that they shared a common passion for ballroom dancing.

Although it was extremely difficult a decade and a half later to pin down the specifics of the amount of personal interaction between Bailey and Helen, compelling evidence *did* exist of a business relationship.

Although Bailey denied it for years, even to police who questioned him soon after Helen disappeared, he later grudgingly confessed that he had been instrumental in the sale of three racehorses to Helen.

It began one day in 1974, a little more than a year after the two met, when they were attending the races at Florida's Gulfstream Park. Helen got caught up in the excitement, Bailey said, and mentioned to him that she wouldn't mind owning a few racehorses.

"What prompted your sudden interest?" he asked, surprised.

"Oh," Helen said casually, "Frank used to own some and I thought it might be fun."

Bailey's pulse quickened. "And how much," he asked shrewdly, "would you be willing to pay for some good horses?"

Helen shrugged. "Maybe a hundred thousand dollars," she replied.

To Bailey, those words were like offering a water jug to a man who had had no liquid for three days. "I handle show horses, not racehorses," he said. "But my brother P.J., the jockey, might be able to help."

Several months later, in March 1975, P. J. Bailey sold Helen Brach two mares—which she subsequently named Brach's Sweet Talk and Vorhees's Luv—for fifty thousand dollars. Neither of the Bailey brothers mentioned to Helen that they had bought the two for nine thousand dollars, thereby realizing an enormous profit on the resale, or that P.J. had split the return with his brother.

By the same token, several months later, Helen bought a South American stallion named Potenciado from P.J. for $45,000. P.J. had paid $8,500 for the horse. Again, P.J. split the money with his brother and again they did not bother to mention this to Helen.

It has never been documented that either of the Baileys ever sold her any other horses, but, Miller would later claim, Richard Bailey did. It would become increasingly important to Miller's budding case to be able to prove that Helen *did* buy additional horses, specifically broodmares, from Richard Bailey. If she had, what happened to her would closely parallel the scam Bailey perpetrated against Carole Karstenson just a short time before. Miller's theory, viewed deductively, made sense. If the prosecutor could prove the additional horse sales, it also would provide a motive for Helen's murder—that is, Helen became extremely angry with Bailey because she found out he was cheating her on the horses and threatened to go to the state attorney's office with her information. Bailey, therefore, Miller's reasoning went, had her abducted to shut her up.

11

An Eventful Day
February 17, 1977

S TARTLED OUT of a deep sleep by the call from the Kohler Hotel switchboard, Helen Brach lay half-awake in the unfamiliar bed, staring into the blackness. Definitely not a morning person, she considered rolling over and closing her eyes, ignoring the crack-of-dawn appointment, and later demanding that Mayo Clinic doctors schedule their meetings at a decent hour. It was a tempting but passing thought. Helen Brach may have been wealthy, pampered, hedonistic, and, according to some, more than a tad eccentric, but she was also remarkably self-disciplined.

Reluctantly, she concluded that meeting with Dr. Karl Anderson to review a report on the current state of her physical well-being took precedence over a couple of hours of sleep. After all, the whole thing had been her idea.

Tossing back the covers, she swung her legs out of bed and wormed her feet into the slippers she had carefully set in place the night before. Gathering her gown around her, she padded somewhat stiffly across the room, the consequences of a mild problem with her legs that she had been suffering from for decades. Standing before the large picture window, she carefully edged the drapes aside.

It looked cold outside, but that was hardly a surprise. The winter had been long and frigid, one of the worst that anyone could remember. Although it was too dark for her to tell for certain, she instinctively knew that it was going to be another gray day. In February in Rochester, Minnesota, that was a safe bet. But it didn't matter, because she knew she was going to be leaving soon for Florida.

With a sigh, she let the drapes slide back into place and turned toward the clean but characterless hotel bathroom. A hot shower would make her feel better.

For a woman almost sixty-six, Helen Brach was physically well pre-served. Her long, thick hair was still more auburn than gray, which was fortunate, because she was old-fashioned enough to resist dyeing it, even though she occasionally liked to see herself as a blonde. But that dilemma was easily solved by wearing a wig, which she sometimes did, especially for social engagements. She had put on a few pounds, but at five-five she was hardly petite, so she could carry a little weight better than many of her friends.

She had checked herself into the clinic a week earlier for a complete physical, knowing it meant seemingly endless days of prodding, pok-ing, and palpating. That she was concerned about her health was char-acteristic of her. At her age, she felt it didn't hurt to be careful. And the Mayo doctors, she knew, were among the best in the world.

What was unusual about her visit to the clinic was that she had made up her mind so abruptly to schedule the examination. Basically a de-liberate, reflective person, a bit of a procrastinator, if the truth be told, Helen definitely was not one who normally surrendered to impulse. But Richard Bailey had convinced her that a thorough physical by the Mayo doctors was a good idea. "My family's been going there for years," he had told her. "I've been there myself. Let me make the arrangements for you." And he had. More easily than she thought possible, he had taken care of all the details, using his contacts to place Helen at the top of the clinic's long waiting list.

After the meeting with Dr. Anderson, who would give her the re-sults of all the tests that had been performed during the weeklong ex-amination, she planned to return to Chicago and then go on to Florida. But first she needed to make a decision about carrying through on a sug-gestion from an old friend.

Just before leaving for Rochester, she had stopped to see William Katz, a memorial engraver she had met years before when she was look-ing for someone to do the work on the mausoleum she was building in Ohio. Their personalities had clicked and almost immediately they be-came fast friends. Katz had become a confidant and they spent consid-erable time in each other's company. Over the years, Katz had visited her in Florida and Ohio, and she had been a frequent guest in his home. When she went to see him in early February, just before leaving for Rochester, she was troubled and wanted his advice. Sitting in his cramped office in a chair surrendered by Katz's son, Arthur, who lounged against a filing cabinet a few feet away, Helen explained to her old friend how she was certain that she had been cheated in a horse deal and that she didn't know what to do about it. After she outlined the problem, explaining that she felt she had been gulled by a much younger man she had been dating, who convinced her to spend a considerable amount on virtually worthless horses, she asked Katz what he thought she should do. She would like very much to get her money back. The elder Katz, his son related later, after Helen's disappearance and his father's death, suggested she go see a friend of his at the state's attorney's office. Helen, however, said she needed to postpone such action because she was leaving very soon for the Mayo Clinic.

She could go, she knew, when she got back to Chicago and before leaving for Florida. In fact, the night before, she had called perhaps her closest friend in Florida, a man who had been friends to both her and Frank. Whenever she flew into the Sunshine State, it was the custom of the man and his wife to pick her up at the airport. As usual, she had made arrangements with him to meet her flight, but she had called him and told him her trip was going to be delayed. She was not certain how long it would be, she said, but she would call him as soon as she made new plans and give him her arrival time.

For weeks, Helen had made no secret about how much she was looking forward to getting to Fort Lauderdale. A few months before, she had decided to give up her penthouse after the Hirschmans announced they were raising her rent by one hundred dollars a month. Subsequently, she had plunked down two hundred thousand for a condo.

The rent increase had really galled her. She and Frank had kept the penthouse apartment for years and she didn't think a rate boost was fair. It was indicative of Helen's personality that she was willing to sacrifice over a matter of principle. Eighteen years later, Steve Miller would point to the penthouse episode and contend that if Helen Brach had been willing to risk a very long friendship with the Hirschmans for one hundred dollars a month, she would have had no compunction at all about seeking legal redress against a man who had fleeced her out of hundreds of thousands of dollars.

Still, Helen was excited about the venture. Discounting the inconvenience of having to move, the necessity of furnishing a new condo gave her a good excuse for some hard-core shopping.

Shrugging into one of the numerous fur coats she owned, Helen pulled the hotel room door closed behind her and took the elevator to the basement, where there was an entrance to the arcade linking the hotel to the clinic, a thoughtful convenience that helped make the Kohler a popular and easily accessible facility for the Mayo's outpatients.

At about the same time Helen was leaving the Kohler, Richard Bailey was tooling down a Florida highway with one of his Chicago girlfriends, a twenty-something Realtor named Christina Kubot, at his side.

As they zipped down peaceful roads that ran through the heart of Florida's horse country, Kubot noted the lush green pastures bordered by freshly painted white fences. Off in the distance behind the fences were grand farms that were home to some of the country's most expensive horseflesh.

Kubot had met Bailey a couple of years earlier when she was taking riding lessons at Northwestern Stables. Although the facility was owned by a man named Frank Jayne, Jr., Bailey seemed always to be there, chatting with the customers, especially the female customers, and strutting around as if he owned the place. After chatting with her a few times, Bailey had pulled her aside one afternoon and suggested she go into partnership with him on a string of horses he said he planned to buy. He was short ten thousand dollars to close the deal, he said, and he wondered if she would like the opportunity to invest. If she would put up five thousand, he would put up the other five thousand, which was all the ready cash he happened to have at the time. It was a wonderful investment opportunity for her, he said, and while normally he would not ask someone else to participate, it happened that he was a little short of cash at the time. If he did not come up with the money, he said dolefully, he would lose the whole deal.

He sounded so convincing to Kubot that she ended up writing him a check. However, when she got home an hour or so later, she began having second thoughts about her rash behavior. Calling a lawyer friend, she asked for advice. "Put a stop payment on the check and forget about it," the lawyer advised. That is just what Kubot did. However, she was so embarrassed by the incident, she quit going to the stables because she feared she would run into Bailey and have to explain to him why she had backed out.

As it turned out, the North Shore is not such a big place. A few months after voiding the check, she ran into Bailey at a neighborhood supermarket. She was tremendously relieved to discover that he acted as if the incident had never happened. Instead of being angry with her for stopping payment on the check, Bailey asked her to visit a stable he had recently purchased. Too embarrassed to say no, she agreed. And then he asked her to dinner. From then on, they dated fairly regularly off and on. Bailey never again suggested she invest in any of his enterprises, but he did throw some cash *her* way.

The year before, after they began dating, Bailey had asked her to handle the sale on a piece of property for him. She sold it at substantial profit, earning a handsome commission for herself in the process. But Bailey told her the commission was insufficient to show his full appreciation; he would like to do something more. What he did was invite her to join him in Florida, all expenses paid.

She had arrived the night before, February 16, and joined Bailey at the Colony Hotel. On Thursday morning, which dawned clear and beautiful, Bailey had rented a car and asked her to accompany him on a visit to one of the country's most prestigious horse farms, a facility owned by Arthur Winnick, who was renowned throughout the horse world.

Once they arrived at the farm, Winnick himself greeted them and took them on a brief tour of his vast operation. One of the stops they made was at a concrete square that Winnick explained was a helipad, a place where very important clients who were short on time could be helicoptered in to save them the time and trouble of actually having to drive to his remote farm.

"And we could use this on Saturday?" Bailey had asked.

"Absolutely," Winnick had replied.

Soon afterward, the tour ended and Winnick and Bailey disappeared into the farm owner's office to talk business, leaving Kubot to explore on her own.

An hour or so later, she and Bailey were back in the rental car, headed for their hotel in West Palm Beach. That afternoon, they went sight-seeing and lounged around the Colony's pool. Over dinner that evening, Bailey told Kubot how much he had enjoyed her visit but informed her, sadly it seemed to her, that it was going to have to end the next day; she was going to have to return to Chicago.

A little disappointed, although she had come down believing it was going to be a short trip, Kubot told him it was fine, that she had had a wonderful time. "But why does it have to end so quickly?" she asked.

"I have an important client coming in on Saturday," Bailey had said, "and I still have a lot of arrangements to make."

Kubot raised her eyebrows. "It's a woman," Bailey explained, "who I hope is going to buy several horses from Arthur Winnick."

Aha, Kubot thought. That explains the trip to the farm and the conversation about the helicopter. "Will you make a lot of money on the deal if it goes through?" she asked.

Bailey shrugged. "Ten percent," he said. "But that's okay. That still could be considerable."

The next morning, as they were sitting around the pool, Bailey pulled out his camera and insisted on taking a picture of Kubot. "Why don't you get in the picture with me?" she suggested. "We can get someone else to snap it."

"No," Bailey said, claiming shyness. "I want the picture of *you.*" He did not know Kubot would put the picture in a drawer and keep it for more than eighteen years.

Sitting in Dr. Anderson's office, Helen was beginning to get a little impatient. She was eager to get going, to take care of whatever needed to be done in Chicago and then fly to Florida, where it would be sunny and warm.

Five minutes later, Anderson strolled in.

"Good morning, Mrs. Brach," he said brightly, slipping behind his desk. He took a few moments to scan the papers in the folder with her name on it that had been on his desk and then got abruptly down to business.

"Mrs. Brach," he said earnestly, "I have good news for you. You're in perfect health. We couldn't find anything wrong."

Relieved more than surprised, Helen grinned broadly.

"Except," the physician intoned, emitting a slight doctorly cough, "there is one thing."

Helen's smile disappeared. "And what's that?" she asked expectantly.

"You need to lose some weight," he said. "Twenty pounds. And get some exercise, particularly walking, since you seem to have some minor problems with circulation in your legs."

Helen smiled again, not quite as broadly as before. "Thank you, Doctor," she said. "I'm heading south very soon and the climate there is ideal for outdoor exercise."

"Good," Anderson replied, nodding. "It will really make you feel better."

Lifting her mink coat off an adjoining chair, Helen complimented him on the clinic's efficiency and thanked him for his time. Walking straight back to the hotel, she packed the single suitcase she had brought with her, being careful to grab the Northwest Orient folder off the desk. It contained the ticket for her return flight.

After stopping at the front desk to settle her account, she reentered the tunnel that led to the clinic and went directly to one of the boutiques that lined the passageway, a discreet, tasteful emporium she had noticed earlier.

A few minutes later, when the woman who operated the Buckskin Shop arrived to open the store at its posted time of 9:00 A.M., she found Helen waiting impatiently outside.

Breezing through the shop, Helen selected an alabaster soap dish, a powder box, and a handful of towels. Handing the clerk her American Express card, she asked that the purchases be boxed and shipped to her new address in Fort Lauderdale.

Not wanting to seem unfriendly, the clerk chatted amiably as she filled out the charge slip, complaining mildly about the winter. As she prattled on, Helen tapped her foot nervously.

"This won't take but a minute," the clerk said soothingly.

"That's all right," Helen Brach replied somewhat abruptly. "I'm just in a bit of a hurry. My houseman is waiting for me."

Houseman, the clerk thought. What a curious word. It was one that she had never heard before. She guessed it referred to some sort of servant, like a butler. But it was unclear whether he was waiting in Rochester or in Chicago.

Signing the forty-one-dollar charge slip, Helen retrieved her credit card, deposited it carefully in her purse, wrapped her coat around her, and strode briskly out the door. It was roughly 10:00 A.M. on Thursday, February 17, 1977. And it was the last time Helen Vorhees Brach was ever seen alive or dead by anyone who would admit it or could prove it.

Up in Smoke
Chicago, March 4-6, 1977

T HE PRECEDING days had been hectic for Everett Moore. For the last week, it had been one thing after another, and the stress was starting to get to him. Finally, things slowed down a little and the accountant-cum-financial adviser decided to take a day off and get an early start on the weekend. As a result, he was not in the office at all on Friday, March 4. If anyone had called him there, they had not been able to reach him.

That evening, he was slouching around the house, catching up on his reading and enjoying his temporary escape from the madness that always accompanies a new tax season, when the phone unexpectedly rang.

Sighing, putting his *Tribune* aside, Moore rose and walked slowly across the room, looking angrily at the phone, figuring anyone trying him at home in the evening on his day off had to be bringing bad news. His premonition proved extremely accurate.

"Hello," Moore said reluctantly.

"Mr. Moore?" said a voice that sounded vaguely familiar.

"Yes," Moore said rather abruptly. "This is he. Who's calling?"

"This is Jack Matlick," the voice replied. "Mrs. Brach's houseman."

Moore frowned. This was highly unusual. Although he had met Matlick several times, they were hardly intimates. Why, Moore asked himself, is he calling me at home?

"Yes, Mr. Matlick," Moore said, his voice still as cold as a northern wind off Lake Michigan. "What can I do for you?"

"I'm worried about the missus," Matlick said, sounding upset. "She's supposed to be in Florida, but I checked down there and she hasn't arrived."

Although Moore had not known that Helen was in Florida, it hardly came as a surprise. He knew, of course, about her recent condo purchase and figured she probably was eager to get moved in. He failed to understand why Matlick was so disturbed.

"Oh, she'll be there," Moore said soothingly. "Either that or she'll show up somewhere else."

"I'm still worried," Matlick replied. "I wish you'd come out to the house."

"Right now?" Moore asked, peering out the window into the dark, cold night.

"Yes," said Matlick. "Right now. Tonight."

Moore thought about that briefly and rejected Matlick's suggestion. "Look," he said, "if you don't hear from her by tomorrow, I'll come over then."

"Okay," Matlick said reluctantly.

Promising to call the next morning, Moore hung up.

After breaking the connection with the CPA, Matlick reached for the address book kept by the phone in the Brach kitchen. Flipping through it, he found the number he wanted and hurriedly dialed it.

"Hello," he said when a woman answered. "I'd like to speak to Charles Vorhees, please. This is Jack Matlick."

When Helen's brother and closest living relative came on the line from his home in Hopedale, Ohio, Matlick told him essentially what he had told Moore—that he had not heard from Helen and had not been able to track her down, although he believed she was in Florida.

Vorhees, much as Moore had done, mumbled that he didn't see what the problem was. Helen was always off someplace.

"No," said Matlick. "You don't understand. I think your sister has disappeared," he added.

"What do you think I ought to do?" Vorhees asked.

"You'd better get up here," Matlick replied. "You'll have to file a missing person's report." He had been to the Glenview Police Department earlier in the day to try to report Helen missing. But the detective on duty, Sgt. Joe Baumann, told him a missing person's report could be filed only by a relative. By calling Moore, Matlick apparently wanted to discuss the situation before alerting her brother. But after Moore's apparent lack of concern, Matlick had decided to call Vorhees after all.

"All right," Vorhees replied in a monotone, "I'll let you know when I'm arriving and you can pick me up at O'Hare."

The next morning, Saturday, March 5, at about 9:15, Moore tried to reach Matlick but instead got the answering machine. He left a message and waited for the caretaker to call back, which he did about forty-five minutes later.

"Have you heard from her yet?" Moore asked.

"No," said Matlick, sounding even more concerned. "Would you please come out?"

"Okay," Moore reluctantly replied. "I'm on my way."

About an hour later, Moore pulled into the driveway, still wondering what he could possibly accomplish by having come to the Brach residence. The trip, he felt, was more to calm Matlick than anything else.

"Come on in," Matlick said, leading the way inside. "Look at that," he said without preamble, pointing to a mound of mail stacked on an island counter in the kitchen, which Helen had recently had remodeled.

Moore walked over and stared at the pile. Picking up a handful of envelopes, he started sifting through them.

"I've already sorted it," Matlick said tersely.

"You haven't heard from her, right?" Moore asked, putting the envelopes back in the pile.

"No," Matlick answered. "Have you?"

"Not since just before she went to the Mayo Clinic," Moore said.

Well, Matlick replied, she had returned from the clinic, spent a few days at home, and then gone to Fort Lauderdale. He had taken her to the airport himself, he added, dropping her off at about 7:00 A.M. on Monday, February 21. Although Moore did not ask, Matlick added that when he had last seen her, Helen had been wearing a black suit and was carrying a black patent-leather purse. That struck Moore as slightly odd. How many men, he asked himself, remember what kind of purse a woman is carrying?

"How have you tried to reach her?" the CPA asked.

Matlick told him that he had tried her old penthouse apartment and also had rung the building manager, who said he had not seen her. He then called her friends the Stevenses. When Doug Stevens said he had not heard from Helen since mid-February when she called to tell him she was postponing her arrival, Matlick asked Stevens if he'd help him try to find her. Later, Stevens called back and said he had not been able to locate her either.

As Moore pondered what the handyman had told him, Matlick turned and started to leave the room. "Come with me," he said abruptly. "I want to show you something."

Wrinkling his brow, not sure what was going on, Moore followed the caretaker up the stairs and down the hall to Helen's bedroom. Walking straight to the dresser that stood against the far wall, Matlick opened one of the bottom drawers and pointed to a collection of papers that almost filled the space.

"What's that?" Moore asked, his curiosity aroused.

"She told me once that if anything happened to her to destroy those papers," Matlick said.

Moore looked at him in surprise. "Don't touch them!" he commanded. "If you destroy them and she shows up, what are you going to do?"

Matlick shrugged, adding that he thought he should burn them.

"Don't do that!" Moore repeated. Starting to feel uncomfortable in his employer's bedroom, he suggested they go back downstairs.

As Moore was once again going through the mail, the telephone rang. "It's for you," Matlick said, proffering the receiver. "It's that Glenview policeman, Detective Baumann."

Baumann asked a puzzled and increasingly worried Moore if he'd stay at the house for a few minutes while he drove out to ask him some questions. Even though the police had not allowed Matlick to file a missing person's report on Helen, Baumann apparently had decided to do some preliminary investigating on his own.

A few minutes later, the detective showed up and spent about thirty minutes questioning Moore, who repeated what Matlick had told him and pointed out that he had not talked to Helen in more than two weeks. That had been a telephone conversation, he recalled, and she had told him that she was going to the Mayo Clinic for a physical.

Was he disturbed by the fact that Matlick had not heard from her and had not been able to find her? Baumann asked.

"No," Moore answered quickly. "She doesn't have to tell Mr. Matlick or me where she's going all the time."

After the detective left, Moore told Matlick that he was leaving, as well. He was somewhat worried, he said, but he thought it was too soon to get overly excited.

"If you say so," Matlick said, looking doubtful.

Moore's interest grew the next day, Sunday, March 6, when he received a call at home from Belton Mouras, the director of the California animal rights organization that was Helen's favorite charity. Mouras explained that he had been trying to call Helen to remind her that it was time to renew her annual donation to the Animal Protection Institute but that he had been unable to reach her.

Mouras, who was telephoning on a Sunday from his office in Sacramento, sounded even more upset than Matlick.

"Well, what do *you* suggest we do?" Moore asked.

Mouras proposed hiring a private detective. "We have an office in Fort Lauderdale and the manager can take care of it."

"Okay, that sounds good," Moore said, but his tone implied that he thought it was not a situation that called for such dire action. The accountant was somewhat puzzled by the flurry of concern. Helen, he knew, was eccentric and very private. He did not think she would take lightly the knowledge that other people, even if they were the ones who were closest to her, had been probing into her life.

Moore had known her a long time and considered her a relatively stable, dependable woman who lived a rather quiet life. As her accountant, he also knew she was careful with her money—not tight, but *careful*. She could be generous with others and she did not deny herself the luxuries she had come to appreciate while married to Frank. Despite her eccentricities—her seemingly overblown protective attitude about animals, her love for cars—she was not given to impulsive behavior. On balance, he felt, she could well afford however many vehicles she wanted to buy. And as for dogs and cats, a lot of people of all ages and both sexes shared her beliefs. Where he thought Helen went a little off the deep end was with her apparent preoccupation with death and the afterlife.

He knew, for example, that she had spent a half a million dollars on the elaborate granite and marble tomb in Unionport. Capping the mausoleum was a $75,000 frontispiece carved from a chunk of marble that she had personally selected during a special trip to Vermont. In his view, that *was* a little excessive.

But it was not this that set some to wondering. What made Moore and others slightly skeptical of Helen Brach's rationality was the fact that she was a staunch believer in being able to communicate with the departed via automatic writing. But, all things considered, Moore decided it was too early to panic. If she had any enemies or if there was anyone who wished to harm her, Moore did not know about it. Just because Helen had been incommunicado for a few days was no reason to call out the troops. In fact, he was so little troubled that he did not call Matlick or the police to ask about her for several days afterward.

About the time Moore was talking to Mouras, Matlick was on his way to O'Hare to pick up Charles Vorhees, who was flying in from Ohio. Some of those close to the case would later be curious about why it took Helen's brother thirty-six hours to respond to Matlick's request to come to Chicago, but no explanation was ever offered. It was not because Vorhees did not know Matlick or had reason to mistrust his information. In the eighteen years that Matlick had worked for Frank and Helen, Vorhees had met him a number of times and his sister had indicated to him on several occasions that she placed great trust in him.

Normally, Vorhees and Matlick saw each other several times a year, usually when Vorhees was visiting his sister or when Helen dispatched her caretaker to Ohio on a special errand of one type or another. The two men, however, had little in common and were not friends. Matlick had at least a nodding acquaintance with Richard Bailey, who called on Helen regularly at her home.

A self-effacing man of fifty-nine, seven years younger than his sister, Vorhees had been a railroad-car inspector for Conrail for thirty-seven years. Except for his fairly regular visits to Helen in Chicago and Fort Lauderdale, he had never traveled outside of his community of twelve hundred or met many of Helen's friends.

Matlick's call caught him somewhat by surprise, he told police, because he had no inkling that anything might have been wrong. He had talked briefly to his sister about two weeks before when she made a quick call to him from the Mayo Clinic, apparently just to let him know where she was. Other than that, he had not talked to her since January, when she stopped for a brief visit in Ohio on her way back from New York. It was not unusual, he added, for him not to have talked to his sister more than two times in just as many months.

Edging through the crowded airport terminal, Vorhees spotted Matlick and began walking toward him. The last time they had seen each other had been in mid-December, when Matlick drove to Ohio with the carload of Brach's candy Helen delivered to him every year so he could distribute the sweets as holiday presents in Hopedale.

After exchanging brief greetings, they went straight back to Helen's house. Once there, Vorhees deposited his suitcase in the room he customarily occupied when he visited Chicago, then returned to the parlor, where Matlick was waiting somewhat impatiently.

Matlick got right to the point. "There are some things your sister wants destroyed," Matlick said.

"What things?" Vorhees asked, only mildly curious.

"Her writings and her diaries," Matlick responded.

Vorhees was not surprised. He had known for years about his sister's belief that she could communicate with her departed family members. When she had told her brother about the automatic writings, he had scoffed at her, so she never mentioned it to him again. But he knew she kept at it. He also knew that she religiously wrote in her diary. As recently as the previous January, when she had visited Ohio, Vorhees had seen her scribbling away in a book with a white simulated leather cover.

Grabbing an empty cardboard box and shoving a pair of pliers into a back pocket, Matlick led Vorhees to the upstairs bedroom, as he had done with Moore the day before. And, as before, he opened one of the bottom drawers and pointed to the pile of papers that Vorhees assumed were the automatic writings.

As Matlick began loading the papers into the box, he explained that he figured it was better to destroy the papers immediately before the police could see them. If they were to give them to the detectives, Matlick said, they probably would be leaked to the media. And that, they agreed, was the last thing that Helen would have wanted.

Opening another drawer, Matlick pulled out two ledgerlike books, one brown and one green. On the cover of each was a notation that said "Five Year Diaries." To Vorhees, they appeared to be her old journals.

He did not see the white diary in which he had witnessed Helen writing in several weeks before.

As he watched, Matlick took the pliers and ripped off the small locks.

"Why did you do that?" Vorhees asked, surprised.

Matlick looked at him blankly. "The locks won't burn," he replied.

Later, each would swear that neither of them attempted to read what was inside.

After putting the journals in the box on top of the papers, Matlick picked up the carton and led the way downstairs.

Exiting the main part of the house, they crossed a small open space, where they stopped in front of a closed door. "This is the furnace room," Matlick explained, opening the door.

While Vorhees waited outside in the cold, Matlick went in with the box. He came out a few minutes later, saying he had fed the material into the fire.

After that, the two of them went to dinner. When they returned to the house, Vorhees, who did not touch tobacco, went into the den and turned on the television. Matlick, a chain-smoker, stayed in the kitchen and lit one cigarette after another.

The next morning, Monday, March 7, they went to the Glenview Police Department so Vorhees could file a missing person's report.

13

A Mysterious Weekend

T HAT'S RIGHT: Helen Brach, who normally traveled with a mountain of luggage, didn't even pack an overnight case. Yes, she had an injured hand and she was accustomed to having people do things for her, but she asked to be dropped at the curb at O'Hare, electing to fend for herself. Sure, it was cold, but Helen insisted on walking coatless into the airport.

"You mean in the middle of February in Chicago she didn't even keep her coat?" Joe Baumann asked.

"That's right," Matlick said, nodding vigorously. "When we got to the airport, she gave it to me and asked me to take it back to the house."

Baumann scratched his head, pondering his strategy. Once Charles Vorhees had gone through the formality of filing the missing person's report, Glenview police formally began an investigation. And the first person Baumann had wanted to talk to was Matlick.

"I want to make sure I understand this," Baumann said slowly. "Start over from the beginning and tell me exactly what happened."

Matlick shot him an exasperated glance. "Okay," he said, "I'll go through it again."

On Thursday, February 17, he said, Helen returned to Chicago, as planned, on a Northwest Orient flight from Rochester, arriving at O'Hare at about 4:00 P.M.

He picked her up in his Jeep, rather than driving one of Helen's more luxurious vehicles, and they went straight back to the house, arriving about an hour later because of heavy traffic. She was slightly irritated because he had shown up in his work vehicle, but otherwise she seemed more bubbly than normal, perhaps, he suggested, because she was excited about going to Florida.

At 5:30 he called his wife at the farm in Schaumburg and told her that he was not going home that night, as he usually did when Helen was home. Instead, he was going to remain in Glenview through the weekend. The trip to Florida was going to be different this time because Helen was moving from an apartment to a condo and she had a lot to do.

Later that evening, according to Matlick, Helen injured herself. As she was packing a trunk, he said, the lid fell on her right hand. Rather than allowing him to take her to the emergency room at nearby Skokie Valley Hospital, she decided to treat it herself by soaking it in ice water. The incident effectively brought their packing to a halt.

The next day, Friday, Helen wrote a series of checks, clearing up some items that she wanted to have settled before she left for Fort Lauderdale.

The rest of that day, all day Saturday, and part of the day Sunday, they bustled around getting things ready for the Florida move. On Sunday afternoon, a man whom Matlick had never seen before arrived to pick up Helen to take her to dinner.

"Do you have any idea who that was?" Baumann asked.

"No," Matlick said, adding that Helen had not introduced them and he did not feel it was his business to ask.

Baumann nodded, making a note. "What time did they get back?"

Matlick cocked his head, thinking. "It must have been at least midnight," he said.

"And what did you do while they were gone?" Baumann asked.

"Finished tidying up."

"Were there any phone calls?"

"Oh, yes," Matlick said. "Richard Bailey called."

That aroused Baumann's curiosity. When he had tried to question Bailey about his relationship with Helen, Bailey had been very abrupt, volunteering almost no information.

"What did he want?" the detective asked.

Matlick gave him a puzzled look. "He wanted to talk to Helen, of course."

"And what did you tell him?"

Matlick smiled. "I told him she was out on a date."

From the tone of his voice, Baumann could tell that Bailey and Matlick were not the best of friends.

Baumann leaned back in his chair. "Sorry," he said. "Go on with your story."

Early Monday, Matlick continued, *very* early by Helen's standards, she said she was ready to go. They got into her salmon-colored Cadillac sedan and Matlick drove to O'Hare. Since Helen had no luggage, he left her at the curb. It was about 7:00 A.M., maybe earlier. Before he drove away, Matlick said, Helen slipped out of the fur coat she had donned when they left the house and handed it to him. "Take this back," he quoted her as saying. "I won't be needing it in Florida."

And that, he said, was the last time he had seen or heard from her.

Baumann, who had been taking careful notes during Matlick's narrative, was curious about several of the caretaker's claims, but he decided to wait until he had a chance to do some more digging. However, there was one question he wanted to pose. "Did you and Mrs. Brach have any arguments or disagreements?" Baumann asked.

Matlick looked abashed. Well, he admitted uneasily, there had been one thing. While they were packing on Friday night, the subject of a 1963 Cadillac she had given him two years previously came up. They got into a spirited discussion, Matlick confessed, when he told her that he had had to sell the car because he needed the money to pay off a gambling debt. She was angry at the time, but by Monday she had cooled off and seemed to have forgotten about it.

"Is that it?" Baumann asked.

"That's it," Matlick replied.

In the following weeks, police began coming up with interesting unexplained tidbits, all of which suggested that the caretaker might have been a little less than truthful in his original statement.

For one thing, detectives were unable to prove Matlick's claim that Helen had returned by air from Minnesota. They found a Rochester taxi driver who, when shown Helen's picture, said he thought he had taken her to the airport but wasn't entirely certain. By the same token, members of the crew on the flight on which she had a reservation were unable to identify her positively as a passenger, even though her ticket had been used. Plus, although he searched the house carefully, Baumann had not been able to find the suitcase that Helen had taken to the clinic.

There was also the issue of Matlick's reference to an argument he and Helen had had over an old Cadillac that Helen had given him earlier. In his statement, Matlick said the quarrel started when he told her that weekend that he had to sell it to satisfy a gambling debt. But, when Baumann checked the records, he discovered that Matlick still owned the car. In fact, the title was still in his name as late as May 26, some ninety days after he allegedly told Helen that he had sold it. And even then, ownership had not gone very far. Rather than selling it, Matlick had simply transferred the title to his wife, Theresa.

A woman who had been a friend and business acquaintance of Helen's for thirteen years, Molly Goldstein, told Baumann that she was highly dubious of Matlick's claim that Helen would have elected to treat an injured hand herself. Helen was so health-conscious, Goldstein felt, that she would immediately have called an ambulance and demanded to be transported to the nearest hospital.

Another friend of Helen's, Joan Romance, said she dropped by unannounced at the Glenview estate on Friday, February 18, hoping to have a cup of coffee with Helen and catch her up on the neighborhood news. But when she pulled into the driveway and got out of her car, she was intercepted by a strange man who asked her what she wanted. She was there to see Helen, she said. Apparently taken by surprise, the man stammered that Mrs. Brach was not at home, but he offered to summon Matlick for her. Before she could respond, another man she did not know walked up and told her that Helen had not yet returned from Rochester but that she was expected the next week. As they were talking, she heard a noise from inside the house. When she asked what the noise was, the second man said there was some minor remodeling being done and that the house was a mess.

When he checked with the telephone company, Baumann learned that several outgoing calls had been placed from the Brach house during the crucial weekend. One, which Matlick later admitted making, had been to Marshall Field, the department store. Matlick had requested rush shipment of a meat-grinder attachment for a blender. Another call had been placed to the home number of the physician who had treated Helen's late husband, a man Helen had not talked to since Frank's death seven years before. The doctor said he had not been home that evening and whoever had called failed to leave a message. A third call was to the number of Everett Moore, and a fourth was made by Matlick to a cleaning and decorating service to ask them to send someone as soon as possible to repaint two rooms and replace a rug. What was curious was that Helen, who virtually lived on the telephone, never called any of her friends that weekend.

Several incoming calls also were noted. One was from Belton Mouras, who telephoned on Sunday morning. He told the detective that he had been careful not to make the call before 9:00 A.M., Chicago time, because he knew that Helen was rarely up before then. Matlick had answered the call, Mouras said, and told him that Helen was en route to Florida. This contradicted Matlick's claim that he did not take Helen to the airport until the following day.

A number of Helen's friends and usual telephone companions said they had tried to reach her over the weekend, but each had been told by Matlick that she was unavailable. Investigators were unable to find a single person who had called and actually been able to talk to her.

When he checked with the airlines, Baumann discovered that the first flight from O'Hare to Fort Lauderdale on February 21, the Monday after she checked out of the clinic, was not until mid-morning. Helen did not have a reservation on that flight or on any other that day. Baumann asked himself why Helen, who was not normally an early riser, would have opted to leave for the airport so early when there were no flights until ten and since she had no reservation. Undoubtedly, as a regular traveler to Florida, she had a good idea of the flight times. Just getting to the airport by seven must have been an inconvenience for her. That was compounded by the fact that she would have a wait of at least several hours before the first plane left. If she could not get on it, she would have had an even longer wait.

It was also unusual that Helen, a woman who was accustomed to being driven everywhere, had not called her Fort Lauderdale friends and arranged for them to meet her, since Matlick had confirmed that they were very accommodating.

And why would a woman who habitually traveled with more luggage than a baseball team leave for an extended stay in Florida without a single suitcase?

Finally, there was the question of the checks. When the detective went to Continental Illinois National Bank to try to verify Matlick's assertion that Helen had signed a stack of them that weekend, he discovered that two of them—one for three thousand dollars and another for two thousand—had been written to Matlick and a third, for one thousand, made payable to cash, also had been cashed by him. All told, there were fifteen checks totaling $13,117.40.

14

Unanswered Questions

B AUMANN SHUFFLED the checks around on his desk, laying them out in neat rows and studying them one at a time. His intuition told him they were important, but he wasn't sure how. Gathering them up, he put them back in the folder and headed for the door. "I'm going down to Helen Brach's bank," he told the officer at the next desk. "I don't think I'll be long."

The officer at the bank studied the checks. "Excuse me just a minute," he said. When he returned, he had a card with Helen Brach's signature on it. Holding it up to the signature on one of the checks, he shook his head. "It isn't even close," he said.

That disclosure gave Baumann a good excuse to go back and question Matlick some more. "Why," he asked the caretaker, a hint of roughness in his voice, "would the bank tell me it isn't Mrs. Brach's signature on these checks if you claim you saw her sign them?"

"That's easy," Matlick replied glibly. "It doesn't look like her signature because she was writing with her injured hand."

Baumann nodded. "Then you wouldn't mind if I get a sample of your handwriting, would you?"

"Not at all," Matlick said, asking Baumann if he could borrow his pen.

"One more thing," Baumann said, pocketing his Bic. "These checks to you—what were they for?"

Matlick looked at the checks. The one for three thousand was his Christmas bonus. Mrs. Brach had just been late in giving it to him. The one for two thousand was meant to cover the payoff on another vehicle that Matlick had purchased.

"Okay," Baumann said, "I'll get back to you."

When the detective took the checks to an expert and asked him if writing with an injured hand could account for the noticeable departure from her normal signature, he was told absolutely not. The signatures on the checks bore no resemblance to Helen Brach's, the expert said, and the difference would not have been that great even if her hand had been tender.

Baumann showed him the handwriting sample he had gotten from Matlick. "Could the person who wrote this have signed the checks?"

The expert looked at the sample and at the signatures.

"Definitely not," he said.

When asked to go over his story about that weekend yet again, Matlick kept his tale essentially unchanged; he continued to insist that events had transpired just as he had laid them out earlier.

At that point, Baumann carefully considered his next move. There certainly were enough questions about Matlick's statement to make him worth looking at further. There were also questions about Bailey, but there wasn't much Baumann could do about that. By remaining silent, Bailey had successfully channeled the police's attention toward Matlick, who was, after all, the only person to claim that Helen had returned safely from Rochester and was alive at least until the following Monday. Efforts to track down the mysterious Sunday-night dinner date had proved futile. The only thing Baumann was sure of was that the dinner date had *not* been Bailey. When asked where he had been, Bailey had flourished receipts showing he had been registered at a Florida hotel beginning the day before Helen left the clinic.

The more he considered whether Matlick might have been involved, the more Baumann kept asking himself why.

What had he gained other than a few thousand dollars? And a few thousand was definitely not worth a murder charge, given the fact that the victim was worth millions.

What could Matlick's motive have been? A disagreement about a vehicle that had originally been a gift did not seem enough to turn a trusted employee of almost twenty years into a killer.

If he was lying about Helen being home that weekend—and that seemed increasingly likely—why? Was he protecting someone? If so, whom? And, just as important, why?

For that matter, Baumann wondered, why would *anyone* want Helen Brach dead? She was a harmless, incredibly rich eccentric who lived in a world considerably different from that of most people, a world largely populated by others in more or less the same circumstances.

If she had been kidnapped, there had been no demand for ransom, no contact at all from the abductors. That, too, was strange.

It seemed unlikely that she had been killed by someone who thought they could get immediate access to her money. The bank had told him that except for those fifteen checks, no other withdrawals had been made against Helen's account. And her credit-card reports showed no charges since the forty-one-dollar purchase she had made at the Buckskin Shop on February 17.

Maybe it was inheritance, Baumann thought. Whom was she going to leave her money to?

What he soon found out about that was that he was not going to find out at all.

When he went to see the lawyer he believed had drawn up Helen's will, John Conway told the detective to go whistle. As far as he was concerned, Helen Brach was alive; no body had been found and no convincing evidence had been presented to show she was dead. That meant that he was bound by lawyer/client confidentiality not to say anything about her heirs.

Although an attempt was made to force Conway to turn over the will by asking for a court order mandating him to do so, Conway told the judge the same thing he had told Baumann: no way.

The judge reacted angrily. Declaring Conway in contempt, he ordered him to pay a one-thousand-dollar fine and serve ten days in jail, although the jail sentence was later withdrawn. Conway appealed the contempt charge.

But the judge's ruling offered no relief to Baumann. He still didn't have a motive for Helen's disappearance.

From his perspective, the detective had only one avenue left. Calling Matlick, he asked him a simple question: "Would you be willing to take a lie-detector test?"

"Sure," said Matlick.

While polygraph examinations are not normally admissible as evidence of guilt in Illinois courts, detectives like them because it makes their job easier. If a suspect flunks a polygraph, that fact won't put him in prison. But if he passes, it helps eliminate him and investigators can focus their attention elsewhere. In Matlick's case, Baumann's plan flopped. The caretaker ended up taking *two* tests, both of which were graded "inconclusive."

Baumann was stumped. There was no direct evidence that Matlick had any connection with Helen's disappearance. Many of the claims that he had made may have been questionable, but there was nothing totally incriminating, either.

After a reporter found out about Matlick ordering the meat-grinder attachment from Marshall Field & Company, there was speculation that Helen had been killed in her house and her body ground up and fed to her dogs.

But Baumann had determined that the type of equipment that Matlick had ordered—an attachment that fit on a blender—would not have been up to the heavy-duty task of grinding up the body of a woman who weighed 138 pounds.

And the fact that Matlick also had ordered in a decorator sounded encouraging until the men who did the work told Baumann they had not noticed anything unusual in the space they had been commissioned to renovate.

While checking at the bank, Baumann also learned that Matlick had visited Helen's safe-deposit box on February 21, but that was hardly inculpating, since Helen herself had earlier given authorization for him to have access. When asked why he had been to the box, Matlick said Helen had asked him to put some jewelry there.

There was no way of verifying that or of determining if he took anything out, since there was no list of the contents.

In the absence of a viable suspect, a motive, or a body—in fact, any strong evidence at all that a crime had been committed—Baumann was up against it. All he could do was hope for a break.

For Baumann, it never came. The trail grew colder and eventually, in the absence of any new revelations, the investigation sputtered to a complete stop.

Sporadically, it looked as if the probe might be revitalized. A little more than a year after Helen's disappearance, expectations soared when the nude body of an elderly woman was discovered in a wooded park on Chicago's South Side. Although authorities hoped to prove the body to be Helen's, the medical examiner declared it unidentifiable because of severe decomposition. While refusing to say who it might be, he said it was *not* Helen Brach. He said he reached that conclusion because the mystery woman wore dentures, whereas Helen had not.

After a flurry of publicity, the body was buried in potter's field. A dozen years later, in 1990, because of renewed interest in Helen's disappearance, the body was exhumed so experts, using more advanced technology, could reexamine the corpse, especially the dental work. However, when forensic experts opened the casket, they discovered to their considerable surprise that the head was missing. The medical examiner's office has not been able to explain the odd development, positing that it might have been sent to an outside lab for analysis. But so far, no one has been able to find any record indicating which lab it might have been sent to. A number of people knowledgeable about the case believe that the body was indeed Helen's and that the head was stolen from the morgue by lackeys working for those who killed her.

Investigators also thought they were onto something in 1979, two years after Helen's disappearance, when two boys on their way to school found a message painted in red on the road near Helen's estate. It read: RICHARD BAILEY KNOWS WHERE MRS. BRACH'S BODY IS! STOP HIM! PLEASE!

When questioned about why someone might want to point a finger at him, Bailey confessed he had found similar messages defacing property in and around his stables.

"Show them to us," the investigators urged.

"Too late," Bailey replied. "I painted over them. They would have been bad for business."

Who did he think had been the graffiti artist? Bailey shrugged. Most likely a competitor. The horse business was cutthroat and everybody was always trying to gig everyone else.

The investigators pressed. Could he name someone he thought it might *possibly* be?

Bailey supplied a few names.

Gradually, after Baumann and other investigators who had become involved ran out of leads, the criminal investigation wound down. The FBI, which had been contacted soon after Helen disappeared, declined an invitation to get involved, claiming there was no evidence a federal law had been violated. Later, one of the lawyers immersed in the civil proceedings stemming from Helen's disappearance would claim that was hogwash, since there was ample evidence that checks had been forged, and *that* was a federal crime. But second-guessing the FBI was as futile as Monday-morning quarterbacking the Bears. The FBI had *not* entered the investigation and that was it. It was likely that no one would ever know exactly why.

*   *   *

As the criminal investigation phase slid into the shadows because it had nowhere else to go, the examination of Helen's fate became an exercise in civil law. The first shot in that battle had been the attempt to force Helen's lawyer, John Conway, to produce her will. But that went nowhere when Conway elected to face a judge's wrath rather than turn it over.

In the wake of that incident, a much more protracted and bitter fight began shaping up over a dispute regarding Helen's money and who had authority to control it.

While lacking the pizzazz of a juicy criminal disclosure, the money issue was fascinating because of its uniqueness: Who has the right to make decisions for someone who simply is not there? If a person is dead, the issues are settled at probate; if they are alive, they are adjudicated in a civil court. But Helen Brach was neither alive nor dead. She was just absent.

On one side in the looming war was the Continental Illinois National Bank & Trust Company, which administered a $7 million trust set up for Helen by her late husband. On the other side was Everett Moore, who, in the weeks immediately following her disappearance, had been named administrator of her estate. As administrator, he would seem to be the man delegated to keeping Helen's financial affairs in order so everything would be up-to-date in case she should reappear. As long as she was not officially dead—a decree that could not be issued until she had been missing for seven years—she had to be considered alive, either voluntarily incommunicado or suffering from some ailment that prevented her from picking up her life where she had left off.

Basically, the fight was over what should be done with the $300,000 in interest that Frank Brach's trust earned every year. Continental Bank, which was responsible for administering the trust (as opposed to Moore), felt that money should remain in the trust account and be available for investment by the bank however its officers deemed suitable. Moore, on the other hand, who was responsible for all of Helen's other money, thought the trust interest should be considered as Helen's income and funneled to her nontrust account. In that case, *he* would have the authority to invest it.

What contributed toward making this such a contentious issue was that there were different beneficiaries from the two accounts. If Helen were eventually to be declared dead, the money from the trust would go one way, while the funds from the Moore-administered account would go another. There was a genuine fear on the part of the judge who had been asked to settle the issue that if the interest money got comingled, the situation probably would never be straightened out.

Since the two sides could not agree on what should be done, Chancery Division Judge George Schaller decided that a neutral party was needed to represent Helen, since the bank and Moore were both, in opposing ways, representing their own interests. In law, such a non-partisan party selected to represent an individual is called a Guardian Ad Litem—literally, a temporary caretaker who would serve only until that specific dispute could be settled. In this case, the GAL selected by the judge was John Cadwalader Menk, a man with thirty-five years of experience in Chicago's civil courts and a former president of the influential Chicago Bar Association.

Feisty and fractious, Menk was a seasoned fighter, a man who would not be intimidated by the high-priced legal talent each of the opposing sides had retained.

While Moore and the bank had the advantage in the number of lawyers they could hire to present their respective viewpoints, Menk had the edge in authority. As GAL, he had virtual carte blanche to do whatever he thought necessary to resolve the situation, including conducting what amounted to a criminal investigation under the guise of a civil action. In addition, he had something the police did not: subpoena power. If Menk wanted to interview someone connected to Helen's disappearance, he could do so while that person was *under oath.*

Since Menk was not one of those lawyers who would be content to sit back and assume the role of passive referee, he took it upon himself to try as best he could, independent of any law-enforcement investigation, to try to determine what had happened to Helen Brach. Almost immediately, as a means to this end, Menk scheduled a series of deposition hearings.

The criminal—as opposed to civil—equivalent of this procedure is an interrogation. It amounts to summoning someone and subjecting them to a rigid question-and-answer session. The main difference between a deposition hearing and a police interrogation is that the responses to questions posed by someone such as Menk carry the responsibility of truth. Since the person being deposed has to swear that the answers being given are accurate, statements made at a deposition hearing are akin to testimony given in court; they have a definite engraved-in-stone aspect. Any variation between that testimony and later conflicting statements can open that person up to criminal charges. Another difference is that the transcripts of deposition hearings, unlike police interrogations, become public record. A third difference is that the questioners are not hard-bitten, blunt policemen, but high-priced civil lawyers clad in expensive three-piece suits.

And a fourth difference lies in the surroundings where such hearings are held. The Brach deposition hearings were conducted not in a cramped precinct interrogation room, but in Menk's posh offices on the eighty-fourth floor of the Sears Tower, a location with a view of Chicago that could be equaled only from a low-flying airplane or helicopter. The benefits of the view and the luxurious surroundings, however, were lost on the four men Menk questioned about Helen Brach. One at a time, over a period of a year and a half, they trooped to Menk's well-appointed suite to settle uncomfortably behind a large, highly polished table and face a battery of lawyers, some of them openly hostile. The first to appear was Jack Matlick.

15

Stranger and Stranger
January 1978

Jack Matlick let his eyes sweep slowly around the room, glancing challengingly at the seven freshly barbered silk-stocking lawyers hovering over their pads of crisp yellow paper, expensive fountain pens poised in expectation.

A few minutes before, at precisely 2:30 in the afternoon on Wednesday, January 11, 1978, Matlick had ambled into Menk's Sears Tower suite 8420 in response to a formal order to appear and face a grilling about his possible role in his former employer's disappearance. Now that he was here, looking decidedly out of place among the pinstriped crowd in his off-the-rack suit and stained, out-of-fashion tie, he radiated defiance.

With a nod at Menk and the others, he rolled back one of the comfortable conference-room chairs and plopped into it. Crossing his calloused, work-hardened hands on the table in front of him, Matlick jutted his chin and waited for the inquisition to begin.

Staring back at him from their seats along the length of the table were Richard C. Robin, James S. Stanhaus, and Arthur M. Gorov, all of whom represented Continental Bank; Robert E. Pfaff, who was there on behalf of Frank Brach's grandchildren, Frank Brach III and Brian; Edgar G. Ballard, Jr., who represented Frank's daughter, Joyce Brach Whartmann, and John H. Conway, attorney for Everett Moore. At the head of the table was the chief inquisitor, the stern-faced Menk.

The questioning started amiably enough with Menk asking Matlick a series of background questions: when he went to work for the Brachs, what his duties were for Helen, and who else had worked in the house and when.

At one point, Matlick rambled, there had been, in addition to himself, a live-in housekeeper and two part-time employees who came in two or three days a week. The housekeeper had retired in 1966, four years before Frank died, although she occasionally came back to help Helen on special occasions. There was another woman, whose name Matlick could not recall, who worked there only for about eight months; she was replaced by a woman named Louise Mathes. Mathes had asked for a leave of absence in late 1975 or early 1976 while she underwent surgery on her eye. Although she remained on the payroll, she had not been back on the job after her surgery and Helen had hired a woman from Florida to fill the job. But as of the previous February, when Helen disappeared, the new housekeeper had not yet arrived. From the time Mathes left in 1976 until Helen disappeared in February 1977, he had been the only full-time employee.

In addition to his work at the Brach residence, Matlick added, he also was manager in residence at the Schaumburg property, which was leased to someone else, a person who actually did the farming. Until Helen disappeared, he had commuted between Schaumburg and Glenview, but after her disappearance, he had moved to the Glenview house so someone would always be there.

At least, he added a little bitterly, that had been the situation until a month before, when Everett Moore had fired him. Moore, though, was letting him stay at the Schaumburg house rent-free until he could find a new job.

Menk exhaled softly. Now that the preliminaries had been taken care of, he could get to some serious questions. Betraying his background as a civil lawyer who dealt on a daily basis with money matters, Menk was particularly curious about Helen's financial situation, since he hoped that would give him a clue about who might have wanted to abduct her.

"Do you have a copy of Mrs. Brach's will?" he asked Matlick.

If the caretaker was surprised by the question, he didn't show it. "I do not," he answered without hesitation.

"Do you have any papers of any kind which make any reference to Mrs. Brach's will?" he asked.

"No," Matlick replied.

"Do you know if Mrs. Brach *made* a will?" he asked, aware of the irony that hung heavily in the room because of the presence of John Conway, the lawyer who was believed to have helped Helen draft her will but who had accepted a contempt sentence rather than reveal any details about the document.

"Yes, sir," Matlick answered crisply.

"How do you know that?"

"For the simple reason that she *said* she made it," Matlick replied.

Did he know who the beneficiaries were?

"Yes," Matlick answered forcefully. "She told me exactly. She said she would make her brother a millionaire but that she did not want his wife to have any of her money. *Her money,*" he added for emphasis. "All right? So instead of giving him the money, she was going to set up a trust fund for him and the rest was to go to the animals."

"Animals?" Menk asked.

"Yes," Matlick said. "The felines, the dogs, this sort of thing. She had a soft spot for animals. She sent donations, I guess, all over the United States, from the way the mail came in. Her opinion was, there's always somebody to take care of the human beings, but there's very few that look out after the animals."

Anxious to pursue the will issue, Menk kept after him.

"Did she ever tell you where she put the original will?" he asked.

Not the original, Matlick replied, but he had seen a copy—uncovered it, in fact, when he was cleaning out the house about six months after Helen disappeared. It had been in an envelope in the nightstand in her bedroom.

Did he read it? Menk asked, his interest quickening.

"No," said Matlick. "I just glanced through it."

Was he a beneficiary? Menk asked carefully.

"No!" Matlick shot back. "No way. I was no beneficiary."

Menk was prepared to ask another question when Matlick added, "I took the copy to the police station to show them. That's when the newspapers broke that I was a beneficiary."

Menk's eyebrows arched. This was information he'd never heard before.

"You took a copy of the will—"

"Right—"

"—to the police station?"

"That's right."

The lawyer shook his head. There had been no mention of this in any of the investigator's reports he had seen. Had he overlooked it? Had the detectives failed to put it in? Or had Matlick just made it up? Scribbling a note to himself to follow up on the subject, Menk turned back to the witness. "What did you do with the copy?" he asked.

"It's in the house, where it belongs," Matlick replied, adding that he had returned it to the drawer in which he had found it.

Menk paused, searching his memory. He was certain now that none of the police reports had mentioned a will. And neither had Howard O. Roos, a private investigator hired by Everett Moore to make an inventory of the contents of the house after Matlick was told some three weeks earlier to vacate the premises. Roos, Menk remembered, had emphasized how thoroughly he had been through the house, spending an entire day there. Riffling through his file, he found a copy of Roos's report. The PI claimed he had examined "every crawl space and the attic space" as well as "every drawer and cabinet" and he reviewed "every writing" he could find. There was no mention of a will.

"You didn't destroy it?" Menk asked Matlick, speaking slowly and distinctly.

"I did not!" Matlick replied, as if his honor had been attacked.

"Did you destroy any of her records?"

"No records! No, sir," Matlick said emphatically.

Realizing that he had not asked the question the right way, Menk backtracked. "Did you destroy any of her *papers*?"

"Yes, sir. I destroyed two old diaries and some automatic writing."

The lawyers exchanged puzzled looks. None of them had ever heard of automatic writing and Matlick lacked the ability to articulate precisely what he meant. "It's a writing that she made—" he began.

"Is it a culture?" asked Merwin Auslander, Matlick's lawyer.

"They teach it in the colleges," Matlick stammered. "You know, automatic writing."

Suddenly, the deposition hearing had taken on a game-show quality, a situation that would have been laughable if the purpose had not been so serious.

"Shorthand?" asked the attorney representing Frank Brach's daughter.

"What does it look like?" asked Auslander.

"Describe it," Menk prodded. "Are there words and sentences?"

Matlick, looking confused, responded monosyllabically. "Yes."

"Then what makes it automatic?" Menk urged, frustrated.

"She'd sit down and pick up a pen and write. Whether it is spiritual—"

"Oh!" Auslander exclaimed. "I see! Something like the occult. I *have* heard of it now. Under hypnosis, people supposedly do these things."

"Let me find out," Menk interrupted. "I'm uneducated on the subject."

"I can't believe this," mumbled Gorov, one of the other attorneys.

"You'd *better* believe it," Menk told Gorov in an aside. Turning to Matlick, he asked, "Is it writing that you could read?"

The handyman shrugged. "Yes and no. Sometimes you could read it and sometimes you couldn't."

And where did she get the messages that she wrote down? Menk wanted to know.

"She didn't claim she got the messages anywhere! They were just *there*. And she asked me in case anything was to ever happen, I was to destroy them. And I did just that."

He then described how he and Helen's brother, Charles, had taken a drawerful of papers from Helen's dresser, along with two diaries, and thrown them in the furnace.

What had prompted them to look for diaries? Menk asked.

She had kept diaries for years, Matlick replied. Anyone who knew her at all was aware of that.

"Had you seen them?"

"Sure."

"Had you seen her writing in them?"

"Yes," Matlick said. "Had I read them? No."

"I didn't ask you that," Menk snapped.

"I have seen the diaries," Matlick replied, nonplussed. "The two I destroyed were from way back. They pertained to nothing but to her and Mr. Brach's life together." He knew that, he added, not because he had read them but because that was what Helen had told him.

What about her current one? Menk wanted to know.

"That, we have never located," Matlick said. "Not the police or anybody else. It was a white one and she must have it with her."

Satisfied that he was not going to get any more information from Matlick about Helen's journals, Menk asked about Helen herself. When was the last time he had seen her?

"February twenty-first!" Matlick said promptly. "When I got her to the airport."

Eager to probe that subject, Menk asked Matlick if he had made a flight reservation for Helen before he took her to O'Hare.

"I object to that!" Auslander broke in. "Don't answer that, Mr. Matlick!"

Menk looked up in surprise. "Why?" he asked, puzzled, because to him it seemed a very innocuous question.

"It is irrelevant," Auslander said.

Menk disagreed, prompting Matlick to answer the question.

"We can sit here all afternoon," Auslander replied testily, "but he is not going to answer you."

"I'll take the Fifth," Matlick interjected, picking up on his lawyer's lead.

"You can do what you wish," Auslander told Menk, ignoring his client.

Matlick's head swung back and forth, like a spectator at a tennis match, as his lawyer and Menk fought over his right to refuse to answer under the Fifth Amendment.

"If you'll be quiet a minute . . ." Menk said to Auslander. "As far as I'm concerned, you—"

"A judge might very well overrule me. . . ."

"You have a very bad habit of interrupting," Menk said angrily. "I don't interrupt you. Don't interrupt me. I don't like it."

"Well," Auslander replied, "we'll just plead the Fifth Amendment entirely."

They continued to bicker for another ten minutes, until Menk reluctantly changed the subject.

"Did you make a thorough search for any other diaries?" he asked.

Matlick looked at Auslander.

"You can answer that," his lawyer said.

"Yes," Matlick replied. "With the police."

After flipping through his notes, Menk decided to charge ahead into another sensitive area: whether Matlick would admit to forging the checks on Helen's account that had been issued that weekend. "Did you prepare a group of checks for her to sign that few days before she disappeared?" he asked as innocently as he could.

Matlick, though, could recognize a train heading in his direction. "I refuse to answer on the grounds it may tend to incriminate me," he said.

"Did you get the proceeds from some of those checks?"

Matlick replied, "I refuse to answer on the grounds it may tend to incriminate me."

After he got the same response when he asked the handyman if he had ever written checks for Helen or if he knew where her checkbook was, Menk surrendered in frustration.

Robert Pfaff, the attorney representing Frank's grandsons, took over the questioning. Following Menk's lead, he tried to get more information about the will, but the effort was largely in vain.

Edgar Ballard, Jr., the lawyer for Frank's daughter, Joyce, also took a swing at the will issue and was successful only to the extent that he got Matlick to expand upon what he had done when he found the copy in Helen's nightstand. In response to a question about whether he had skimmed through it, Matlick grew irascible. "That's correct!" he growled. "At that time, I was supposed to have been in her will and that's when I glanced through it. That's when I went over to the police station and presented it to the chief to show him that I wasn't in the damn will, as the newspapers had stated it."

James Stanhaus, one of the lawyers representing Continental Bank, tried to pump Matlick about the diaries, asking him why he and Charles Vorhees destroyed the two journals they had found if they were, as he had said, old ones that had no application to current events.

"Because they pertained to the personal life of Mrs. Brach and Mr. Brach," Matlick said agitatedly. Besides, he added, Helen had told him explicitly that's what she wanted done if anything ever happened to her.

And the automatic writing? Stanhaus asked. Why had he destroyed those papers?

"Because she didn't want anyone else reading it," the recently fired caretaker replied.

With only one final, bitter exchange between Menk and Auslander over whether Matlick would waive his right to examine and sign the transcript of the interview, the session dissolved, to no one's satisfaction, except possibly Matlick's.

The man who, by his own admission, was the last known person to see Helen Brach alive scooped up his topcoat and strolled out of the lawyer's plush skyscraper office, certain that would be the end of his official involvement in the case of Helen Brach. He was right. As of this writing, no criminal charges have ever been filed against him in connection with Helen's disappearance. Not long after giving the deposition, he left Chicago and returned to his native Pennsylvania.

Matlick may have been satisfied with the results, but Menk was not. Convinced that the handyman had raised more questions than he had answered, Menk contacted the Glenview police and asked if they could verify that Matlick, as he claimed under oath, had shown them a copy of Helen's will.

"What will?" replied the Glenview police chief. "We never saw any will."

Now *that* was curious, Menk thought, hanging up.

Within a few days, the lawyer had prepared a formal request, asking Judge Schaller to authorize him to search the Glenview residence. He wanted, he said, a for-the-record examination of the premises to see what could be found. At the very least, he hoped to recover the copy of the will that Matlick had mentioned. And if he was really lucky, he might find the diary Helen had been keeping when she disappeared or some of Helen's automatic writing that Matlick and Charles Vorhees may have overlooked. Menk figured there was little chance of that, though, since Matlick had been in the house alone for more than nine months, which would have been more than enough time for him to look for and destroy such material. Besides, Moore's private investigator, Roos, had been through the house just after Matlick vacated it and he had come up empty-handed. Still, he figured, it didn't hurt to try.

Schaller approved Menk's request on January 27, but the search itself would not take place for another eight weeks. In the meantime, Menk went ahead with his original plan to take depositions from the major players. Next on his list was Helen's brother, Charles Vorhees, the only person still alive who possibly knew the missing heiress better than Jack Matlick.

16

"Burn This!"
March 1978

O N MARCH 1, precisely seven weeks almost to the hour after Matlick had vacated the same chair, a highly agitated Charles Vorhees, flanked by his two attorneys, sat squirming under the gaze of the Menk-convened panel.

Moore's lawyer, John Conway, was there again, as was Edgar Ballard, Jr., who represented Frank's daughter. James Stanhaus, who represented Continental Bank, and Arthur Gorov, another lawyer involved in the Continental Bank/Moore dispute, also had returned. New to the group was Robert E. Elliott, Jr., another Continental Bank attorney.

Shuffling the stack of papers in front of him, playing for time, Menk surreptitiously eyed the fidgety witness. What he saw was a gawky, confused-looking refugee from the Ohio hill country, an unsophisticated blue-collar worker who looked as nervous among the gathering of polished Loop lawyers as a rabbit who had inadvertently wandered into a coyote den. Although both he and Matlick had limited educations, Vorhees lacked Matlick's street smarts and innate cunning. Matlick was a canny urbanite, a man sharpened and made wary by the need to survive in a large, cold city. Vorhees appeared to Menk to be a guileless country bumpkin.

Watching carefully as Vorhees's gaze flicked nervously from one panel member to the next, never pausing long enough to establish eye contact, Menk's wonderment grew. Why is he so flustered? Menk asked himself. What reason does he have to be so jittery? As far as he knew, Vorhees was not a suspect in his sister's disappearance. Other than Matlick's claim that Helen's will would make him a millionaire, an assertion that Menk was prepared to accept with a grain of salt, in lieu of the actual document, Vorhees would have no apparent motive for being involved. Yet something was causing him undue disquiet.

As he contemplated Vorhees's skittishness, Menk's intuition, honed from years of combat in Chicago's mean courts, began to take over. His behavior, Menk concluded, went beyond what would be expected of someone who was merely uneasy about suddenly finding himself in strange surroundings. "I got the impression," Menk said, years later, "that Charles Vorhees was quite frightened. And it wasn't just because he was in an unfamiliar location with a group of people he didn't know." Menk has never been able to figure out exactly what it was that had Vorhees so spooked.

Unlike his strategy with Matlick, who Menk had perceived could more than hold his own under interrogation, the GAL approached Vorhees gingerly, beginning the session with a series of nonthreatening questions about where he lived, what he did, and how he got along with his sister.

The only interesting tidbit the preliminary quiz turned up was the fact that Vorhees had been receiving roughly ten thousand dollars a year from a special trust that Helen had set up for him a dozen years earlier. While money was always a strong motive for murder, Menk did not sense that greed was one of Vorhees's personality traits. Even if Matlick's belief that Vorhees would stand to reap considerable financial gain from Helen's death was correct, Menk could not comprehend a circumstance under which the mild-mannered Vorhees would be a participant in a cold-blooded assassination plot against his own sister.

About thirty minutes into the session, Menk began getting around to what he considered more serious issues, especially Vorhees's apparent acceptance of Matlick's highly improbable story. Didn't he wonder why Helen, a notorious late riser, would ask to be dropped off at the airport so early in the morning?

"Did he tell you what time he took her to the airport?" Menk asked.

"Yes," said Vorhees. "At about six o'clock in the morning."

"Did he tell you why he took her out so early?"

"That's when she wanted to go."

"Why would she want to go then," Menk queried, "when the first flight wasn't for several hours?"

"Jack said she liked to go to the airport and walk around and shop," Vorhees said.

"*Shop?*" Menk asked incredulously. "At six o'clock in the morning?"

"I don't know," Vorhees responded. "That's what he told me."

Had Matlick also told him why he didn't go inside with her, considering that she had no reservation?

"He said she told him not to," Vorhees replied.

According to Matlick, although it was bitterly cold, Helen took off her fur coat and gave it to him, ordering him to take it back to the house. "Did you ever ask Jack about that?" Menk wanted to know.

Vorhees said he had not. Neither had he asked if his sister had been carrying a suitcase, nor what airline she intended to fly. He also admitted that he had not suggested they look through Helen's things to try to find out what might have happened to her; nor had he raised any objection when Matlick proposed they destroy the automatic writings and Helen's diaries.

What had he said when Matlick told him he wanted to burn the material? Menk asked, unable to fathom Vorhees's passivity.

"I said all right," Vorhees replied.

"All right *what?*" Menk pressed.

"I *said,*" Vorhees explained, " 'If that's what she wants.' "

"How did you know that's what she wanted?"

"I had no reason to distrust Jack."

Had he suggested they tell the police first?

"No," said Vorhees.

"Did that thought cross your mind?"

"No, it didn't," Vorhees said, adding that Matlick had not wanted the police to see the papers because he believed if they gave them to the police, the police would turn them over to reporters.

"Did you think those papers might be helpful to the police in their investigation? Did it occur to you that they might be?"

"No, it didn't," said Vorhees. "I didn't think anything had happened to her."

Then why destroy them? Menk asked.

"I told you. They were personal."

"Well, assuming she might turn up?" Menk pressed.

"They were still personal," Vorhees added doggedly.

Confounded by the logic, Menk asked Vorhees if Jack had offered an opinion on what may have happened to Helen.

At first, Vorhees said, Matlick believed Helen had amnesia, but about two weeks later he had changed his mind.

"What did he say then?"

"He thought she was dead."

In a long series of terse responses, Vorhees revealed that there had been a note on top of the stack of automatic writings that Matlick had shown him. Menk perked up; Matlick had not mentioned a note in his deposition.

What did it say? Menk wanted to know.

"Burn this!" Vorhees said.

"In whose handwriting?" Menk asked with interest.

"My sister's."

"Is that all it said?"

"That's all it said."

"Was it addressed to anybody?"

"No."

"It said, 'Burn this!'?"

"Right."

"That's all?"

"That's all."

Eager to pursue the issue that Matlick had raised earlier about the will, Menk asked Vorhees if Matlick had mentioned the document to him.

"No," he said, although he had read about it in the newspapers and in his copy of Matlick's deposition.

Nodding at Conway, Helen's lawyer, who was sitting across the table, Menk asked Vorhees if he had asked him about a will?

"No," Vorhees said.

Had he asked Everett Moore?

"Didn't ask anyone," Vorhees replied tartly.

Had Helen ever told him that she had prepared a will?

"No."

Had Matlick ever said anything to him about the will since it was in the newspapers?

"I haven't talked to him," Vorhees replied.

Didn't the fact that Matlick claimed that Helen was going to leave him a millionaire make him curious enough to ask about it?

"No," Vorhees replied.

"You are not interested enough to ask, I take it," Menk commented.

"If [Conway] won't show it to the court, he sure won't show it to me," Vorhees replied dryly.

Interviewing Helen's brother, Menk was coming to understand, was both difficult and frustrating. His short, sullen answers made Matlick seem verbose. Every answer had to be dragged out of Vorhees, every question presented in such a way that Vorhees could answer in as few words as possible. He almost never elaborated upon a response and sometimes Menk had to go over the same issue several times to get what he considered a decent answer.

"Did you see any other papers of hers in the bedroom besides these automatic writings and the diaries?"

"No."

"Of course, those were the only two drawers that Matlick opened."

"That's right."

"Then he told you to come downstairs."

"That's right."

"Were you doing pretty much everything he told you to do?" he asked, curious to see if that would get his attention.

It did. "We were doing it together!" Vorhees snapped.

Menk persisted. Had he done everything Matlick had told him?

Vorhees's response was probably his longest of the day. "He didn't say, 'Come downstairs.' When we got the papers, we walked downstairs. He didn't say, 'Follow me.' "

"It was his idea to go up to the bedroom, wasn't it?"

"Right."

"He got the box and the pliers and opened the diaries, right?"

"Correct."

"And he said, 'Let's go downstairs'?"

"Do you say, 'Let's walk out into the other office'?" Vorhees replied sarcastically.

"And you went along?" Menk asked, ignoring the tone.

"I went along."

"So when you got down to the kitchen, then what did you do?"

"Went out to the furnace."

It took Menk twenty-one more questions to determine that Matlick, unaccompanied by Vorhees, took the box containing the papers into the furnace room and returned without the papers, leaving Vorhees to assume that he had burned them. Then it took another fifteen minutes for Menk to establish that the two men had virtually no further conversation from then until the next afternoon, when Vorhees returned to Ohio. All told, Vorhees had spent less than forty-eight hours in Chicago.

He came back, Vorhees said after another long series of questions, toward the end of March to talk to the police again. But from then on, for the next year, except for a quick trip to sign a document allowing Moore to be named administrator of Helen's estate, he had not revisited the city.

Had he tried to follow developments by telephoning Moore or Helen's attorneys? Menk asked.

"No," Vorhees said.

How about the police?

"I have talked to them several times and they have been down to Ohio," Vorhees said.

"When were they down to Ohio?" Menk asked.

"Last spring sometime, I think it was," Vorhees said, meaning almost a year before.

Baffled by Vorhees's passivity, Menk decided to make one more attempt to see if he had talked to *anyone* about his sister and her possible fate.

"Did you ever talk to the investigator that was hired by Mr. Moore?"

"He called me once."

"When was that?"

"When he first hired him."

"That was how long ago?"

"Three months."

"He called you in Ohio?"

"That's right."

"What did he want to know?"

"He didn't want to know anything. He called me and told me he was hired and was going to go to Florida and check for my sister and get in touch with me later."

"Did he?"

"No."

Did he go to Florida?

"I don't know."

Menk threw up his hands. "I think that's all the questions I have," he said.

❧

Gorov and Ballard also tried questioning Vorhees, but they had no more luck than Menk. The best Ballard could do was elicit a detailed—for Vorhees—response to a request to expand on his explanation of how Helen did her automatic writing.

"Well," Vorhees answered in exasperation, "she tried to explain that you relax and let everything go limp, or something, and hold a pencil in your hand; pretty soon your hand automatically will start writing. That's all I know."

Taken as a whole, Vorhees's deposition was not as remarkable for the information it imparted as for the portrait it painted of the man being deposed. After some two hours of questioning by Menk and two other lawyers, Vorhees emerged as a man who did not reveal any of his grief over the loss of his only sibling. Rather, he seemed a curiously cold man, a man who seemed to have little interest in investigating what had happened to his sister or in the possibility that he stood to become a millionaire. It was strange, Menk thought. Very strange indeed.

But Menk had little time to consider the intricacies of Charles Vorhees's personality quirks. A short four weeks later, roughly fifty-eight weeks after Helen left the Mayo Clinic, a group that included Menk and four other lawyers, plus Detective Baumann, gathered at the Wagner Road house, court order in hand, ready to do whatever was necessary in an effort to find any scraps of information pertaining to Helen's disappearance. Since investigators had so far been unable to explain satisfactorily why she had vanished, much less when or how, Menk figured anything the group discovered would be a bonus. Like partygoers on a treasure hunt, the searchers began their quest promptly at 10:00 A.M. They were successful almost immediately.

In the kitchen, one of the first rooms to be searched, they found an eleven-by-fourteen manila envelope in a cabinet drawer. Helen's name was on the front of the envelope and her lawyer's name and address was in the upper left-hand corner. Inside was a copy of the mysterious will. The five-page document was unsigned and undated except for a notation on the edge of one of the pages that read "1974."

Encouraged by this discovery, the searchers spread out in a systematic exploration of the rambling house. Although they found no diaries or anything that resembled the automatic writings that Matlick had described, they quickly discovered an item that was almost as interesting. In an upstairs room that apparently had been used to store miscellaneous clothing was a two-suiter suitcase that still had a Northwest Orient airlines claim check dangling from the handle.

They had discovered this important piece of evidence with such ease that Menk could not believe that the previous searchers had failed to find it. When they saw it, it was standing upright in plain sight, seemingly ready to be carried away.

Excitedly, they laid it on its side and flipped the latches. Inside, along with a neatly folded nightgown and a pair of slippers, was a packet of unused checks and a collection of papers bearing dates coinciding with Helen's trip to Minnesota: receipts from the clinic, the Kohler Hotel, and a hotel shop. When police later asked the airline to run the number on the claim tag, Northwest said its records showed the marker was used on a piece of luggage shipped on a flight from Rochester to O'Hare on February 17, 1977.

The significance of the suitcase was that it seemed to offer undeniable proof that Helen had returned from Rochester on the day she was discharged from the Mayo Clinic. But as far as Menk was concerned, it did *not* prove that Helen was the one who had checked the suitcase and had taken the Northwest Orient flight. Rather than being elated by the discovery, the lawyer was furious. He felt he had been set up in an effort to allay his suspicions and bolster Matlick's story that Helen had indeed returned from Rochester. Menk was certain the suitcase had been brought to Chicago by someone other than Helen.

Also, the same intuition that caused Menk to conclude that Vorhees had been scared stiff during his deposition also told him that something really fishy was going on. It was simply *too* convenient that two pertinent items had been missed in two earlier searches by qualified, competent investigators yet were so easily discovered when the court-authorized searchers appeared. Someone was playing games with the evidence, Menk concluded, and he didn't like it.

"It was an Easter-egg hunt," Menk bellowed when reporters asked him about the results of the search. "Those items had been *planted* there for us to find."

The question, however, was *who* had done the planting. Who, Menk asked himself, would be so eager to try to prove that Helen had arrived back in Glenview and had not disappeared from the vicinity of the clinic as everyone but Matlick claimed? The planted suitcase seemed clearly a way to attempt to corroborate Matlick's story. So, too, did the will, although it was discovered in a kitchen drawer rather than in the nightstand, where Matlick said he had put it. But Menk was convinced the will and the suitcase were red herrings. Someone had tossed the investigators a couple of bones in an effort to persuade them to quit digging. It was an interesting ploy, Menk figured, but he wasn't buying it.

To see if he might find an overlooked clue that might help him solve the riddle, Menk flew to Rochester to question personally the last person who could positively confirm a contact with Helen Brach before she disappeared.

As Helen herself had done, Menk waited in front of the Buckskin Shop for the proprietress to arrive and open the door. Once she did, Menk asked her to recount for his own edification as many details as she could remember about Helen's visit to the store on February 17. When the middle-aged shopkeeper got to the part where she said Helen had told her she was in a bit of a hurry, Menk stopped her.

"Tell me *exactly* what she said," Menk asked.

When she did, Menk repeated it. Then he asked her, "Are you *certain* that the woman told you she was in a hurry because her 'houseman' was waiting for her? Are you sure that was the word she used—houseman?"

"Oh, yes," the woman replied easily. "I'm positive."

"Why are you so sure?" he insisted.

"Because I had never heard the word before," the woman replied. "I repeated it to myself several times after she left because I wanted to remember it."

On the flight back to Chicago, Menk could not help noticing how desolate the countryside was, how uninhabited, how densely wooded. It would be awfully easy, the lawyer reckoned, to hide a body just about anywhere out there.

By the time he got back to his home in his North Shore suburb, Menk had convinced himself that Helen Brach had never taken that Northwest Orient flight and had never spent that weekend in Glenview. He felt sure she was met outside the clinic in Rochester by someone who led her to her death. The problem was, he still did not know who. Or why. Or how.

17

Taking the Fifth
June 15, 1979

J OHN MENK rubbed his eyes and thought longingly of his bed. Through the window of his skyscraper office, the streets of Chicago looked like a basketful of sparkling pebbles that had been tossed on a dark blanket. Without looking at his desk clock, he knew it had to be late. If he had the option, he would be home with his wife, but there was work he had yet to do.

Sitting on his desk, like a ghost that had come to haunt his thoughts, was a stack of papers dealing with a legal claim by a woman named Carole Karstenson in which she alleged that she had been cheated out of a considerable sum of money by Richard Bailey. Menk had used the same tactic that Steve Miller would follow later: In his investigation of Bailey, he scoured local courthouses to see if any suits had been filed.

In the months following his trip to Rochester, the lawyer, a tall, slim man with dark hair and a closely clipped mustache, had not been able to mentally shelve the details that he knew about Helen Brach's disappearance. He had never ceased pondering the possibilities of desire, opportunity, and motive: Who would want Helen Brach dead and how could it be accomplished?

After countless days and nights of turning over all the possibilities, he had developed a theory about the case. If his hypothesis was correct, it had not been Jack Matlick who picked her up, despite what Helen may have implied to the woman in the Buckskin Shop. While it may have been someone she knew, it had not necessarily been Matlick; she could have simply *thought* it was Matlick. In other words, she could have believed it was Matlick coming to pick her up and it turned out to be someone else. But who?

The puzzle had greatly troubled Menk; it was like trying to remember the name of a song whose melody kept repeating. He felt he should know, should be able to figure it out, but the answer kept evading him. Then he learned about Karstenson's lawsuit. According to the court documents, the widowed Karstenson had fallen under the influence of a charming rapscallion who was interested only in her bank balance. She thought he loved her as she loved him, but he didn't want her heart; he wanted her money.

Menk flipped through the documents, searching for the high points. He became increasingly angry as he read about the cold-blooded manner in which Bailey allegedly had swindled Karstenson out of more than a quarter of a million dollars. But when he got to the allegations where Karstenson described how Bailey continued his pursuit of her money even while she was lying in the hospital too weak to move, believing she was on the verge of death, Menk bolted upright. "Good God! How callous can a person be!" he exclaimed.

Menk's adrenaline began pumping, his exhaustion forgotten, when he realized that the hospital Karstenson had been in when she thought she was on the verge of death was the Mayo Clinic and that she had been admitted only because Bailey had pulled the right strings. There was too much coincidence there, Menk felt. Two women, both connected to Bailey, had both been admitted to the Mayo Clinic on Bailey's recommendation. Karstenson claimed she was swindled by Bailey. Had Helen Brach also been taken in by the con man? Menk wondered. If she had been, why had she not filed a lawsuit as Karstenson had done? From what he knew about Helen Brach, she certainly was not bashful when she thought she had been taken. The more Menk thought about the possibilities, the more anxious he became to get Bailey into his office and ask him some questions. However, that would have to wait.

Giving him hope was the Karstenson lawsuit, a document that unequivocally accused Bailey of masterminding a swindle of considerable, if not monumental, proportions. He couldn't wait to hear what Bailey had to say about *that.* And then, too, there was the graffiti issue. It had been only sixty days before that the schoolboys had found the spray-painted message on the road near Bailey's stables insinuating that Bailey was involved in Helen Brach's disappearance. That would be an interesting subject to discuss as well, Menk felt. In fact, he had a long list of questions he wanted to ask the stable owner, roughly a hundred in all.

Menk fully realized that the chances of his breaking Bailey down, Perry Mason–style, and getting him to confess were about the same as that of Lake Michigan freezing over in June. Still, he hoped to be able to maneuver him into some relatively small admissions that detectives could use as a wedge to get the stalled criminal investigation moving once again. Although he had been practicing law for a third of a century, Menk had never run across a witness as uncooperative as Richard Bailey.

Bailey's deposition hearing was scheduled in Menk's Sears Tower office for Friday, June 15, 1979. At a few minutes before two in the afternoon, Bailey strolled in, looking relaxed and comfortable, decked out in an expensive but flashy sport coat and an open-necked shirt, the better to display an abundance of chest hair. Accompanying him, smiling as they shared a small joke together, was his lawyer, a mild-looking but tough-talking woman in her early forties. Her name was Jo-Anne Wolfson.

Known throughout the Chicago legal community for her hardball style—no little accomplishment in the male-dominated field of criminal law—and the fact that she came from a prominent legal family (one brother was a judge and another a high-profile member of the bar), Wolfson also was a riding companion of Bailey's. Years later, after the indictments were announced in 1994, *People* magazine published an old snapshot of the defender and her star client. The photograph, which was not dated, showed the two of them astride horses, Bailey on a big black horse, Wolfson on a smaller sorrel. In the picture, Wolfson is rising out of her saddle and leaning toward Bailey, their lips about to touch.

Also present for the hearing was the counsel for parties involved in the legal dispute: attorneys for Moore and the bank plus James C. Leaton, one of the lawyers representing Charles Vorhees. Absent was Matlick's attorney, Merwin Auslander. By this time, Matlick apparently had left Chicago to return to Pennsylvania, confident that his involvement had ended, since his deposition had been taken more than eighteen months before.

With Wolfson at his side, Bailey raised his right hand and swore to tell the truth. Then he slid into a chair, smiled at Wolfson, and turned toward Menk, looking more like an interested spectator than a participant. While waiting for Menk to begin, he eyed the lawyers, looking like a shark about to attack a group of wildly flapping swimmers.

Although he expected Bailey to be hostile, Menk quickly learned just *how* difficult the session was going to be, how Bailey would determinedly remain part of the background.

Unaware of the obstacles he was going to face, Menk led off by asking Bailey the simplest of questions: "What is your name?"

Bailey made no attempt to reply.

Wolfson, after a dramatic pause intended to get the attention of the group, said, "I will stipulate this is Mr. Richard Bailey."

Menk stared at her. "Well," he said firmly, "the witness is going to have to say that for himself. He's a big boy now."

The response was the same: Bailey sat without speaking, staring back at the questioner as if he were speaking Vietnamese.

Again, the dramatic pause, and then again, Wolfson spoke for her client. "I don't think there is anything in the rules that says *he* has to make the utterance. But," she added in a condescending tone, "if it would make you happy—"

"It has nothing to do with 'happy,' " Menk said. "That's the way it is going to be."

For the first and next to last time at the hearing, Bailey spoke. "Richard Bailey," he said listlessly.

"Richard *J.* Bailey?" Menk asked, emphasizing the *J.*

"No," Bailey answered.

"Where do you live, sir?" Menk asked, not realizing he had reached the end of his dialogue with the witness.

Wolfson answered instead, reminding Menk she had already given Bailey's address when he was sworn in.

"I want to hear it from *him,* "Menk said, fixing her with an icy glare. "I am not taking your deposition, Mrs. Wolfson."

Her response was equally frigid. "I understand that," she said. "Under advice of counsel, I am stating for Mr. Bailey his address."

"I want *Mr. Bailey* to give me his address," Menk persisted. "Mr. Bailey, would you give me your address?"

"Let us proceed," Wolfson said crisply, ignoring Menk's question.

Menk repeated the question and Wolfson repeated her answer.

Turning to Wolfson, Menk asked, "Are you advising him not to give his address?"

"I have already made my statement for the record. His address is a matter of knowledge and record."

"It doesn't matter," Menk said stubbornly. "I want *him* to tell me his address."

Wolfson's response was the same: "Let's proceed."

"What is your business address?" Menk asked, trying to break the logjam.

Wolfson fielded the question. "I am advising Mr. Bailey, and under advice of counsel, he is exercising his Fifth Amendment privilege."

Two of the other lawyers—Leaton and Arthur M. Gorov—interrupted, asking to be heard. Gorov tried to convince Wolfson that someone claiming the right to remain silent under the Fifth Amendment had to make the statement on his own rather than through his lawyer. But he fumbled when he tried to cite the specific Illinois appeals court decision.

Wolfson, like a professor addressing a dense student, rattled off the case.

Gorov looked flustered. "It is my understanding," he said loudly, trying to save face, "that *he* must make that statement as to each question that is asked of him. He cannot sit mute."

"That is not *my* understanding of the court's ruling," Wolfson shot back.

Menk and Gorov looked at each other and shrugged.

"Mr. Bailey," Menk said, "did you know Mrs. Helen Vorhees Brach?"

Wolfson answered for him, again claiming that he was exercising his Fifth Amendment privilege by refusing to answer on the grounds that it might incriminate him.

Menk paused. He knew by now that whatever he asked Bailey, Wolfson was going to make the same response. Still, he had to ask the questions; he had to build a record.

"When did you last see Mrs. Brach?"

Wolfson said her client was refusing to answer.

Was he involved as a defendant in a lawsuit brought by Carole Karstenson?

"I am advising Mr. Bailey, and under advice of counsel, he is exercising his Fifth Amendment privilege," Wolfson said.

Leaton spoke up, revealing his frustration. "Mr. Menk," he asked sarcastically, "I wonder if you could ask the witness or his attorney if the witness has any defect of speech or hearing that would justify the attorney answering in his behalf."

Wolfson was not amused. "Everybody here has heard Mr. Bailey state his name and respond to the court reporter when he was sworn as a witness," she said. "I think that question is frivolous."

Menk didn't want to let the opportunity pass. Pointing out that Bailey had greeted Helen's attorney, who had arrived late and just entered the room, he said, "At any rate, let the record show that Mr. Bailey said he was glad to meet Mr. Conway, so we did get some statement from him. He *can* talk."

Wolfson ignored him.

"Were you in Florida, and if so, where, at the time Mrs. Brach was at the Mayo Clinic?" Menk asked.

"My client is declining to answer," said Wolfson.

"Do you know if Mrs. Brach is alive at the present time?"

Wolfson responded that her client, exercising his right under the Fifth Amendment, was refusing to answer.

"Do you know if she is deceased at the present time?"

Wolfson said Bailey was taking the Fifth.

Menk then tried to question Bailey about his relationship with Helen and about whether he had sold her any horses. But again he ran up against Wolfson's wall.

In the middle of a question about the spray-painting incident, Menk looked up, saw the smug look on Bailey's face, and stopped. "Do you find this amusing, sir?" he asked Bailey. "I detected a smile."

Bailey surprised the group, including Wolfson, by answering himself. "I see *you* smiling," he told Menk.

"I am just being pleasant," Menk replied, implying that the same could hardly be said for Bailey.

Wolfson, feeling that Bailey had said enough, hurriedly answered for her client. "I think probably Mr. Bailey is trying to be as pleasant as he can, too," she said, smiling slightly herself. "I think the record should reflect that Mr. Menk and Mr. Bailey are very pleasant." Unable to resist the opportunity for the dig, she added, "Mr. Gorov has been pleasant from time to time, too."

For the next half hour, Menk fired questions at Bailey, all of which Wolfson met with Fifth Amendment objections. Finally, he surrendered in frustration. "I have asked a number of questions," he said, "not meant to be all-inclusive by far, but it is clear at this point that the court will have to rule on the matter. There is no need for all the lawyers to be here all afternoon if the response is going to be the same."

Menk turned to Wolfson. Would she confirm, he asked her, that Bailey would continue to take the same position no matter how many questions he was asked?

Wolfson replied that he would.

Seeing no point in continuing, Menk unhappily suggested that everybody go home.

Bailey's deposition hearing, however, was not Menk's last; that honor went to Everett Moore, who proved significantly more voluble than Matlick, Vorhees, and Bailey combined. Because of his talkativeness and because the other lawyers eagerly entered into the questioning, Moore's hearing stretched over two long, separate sessions spaced four and a half months apart. The first hearing was held on October 8, 1979, four months after Bailey's, and the second was on February 18, 1980, one day after the third anniversary of Helen's disappearance.

Moore, of course, was not under suspicion and was more cooperative. Menk's questions to him dealt more with Helen's financial status than with her disappearance, since Moore seemed in no way physically linked to what had happened to his employer. Also, unlike Matlick, Moore had had no contact with Helen since several days before she left Chicago for Rochester. And, unlike Vorhees, Moore stood to gain nothing from Helen's death. In fact, he would lose a job. Also, Moore had no romantic connection with Helen and there was no indication that he ever tried to involve her in a business deal or an investment that was even remotely shady.

Despite the hours he spent answering questions from Menk and the other lawyers, Moore provided only two interesting bits of information. One was that the private investigator that he and Belton Mouras had hired to try to find Helen had discovered that Matlick had a criminal record before moving to Chicago and going to work for Frank Brach. According to Moore, the investigator said he had learned from the Cook County state's attorney's office that Matlick had been arrested in Pennsylvania for delinquency, gun theft, burglary, auto theft, and receiving stolen property, although Moore did not say whether Matlick had been convicted on any of those charges. Later, also in Pennsylvania, he was convicted of auto theft and armed robbery and sentenced to twenty years in prison. Moore could not say how long Matlick had actually served or if Frank or Helen had known about his record.

The other chunk of information provided by Moore that was interesting to Menk was the history of Helen's venture into the horse world. According to Moore, it began in the spring of 1975, when she called him from Florida and told him she was interested in buying some racehorses.

Frank Brach, Moore added by way of background, had owned several horses in the late forties, before he married Helen. Apparently, though, he had talked about them to his wife. Twenty-five years later, Helen herself decided that it might be interesting to have a horse or two.

Moore knew that Helen's investment in the three horses was almost a hundred thousand dollars. Then he added a very interesting tidbit: A few months after buying the three racehorses, beginning early in 1976, Helen bought still more horses and hired a trainer, a man named Pete DeVito, who also would be her adviser on which horses to buy and which to dispose of.

Although Moore, under questioning from Menk, tried to establish the chronology of the horse purchases, the issue quickly got confused; Moore was not sure which horse was purchased when or for how much. He did know, he said, that eventually Helen built a stable of nine, five of them thoroughbred racehorses. After Helen's disappearance, under Moore's direction, DeVito bought several horses and sold others. The intention was to keep Helen's stable at nine horses, which is where it had been on February 17, 1977, when she vanished.

The animals did not turn out to be good investments, Moore admitted. Potenciado, the $45,000 Argentine import, never posted an impressive record, eventually became lame, and was put out to pasture because Helen did not have the heart to have him destroyed. In 1978, after Helen disappeared, Moore sold the animal for one dollar.

"I'd say you gave him away," Menk added dryly.

"Well . . ." Moore replied.

Menk cut to the chase: What had been the net result of Helen's horse investments?

Helen's losses in the first two years had been considerable. On her tax return for the first full year she was a horse owner, Helen claimed a loss of roughly $130,000 on the animals, including depreciation.

Did that seem to disturb her? Menk asked.

"No," Moore replied. "She never seemed to be anxious to get rid of the horses, even though some of them weren't good runners. I think she got a little bit attached to them and, therefore, she wasn't too anxious to sell them." However, he added, sometime in about 1976, she realized that the first three horses she had purchased were duds and she knew she was going to have to do something about them.

How about the profitability of the animals after 1977? Menk asked.

In 1978, Moore said, the year after Helen disappeared, her racehorses brought in $78,000 in purse money, but it cost her $183,000 to maintain them. After deducting depreciation of $35,000, there was still a loss of roughly $70,000 for the year.

And in 1979? Menk asked.

"I know we will not have a profit," Moore replied, adding that the loss would be in the neighborhood of $75,000.

Menk did some quick arithmetic. Since 1975, when Helen bought her first horse, through the 1979 tax year, her investments had resulted in losses totaling more than a quarter of a million dollars.

18

Lurching to a Halt

JOHN MENK picked up the sheaf of papers and carefully squared them on his polished wooden desk. Setting them carefully in the center, he stared at them until the type blurred. Then, reluctantly, he gathered them up and shoved them into his briefcase.

There was, he knew, little else he could do. His term as Guardian Ad Litem was coming to a rapid close; he simply had run out of avenues to explore. Everett Moore's last deposition had been his swan song; there simply were no more people for him to talk to. Although he knew he had done the best with what he had, he wished he had done more. As it was, he was having to pack it in without having come any closer to a final resolution of Helen Brach's mysterious disappearance than he had been when he took the job as GAL some three years earlier.

Before closing his Brach file, however, there was one last chore to perform. Among the papers that he had stuffed into his briefcase was a report to Judge Schaller on his activities over the preceding months, a summary of the interviews, and his analysis. Included in the report was a recommendation for a full-scale court hearing to determine if Helen was alive or dead.

What Menk hoped Schaller would do would be to drag Richard Bailey into a courtroom, put him under oath, and order him to testify, despite his insistence on claiming Fifth Amendment protection.

Menk knew the chances of that occurring were slim. And he was right. Schaller rejected the recommendation, declaring that under the circumstances Bailey's position was correct, that he had the right to take the Fifth.

The judge also rejected Menk's recommendation that Helen be declared dead without waiting the customary seven years for a hearing. Instead, on April 23, 1980, the judge issued an order officially listing Helen Brach as a missing person—that is, a *live* missing person.

That decision had no effect on the standing of the criminal case, but it was significant to the parallel civil case in that it gave Moore the authority to continue to handle her affairs. As far as the court was concerned, it was as if Helen were on vacation on a remote desert island and temporarily out of touch with her family, friends, and adviser. She would remain in that status, Schaller mandated, until seven years had passed from the time she was last seen—that is, until February 17, 1984—almost four years in the future. At that time, if she had not reappeared, it would be up to another court to declare judicially that she was dead.

As a result of Schaller's decision, Moore came out the winner in the dispute with Continental Bank. Even though Continental would continue to administer the $7 million trust, the bank would have no access to the interest income that fund generated. The interest money, instead, would be funneled to Helen's other accounts, just as if she were not missing, and come under Moore's jurisdiction.

Helen's will, the document that Menk had eagerly sought and eventually found, became a nonissue as far as the law was concerned. It would not come into play for another three and a half years, after the seven-year waiting period had expired.

Since Menk's job was finished, Judge Schaller terminated him in June 1980, roughly three years after he was appointed.

That, from Schaller's point of view, was that.

In February 1984, three years and seven months after Menk's job was formally abolished, the voluminous Helen Brach record was passed from Judge Schaller to probate judge Henry A. Budzinski.

Since the court did not have the power to initiate the proceedings on its own, the process of officially declaring Helen dead had to come from an outside source. In this case, it was her brother, Charles Vorhees.

Following the filing of Vorhees's formal petition to have his sister declared dead, Judge Budzinski convened a hearing, thereby jumping with both feet into the quicksand that already had swallowed more people than anyone had bothered to list.

However, the issue facing Budzinski was different from the one that had faced Schaller. Back in 1980, Schaller had to decide if Helen, after being missing for three and a half years, was alive or dead. But by the time Budzinski got the case, no one had heard from her for seven years, the amount of time customarily recognized in Illinois before someone can be taken off the missing person's list, and the decision seemed a straightforward one: Helen was dead and all Budzinski had to do was to certify that.

But that was not all of it. The tough part of Budzinski's task was deciding *when* Helen had died.

Before he could delve into that issue, though, he had to announce formally the terms of Helen's will, the document drawn up by her lawyer, John Conway, in 1974.

The will produced by Conway in 1984, more than six years after being charged with contempt for failing to do the very same thing, was identical to the document found in Helen's house during the court-authorized search in 1978, except that Conway's document carried Helen's signature, whereas the copy found in the house had been unsigned.

Considering the amount of money involved, the will was amazingly simple. It set up a $500,000 trust for her brother, Charles; it specified that $50,000 would go to Jack Matlick in return for his years of loyal service; it directed that Helen's personal property, later valued at some $500,000, was to be distributed "in accordance with (her) wishes which (she) shall make known to them," and it ordered that the bulk of her money, roughly $19.5 million after Vorhees's $500,000 was deducted, was to be used, via the Helen Brach Foundation, "to improve the lot of animals."

With the will out of the way, Budzinski tackled the big issue: When did Helen die? It was a major point for two reasons. First, it would either give official credence to Matlick's story about Helen being home from February 17 to February 21 or brand it a grand lie. But more important, it was big for financial reasons; a lot of money rested on Budzinski's nod.

Charles Vorhees wanted the date of death to be officially set on Thursday, February 17, 1977, since that was the last day on which Helen had been seen alive by anyone willing to come forward and say so other than Jack Matlick.

Vorhees was opposed by Moore, who wanted the date of death to be set at February 21, 1984, exactly seven years after Matlick said he left her at O'Hare.

If Budzinski accepted Vorhees's contention, he would rule that Helen had indeed been dead since the day she left the clinic, thus establishing officially that Matlick's story about her returning home that weekend was a huge fabrication. If Moore prevailed, the date of death would begin immediately and not be predated by seven years, thereby adding credibility to Matlick's claim. But the real issue was money.

If Judge Budzinski agreed with Vorhees, Helen's brother stood to reap considerable financial gain, specifically seven years' worth of interest on the $500,000 in the trust Helen had set up for him in her will. If Moore was successful, none of that interest money would go to Vorhees; it would remain in the fund that he was charged with administering: the Helen Brach Foundation.

It was an interesting move on the part of Vorhees, a man who, judging from what he had told Menk during his 1978 deposition, was so disinterested in his sister's money that he had not even attempted to determine if she had prepared a will at all, nor had he made any aggressive attempt to find out what had happened to her. Making it even more interesting was the fact that in February 1982, Charles had asked Judge Budzinski to allow him to collect an annual gift of ten thousand dollars from the estate. The judge had readily agreed to the request, noting that Helen had established a history of making gifts to her brother.

In his efforts to determine the date of death, Budzinski took testimony from twenty-seven witnesses, including Matlick, over a period of four days. At the conclusion, Budzinski ruled that Matlick totally lacked credibility and discarded his claims about Helen spending the period from February 17 to February 21 at home.

Regarding the seven-year period in which Moore hoped to prove that she had been alive, Budzinski said: "The evidence takes this case out of the category of an ordinary disappearance and would lead the unprejudiced minds of reasonable men, exercising their best judgment, to the conviction that death did intervene before the expiration of seven years." In other words, in his opinion, Helen died or was killed the day she left the clinic.

As a result of Budzinski's ruling, Charles Vorhees came away the big winner, going home with a $500,000 trust and seven years' worth of interest on that amount, plus the $30,000 or so he had already drawn against her estate through annual "gifts." Although Moore lost the fight over the date of death, he also was a winner to the extent that the court later said that proceeds from the sale of Helen's personal property—material that included a store of expensive jewelry, twenty fur coats, and the lavender Rolls-Royce—should go to the Helen Brach Foundation rather than, as Vorhees had asked, into his pocket.

While Budzinski's ruling effectively settled the money and death issues, several other skirmishes were still to come.

A year after the probate judge's decision, the Illinois attorney general's office accused Moore of mishandling Helen's funds to the tune of some $850,000. A good part of that money, the agency said, resulted from Moore botching an account set up specifically to provide funds for the purchase and maintenance of Helen's horses. The CPA's authorizations for spending on Helen's Florida condo and his fees as Helen's financial adviser, both before and after she disappeared, also came into question. As a result, Moore was forced to step down as director of the Helen Brach Foundation on February 25, 1987, ten years and eight days after Helen disappeared. He also agreed to return an unspecified amount of money to the estate.

Jack Matlick never got the fifty thousand dollars set aside for him in Helen's will. Rather, in September 1993, a Cook County judge ordered him to *pay* the estate ninety thousand dollars—seventy-five thousand as reimbursement for money or salable items that Matlick allegedly removed from Helen's safe-deposit box and fifteen thousand as reimbursement for the forged checks that Matlick claimed had been written by Helen on her last weekend in Glenview. At first, Matlick tried to fight the order, but in the summer of 1994 he agreed to renounce his claim to his share of Helen's estate in return for the estate's dropping a suit against him for having cashed forged checks. No criminal charges were ever filed against the handyman.

In the end, the only one of the four principals that Menk had deposed during his tenure as guardian ad litem to come out unscathed was Charles Vorhees.

After Moore stepped down as director of the Helen Brach Foundation, Vorhees took over as chairman. While his job is almost exclusively honorary, since the foundation is run by a president, the fund has prospered. In order to fulfill its avowed purposes of protecting wildlife, curtailing animal and child abuse, furthering education for the disadvantaged, and helping the disabled, the homeless, and the elderly, the foundation annually awards grants of almost $3 million.

As for the criminal investigation of the mysterious disappearance of Helen Brach, it essentially ground to a stop after Menk's frustrating attempt to question Richard Bailey on June 15, 1979.

Although sporadic attempts were made to breathe new life into finding a solution to the puzzle, such as that by David Hamm, they never went anywhere until Steve Miller, in what seemed simply a search for a new challenge, launched the federal probe in December 1989.

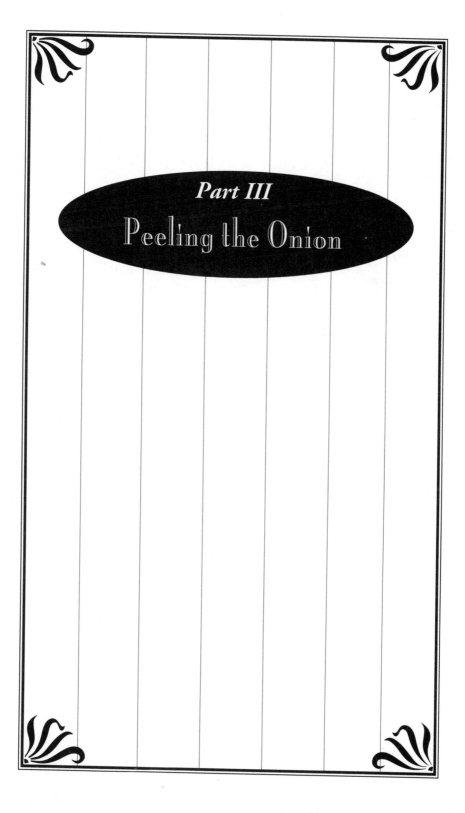

Part III
Peeling the Onion

19

Piece by Piece
1990

E VEN WITHOUT the rain, it was hard trying to see down the nar-
row, dark road that led to Dr. Ross Hugi's house in rural
Mundelein.

"Do you know where we are?" Steve Miller asked anxiously. "We've
been driving around for more than an hour."

Jim Delorto gave him an exasperated look. "I think it's coming up,"
he said, slowing to look for the sign for Indian Creek Stables.

"There it is," he added, leaning forward to peer through the rain-
streaked windshield.

Delorto turned into the driveway and pulled up near the front entrance of the house. The rain was coming down in sheets and the two
men debated about whether to make a run for it or wait to see if it was
going to let up. Finally, they decided to chance the dash.

Trying to dodge the mud puddles, Miller was hopscotching across
the open space, puffing like a marathoner, when he heard a noise that
made the hair raise on the back of his neck. Stopping as quickly as he
could, he looked up to see a large German shepherd—teeth bared,
growling deeply in his throat—barreling straight at him. Two seconds
later and five feet short of Miller, the dog snapped to a halt. Much to
Miller's immense relief, he had run out of chain. "God," he mumbled,
"I think I'm going to have a heart attack."

Still shaking from the encounter with the guard dog, Miller knocked
on the door. When Hugi answered, the prosecutor introduced himself
and Delorto. "We'd like to talk to you. May we come in?"

Hugi stared at the men. "Where have you been for twenty years?"
he asked cryptically. Ten minutes later, the soaked prosecutor and the
equally wet ATF agent were sitting in Hugi's comfortable living room.
Trying to ignore his sopping suit, Miller laid it out for the middle-aged

veterinarian as succinctly as he could. "We've got you cold on the fraud charge," he said, going into detail about the information they had compiled against him.

As Miller spoke, Hugi's face grew increasingly pale. Then Miller got to the punch line: "It's up to you. Would you like to tell us all about it, or would you rather take your chances with your colleagues before a jury?"

It took Hugi less than a minute to make up his mind. "The last thing I want," he said solemnly, "is to be sitting in a courtroom next to Richard Bailey. I'll write the book for you," he said quietly. "Chapter after chapter."

For several months, Miller had known that he had enough evidence against Richard Bailey to charge him with fraud. His investigators had uncovered enough details about Bailey's scams against vulnerable women, Miller felt, to get a conviction and ensure that the con man went away for several years.

Slowly, his investigators had built a file on Bailey and his associates, gathering as much information as they could in the hope they would never have to use it in court. If done right, Miller felt, the scammers would see that the odds were stacked against them—that the prosecutor could nail them solid—and they would plead guilty, agreeing to fill in the blanks and testify against their former comrades. "Flipping," Miller called it.

When the investigation started, Miller's team left over from the Hartmann case consisted of ATF agent Delorto, state police investigator David Hamm, and an FBI agent named Bob Buchan. But, through no fault of his own, Miller had not been able to hold the group together. Hamm had decided to retire and Buchan was pulled back after his bosses decided that their particular office did not have jurisdiction in the area the Bailey probe would cover.

To take Buchan's place, Washington assigned another FBI agent, Peter Cullen. A tall, slim man with a ramrod-straight military bearing, Cullen quickly proved invaluable. A former high school math teacher, he had a genius for detail, a trait that became ever more necessary as the Brach investigation grew incredibly complicated.

Once they thought they had all the players sorted out, the investigators began looking for weak spots. Robert Lee Brown and Jerry Farmer, they reckoned, were hard-core. Therefore, the best way to get at them was through Ross Hugi, a professional man who had let his greed get the better of him.

Although his evidence against Hugi was strong, Miller was surprised at how quickly he had collapsed. He not only would tell them everything he knew, Hugi said, but he promised to help lay traps for the others.

Farmer and Brown were different; they weren't giving Miller the time of day. The pivotal man in the group, Miller decided, was Farmer, and he figured he'd bear down on him first. "Find out everything you can about him," Miller told Cullen and Delorto. "Check his background. Check his business. Check his friends. Check his income-tax returns. Check everything you can think of."

In one way, Miller was pleased at how the probe was progressing. But the progress was awfully slow. It also wasn't going exactly in the direction he had hoped. When he decided to look into Bailey, it was because of a possible Helen Brach connection. So far, Cullen and Delorto had made sizable strides in gathering evidence of fraud against Bailey—Miller felt he could take him into court and get a conviction—but there had been precious little verifiable information to turn up that tied Bailey to Helen Brach.

From the very first, Miller had made a conscious, deliberate decision not to review files compiled by the Glenview police during the earlier Brach inquiries.

In his view, investigators from small police departments exhibited a tendency to disregard anything out of the ordinary and give up too quickly. Miller's response had been to do much of his own digging on York. In the Hartmann case, he had depended heavily on Delorto and Hamm, men he felt he could trust. Too many investigators in small police departments, Miller felt, not without sympathy to their plights, were looking for quick solutions. In too many cases, the overworked detectives tended to fall into the habit of relying on avenues that produced rapid rather than accurate results.

So Miller slipped into the pattern that had proved successful for him in the past: doing as much investigatory work as possible in-house. It made the job harder, but it also gave him more confidence in the results.

*   *   *

While Miller hesitated about perusing the Glenview PD records, he felt no compunctions about digging though the material Hamm had collected during the state police probe.

One thing that had particularly caught his eye was a report on an interview with a woman named Cathy Jayne Olsen, Frank Jayne, Jr.'s daughter.

"Let's get her in," the prosecutor told Delorto. "I'd like to hear what she has to say from her own mouth."

As he listened to her, his reservations grew. He had no doubt that she was trying to be truthful, but he wasn't sure just how far he could trust her version of the "truth," since she had told the same story several different ways, not only to various investigators but to a grand jury as well.

Cathy Jayne Olsen had once been a striking-looking woman, but years of drug and alcohol abuse and rough treatment by men had left her scarred and mentally confused.

In a voice deepened by booze, the thirty-six-year-old Olsen told Miller how, when she was working around her father's stable as a teenager, she had been befriended by Helen Brach, a kindly rich lady who had purchased eight or ten broodmares.

Helen had been good to her, had invited her to her Wagner Road home, and had listened patiently as Olsen poured out her troubles, telling the heiress how difficult it was growing up under a strict father.

One day early in 1977, she had confided to the heiress that the broodmares she had purchased were virtually worthless.

While Helen had said nothing to her, she went straight to Jayne and questioned him about the deal.

"I don't know what my father told *her*," Olsen said to Miller, "but he beat me. Told me to keep my blankety mouth shut."

Despite the beating and the warning, Olsen said she again told Helen that she should be wary of the horses they had sold her. "But that time, I made her promise not to tell my father," Olsen said with a grim smile.

Patiently, she explained to the prosecutor what her duties were at the stable. One of her jobs was to medicate the horses. The drugs were kept in a small closetlike room off her father's office. Every day, she would go into the room, close the door behind her to keep from being interrupted, while she was preparing the injections.

Although the room was tiny, it had a small window that looked into her father's office, a result, Miller deduced, of new construction.

About two weeks before Helen disappeared, Olsen said she had been in the medicine closet getting the shots ready when she heard male voices in her father's office. They were talking about Helen Brach. "She knows too much," she heard one of the men say.

Peeking out the window, she noticed that the two men in the office with her father were Richard Bailey and a policeman.

"We have to shut her up," her father said.

"But that wasn't all you heard, was it?" Miller prompted, recalling Hamm's report of an earlier interrogation.

Olsen shook her head slowly. "No," she admitted. "Later, I guess it was after Mrs. Brach disappeared, I was in the closet again and I heard another conversation about her."

"What was the gist of it?" Miller asked.

"I heard the cop telling my father and Bailey not to worry, that she 'had been shut up.' "

Miller continued questioning her, trying to pin her down on times, dates, places, and exactly who said what to whom. But the longer the session went on, the vaguer Olsen's responses became. Finally, Miller had to call a halt.

"What she says is really dynamite," he told Delorto after she had gone, "but how much of it can we trust?"

"She has problems all right," Delorto responded.

"A good defense attorney would eat her alive," Miller said sadly. "We can't rely on her alone. We need some corroborating testimony."

"Okay," Delorto said. "We'll see what we can find."

Operating on the theory that the best way to break the case open was to find a soft spot and keep pounding, Miller's investigators uncovered something in Farmer's background they hoped might convince him to cooperate.

As the investigation broadened, Miller began to realize that he was venturing into areas about which his main snoopers—Delorto and Cullen—knew little, if anything. The horse world, separate from the rest of society, has specific rules and regulations that apply simply because there are animals involved.

To help his investigators wend their way through the maze of laws that deal with livestock, Miller asked for help from the U.S. Department of Agriculture. In response, they assigned a young investigator named Daniel Ivancich, who eventually would become a permanent member of the team.

Using his knowledge of the USDA statutes, Ivancich began focusing on Farmer's business: Was he complying with all the special rules that cover the sale, transportation, and care of horses? Much to Ivancich's delight, he found that Farmer was not.

"Look at this," the young investigator said happily, waving a stack of interview reports under Miller's nose. "I think we've got him."

Once he learned that Farmer regularly exported horses from Illinois to Canada, Ivancich began digging to see if Farmer complied with all the stringent regulations dealing with the export of animals to a foreign country. One of the regulations required that all the animals taken across the border had to be certified free of a highly contagious and deadly horse disease called equine infectious anemia. Each horse allowed into Canada had to be accompanied by a document, called a Coggins paper, signed by a USDA-accredited veterinarian, pledging that the animal was free of EIA.

To determine if a horse was free of the disease, the accredited veterinarian had to draw a blood sample and send it to a USDA-licensed laboratory for analysis. The lab results were returned to the vet, who then was required to submit what was called a United States Origin Health Certificate to a department within the USDA—the Animal and Plant Health Inspection Service—for endorsement. An APHIS vet then would issue an export permit for the horse.

It was a detailed, time-consuming process that irritated the owners of many small horse operations. Apparently, Farmer found it particularly aggravating.

By talking to enough stable hands, grooms, and horse transporters, Ivancich discovered that Farmer had been bypassing the EIA regulation by bribing a veterinarian to issue false certificates on his Canada-bound horses.

The allegedly corrupt vet was a twenty-nine-year-old Illinois woman named Dana Tripp, who was well known on the show-horse circuit both as a veterinarian and as a champion rider.

Miller went to Farmer with his suspicions, hoping it would convince him to flip. After Miller laid out what Ivancich had discovered, Farmer laughed. "Prove it," he said.

Discouraged but not defeated, Miller took another tack. "Let's see what we can find out about Tripp," he directed.

Unknowingly, he had given an order that was going to turn his entire investigation upside down. While Miller had been aiming single-mindedly at building a case against Bailey and his fellow scammers, the entrance of Tripp into the equation was going to blossom into something that would send Delorto, Cullen, and Ivancich down a completely new path. In a matter of weeks, it would lead to the disclosure of events that would steer them away from the Bailey probe for almost two years and lead them down highways they had never envisioned going when Miller decided to try to solve Helen Brach's disappearance.

20

An Unexpected Turn
February 1991

T OM BURNS didn't have much use for small talk. A blunt, down-to-earth kind of guy, he liked to get right to the point.

"Someone told me to call you. What's this about?" Burns asked Donna Brown when he got her on the phone.

Burns had never met Donna Brown, but he knew her husband, Buddy. As a member of the U.S. equestrian team, he had won a Gold Medal in the 1976 Olympics and was still active on the circuit as a Grand Prix performer. He knew the Browns were superrich, with homes in Long Island and West Palm Beach.

"A horse," Brown said. "One I've been trying to sell for weeks, but so far haven't been able to find a buyer."

"Which horse?" Burns asked.

A seven-year-old chestnut gelding with white stockings and a white blaze, Brown told him. "He's called 'Buddy,' after my husband, but his official name is Streetwise."

"How much did he cost?"

"Sixty-five hundred. And he's insured for twenty-five thousand."

Burns whistled. "In that case, my fee is five thousand. You see any problem with that?"

"Nope," said Brown.

"Swell." Burns grinned to himself. "I'll do it right here. Roscoe, Illinois, is as good as anywhere else."

"No!" Brown said emphatically. "Not there. I'll be in touch."

Between January 19 and January 22, 1991, Burns and Donna Brown conferred a half a dozen times by phone. The problem was not with Burns's fee but with the method of execution. Burns preferred electrocuting horses because it simulated death by colic, an illness that was extremely fatal to horses. Brown, however, nixed that plan. Because

Streetwise had a history of suffering from colic, the insurance policy wouldn't pay off if the adjusters thought that was the cause of death. Instead, she insisted that it look like an accident.

At first, Burns balked. He didn't much like that idea. An accident meant breaking a horse's leg and that smacked too much of unnecessary cruelty to suit him. Then Harlow Arlie, a groom at the stable owned by Burns's wife's family, volunteered to help for half of Burns's fee.

Six weeks earlier, Arlie had been somewhat miffed because he had been cut out of a share of the handsome fee Burns was promised for flying to New York and killing the horse Charisma. When Arlie complained to Burns that he was not properly sharing the work, Burns told him he would get a cut on the next one. It happened that Streetwise was the first to come up since then.

Finally, Burns and Brown sketched out a scheme whereby Burns and Arlie would transport Streetwise from Illinois to Florida and the "accident" would occur there. It sounded like a solid plan. What they did not reckon on was that in the equine industry, secrets were very hard to keep.

In their increasingly determined effort to tie Bailey and Helen together, Delorto, Ivancich, and Cullen had immersed themselves in the horse world, talking to everyone they could find, from stable hands to stable owners, to try to tighten their case. By early 1991, the three investigators had spread the word throughout the industry: They were looking for *any* information they could find about illegal activity in the horse world, hoping that such information might lead them back to Bailey and his colleagues.

One of the lower-level horse-world people Cullen had interviewed worked at the Equestrian Oaks Stable in Libertyville, Illinois, just north of Chicago and adjacent to Mundelein, where Ross Hugi operated. Equestrian Oaks was owned by a Libertyville couple and run by their daughter, who was Tom Burns's wife. Both Burns and Arlie worked at the stable.

One of the horse-world people Cullen had talked to was a man who ran an independent rider-training service that operated out of Equestrian Oaks.

After Cullen explained that he was looking for details about horse-world activity, no matter how trivial it seemed as long as it was illegal, the man promised to alert him if he heard anything he thought might be helpful.

For months, Cullen heard nothing from the man. Then, late in January 1991, the trainer called and said he had overheard two men at Equestrian Oaks laughingly discussing a horse's "last meal." Cullen was interested because Libertyville was close to Chicago and he thought something that developed there might somehow lead to Bailey. "Call me if you hear anything else," Cullen told the tipster.

About the same time, another informant called and told Cullen roughly the same tale: A horse was going to be transported from Libertyville to Florida, where it was going to be executed as part of an insurance scam. The man who phoned in that information was, he told Cullen, one of the drivers who would be making the trip to Florida. He was *not* part of the plot, he added emphatically, and he didn't want to be dragged down if things went sour.

In the next few days, Cullen learned that the horse's name was Streetwise, and it was supposed to be killed by a groom named Harlow Arlie and a professional horse hit man named Tom Burns, who was also known as Tim Ray.

Taking the information to Miller, they decided the best thing to do was to wait until Burns and Arlie made their move—that is, keep them under surveillance. They were not sure how or if this connected to Bailey, but it was too good a tip to pass up because of the horse-world connection.

Since Ivancich knew some of the agricultural agents in Florida as a result of his job with the USDA, he volunteered to call them and help set up a plan to trap Arlie and Burns.

At first, everything went according to plan. The Florida agricultural agents were waiting at the agricultural/large animal inspection station when the Burns-Arlie caravan crossed into the state from Georgia and they were able to confirm that a horse named Streetwise was among the animals in the shipment. When the caravan pulled out of the agricultural checkpoint and headed south, Florida agents followed them at a discreet distance, watching as they pulled into a horse facility near Gainesville called Canterbury Farms.

The plan was to sit back and watch until the last possible moment, then rush in and nab the horse killers red-handed. The Florida State Police and the Alachua County sheriff's office were part of the plan and they had men surrounding Canterbury Farms, ready to swoop in

. Harold Barry gave the signal. was the weather and the swift-

ry Farms, the horses were off- nd watered. Then they were to y near West Palm Beach. railer about one hundred yards inoculars as stable hands began One of the horses was Street-

Burns and Arlie seemed about wise, then sound the alarm. At ding across the road on the edge b them. But as he lay in a cold s making it difficult to see, Barry as best he could, he watched as Burns picked up a lead snank, hooked it to Streetwise's halter, and begin walking the animal up the ramp into the cavernous vehicle.

Suddenly, the agent's eyes grew wide in horror. As he looked on helplessly, he saw Arlie materialize like a ghost out of the rain. Without warning, the well-muscled stable hand, as if trying to emulate Hank Aaron going for the fence in right center, swung a crowbar with all his considerable strength, aiming for a spot just above the white stocking on Streetwise's right hind leg. The crack of the breaking leg bone could be heard by the other agents a quarter of a mile away.

Streetwise let out a horrendous scream that sent shivers through the surprised agent's body. As he watched, Streetwise collapsed in a bellowing heap. Then the animal hopped up on his three good legs and tried to gallop away. He made it as far as the rear of the stable before collapsing again. All the while, the animal was wailing like an air-raid siren, obviously in excruciating pain. Burns, as shocked as Barry by what had occurred, grabbed a mobile phone and frantically dialed Donna Brown, telling her to summon a vet to have Streetwise put to sleep.

Tossing the phone aside, Burns and Arlie jumped into Burns's truck and sped down Route 26, only to be quickly stopped by the state police and sheriff's deputies. Unwilling to surrender, Burns vaulted out of the vehicle and took off on foot across a soggy pasture. An officer ran after him, chasing him down and tackling him. While one deputy stood by with a shotgun, another slapped a pair of handcuffs around Burns's wrists and threw him in the rear of a patrol car. He and Arlie were then taken to the county jail and soon afterward they were hauled before a magistrate, who set bond at a hundred thousand dollars.

With Burns and Arlie safely in jail, Barry called Cullen, who called Miller.

It was early Sunday morning in Chicago, one of Miller's rare days at home. Ever since the Bailey investigation began, it had been twelve-hour days, holidays included, and this was a day he had anticipated spending with his family. Not surprisingly, when the phone rang in his home in a northern suburb, Miller winced.

As Cullen explained what had happened in Florida, Miller's enthusiasm did not grow perceptibly.

"Do you think we ought to get down there?" Miller asked.

"It could be a wild-goose chase," Cullen replied.

"Yeah," Miller agreed unenthusiastically. "This guy's much too young to know anything about Helen Brach."

"On the other hand," replied Cullen, "if we don't go, we might be kicking ourselves forever."

"You're right," Miller said. "Let me call the airlines and see what's flying in that direction."

Ten minutes later, he called Cullen back. "Let's get our asses down to Florida," Miller told him. "I'll meet you at O'Hare in ninety minutes."

When they got to the Alachua County jail, they found conditions less than optimal for a hoped-for quiet tête-à-tête with Burns. Miller disgustedly surveyed the situation. "I don't see anyone in here who doesn't look like he'd slit your throat in one second flat," he whispered to Cullen.

The building was suffocatingly hot, nauseatingly smelly, and unbelievably noisy. People were bustling about, moving hurriedly in one direction or another that, as far as Miller could determine, had no reason or pattern. It had all the ambience, Miller decided, of the concession area in Soldier Field during halftime at a Bears game.

Worse than the noise and confusion, from his point of view, was the fact that every single inch of available space seemed to be taken by prisoners, deputies, lawyers, and visiting family members; there was not one room where they could meet privately with Burns, not even a corner where they could huddle in relative privacy.

Then Miller spotted the broom closet. An inmate was returning a mop to the tiny space off the main corridor when Miller caught a glimpse of the interior. It wasn't much bigger than a phone booth, but it would have to do.

Collaring one of the deputies, Miller asked him if it was all right to use the space.

Suppressing a smile, the deputy drawled that it would be fine.

While another deputy went to fetch Burns, Miller and Cullen went to work on the closet. They were busily tossing out brooms, mops, and pails when Burns appeared, with his lawyer in tow.

"In here," Miller said gruffly, pulling Burns inside. As soon as all four of them had crammed into the tiny space, Miller closed the door. In seconds, they were drenched in sweat.

Miller shoved his face only inches from Burns's. "We didn't fly halfway across the country to hear about you breaking a horse's leg," he snarled. "What can you tell us about Helen Brach?"

Burns looked at him in surprise. "I don't know *anything* about Helen Brach," he said, "but I can tell you about killing horses. I've killed horses for prominent people all across the country."

Miller looked at Cullen. Neither of them knew anything about horse killings; all they had heard were a few vague rumors. At that time, neither was particularly interested, either, since they were still gathering information against Bailey and that was their first priority.

Miller looked closely at Burns and decided not to pass up whatever it was being offered to him, even though he was not yet sure exactly what it was. "Will you cooperate?" he asked. "Maybe we can work a deal."

"Oh, yeah," Burns replied with a lame smile. "You bet. I'll gladly cooperate. I'll do anything to get out of this place."

21

"A Dirty Little Secret"

STEVE MILLER pessimistically eyed the stacks of paper that covered his desk, a nearby table, and climbed up his office walls. "How are we ever going to handle this?" he cried, throwing up his hands. "How are we ever going to find anything in *here*," he said, pointing to one pile, "and connect it," pointing to another pile, "to something in *there*?"

Pete Cullen smiled ruefully. "Let me have a crack at it," he suggested. "Maybe I can get it organized."

Until Tom Burns got arrested in Florida on Groundhog Day, February 2, in 1991, Steve Miller's cast of villains was relatively small and well defined. But with Burns's arrest, everything went topsy-turvy. Almost immediately, as he had promised, Burns began spewing out names, places, and events, which sent Cullen, Delorto, and Ivancich scurrying in a dozen different directions at once.

There was no question, Miller decided from the beginning, that he could ignore Burns's information. Although at first it seemed to have no practical connection to the Bailey investigation, it related to serious crimes within the horse industry, events that he could not even consider playing down or passing along to someone else. The material being supplied by Burns was not what Miller had been expecting or looking for, but it had to be checked out and acted upon. At the time, Miller's most fervent hope was that it would somehow tie in with Bailey and the Chicago group.

Soon after Miller expressed his exasperation at the mountain of paperwork that was collecting, information that the four men would never be able to sort manually and make sense of, Cullen disappeared for a week into a small room down the hall from Miller's office. When he

Helen Brach, the eccentric widow of millionaire Frank Brach and heiress to the Chicago-based Brach candy fortune, mysteriously vanished after a brief stay at the Mayo Clinic in 1977. Her disappearance—and presumed murder—would set off a search spanning two decades that would reveal a dark and brutal side to the glamorous world of equestrian competition. (Courtesy of the *Chicago Sun-Times* file)

In 1994, U.S Attorney James Burns announces the indictment of
Richard Bailey in the 1977 disappearance of candy heiress
Helen Vorhees Brach. *(AP/Wide World)*

Richard Bailey was a major figure in the Chicago horse world, whose specialty became wooing well-to-do older women and convincing them to spend thousands of dollars on worthless horses. Prosecutors believe Bailey hired someone to kill Brach when she began to suspect he was conning her. *(Chicago Sun-Times/*Jack Lenahan*)*

Dr. Annette Hoffman, a prominent plastic surgeon who married Bailey, had their marriage annulled, and then remarried him on the eve of his trial. *(AP/Wide World)*

Jack Matlick worked as Helen Brach's handyman and claims to be the last person to have seen her before her death. *(AP/Wide World)*

Kenneth Hansen, a Chicago-area equestrian, was convicted of the murder of three young boys in 1955. *(Chicago Sun-Times)*

"The Sandman," also known as Tom Burns and Timmy Robert Ray, was a professional horse assassin responsible for the deliberate killing of fifteen horses using a method of electrocution that made the death seem to be a result of colic. *(AP/Wide World)*

Barney Ward, a former Olympic rider, was accused of arranging the murders of four valuable horses. *(Doug McGlothlin)*

Marion Hulick, manager of the prestigious Cellular Farms, was
convicted of helping plan the murder of Charisma, a
magnificent, if erratic, thoroughbred.
(Doug McGlothlin)

Extremely wealthy, the handsome heir to a cellular phone fortune, George Lindemann, Jr., had been guaranteed a spot on the U.S. equestrian team for the 1996 Olympics. He was convicted of masterminding the execution of his sister's horse, Charisma.
(Doug McGlothlin)

Steve Miller, the aggressive, capable assistant U.S. Attorney who spearheaded the investigation leading to the indictment of twenty-three figures in the equestrian world. *(Tom Maday)*

Susan Cox, the federal prosecutor who was co-counsel in the case against Marion Hulick and George Lindemann, Jr. *(Author's Collection)*

reemerged, he had a happy grin on his tired face; his red-rimmed eyes were smiling. "I think I've got it," he told Miller.

What the former math teacher had was a spontaneously created computer database that would facilitate the organization of information, allowing material to be indexed, cross-referenced, and called up for immediate scanning. By using the database, he, Miller, or either of the two other investigators, for example, could enter the name of a horse and all the information they had collected about that animal—its age, description, who its owner was, and where it had been stabled—would pop up on the screen. That information could be cross-checked with other details: which vet had been treating the horse and what drugs had been used, what had happened to the horse, and how that particular animal was connected to any of the other persons mentioned so far in the investigation.

Although it was slow in becoming apparent, a number of parallels eventually emerged between the people and animals Burns was giving them information about and the Chicago group. Viewed narrowly, the material told Miller little. But by stepping back and using the computer database to tie the loose ends together, a tapestry began to emerge that both fascinated and repelled the prosecutor. Taken individually, it was just a list of names; taken as a whole, it painted a disturbing picture of what Miller referred to as the horse world's "dirty little secret."

Once Burns decided to talk, Miller noted gleefully, he was hard to shut up. He not only spilled details about the murder of Streetwise, he outlined for investigators a whole series of executions he claimed to have committed during his spectacular nine-year career as a horse hit man.

Affable and gregarious, the pudgy Burns seemed anxious to tell his story, opening his life to Cullen like a book.

It really began, he said, when he was eight years old and his mother and father were divorced. He took it hard, he said, and it set him along a path of rebelliousness that led him to drop out of school in the ninth grade, run away from home, and eventually find a place with a horse-farm operator named Barney Ward in upstate New York.

A former professional football player and Olympic trainer, Ward became a surrogate father to the young Burns, alternately treating him roughly and kindly (all but adopting him and buying him his first car).

It was Ward, Burns said, who gave him his first steady job, putting him to work as a stable hand, shoveling manure and hay for one hundred dollars a week.

After several years of Ward's uneven treatment, and unable to cope any longer with the farm owner's violent mood swings, Burns decided to strike out on his own, heading for Florida.

Soon after arriving in Ocala, he found a job with a lawyer/horse owner named James Druck. He worked around Druck's stable and proved so loyal that Druck soon put him in charge of his horse-show van, a mobile tack shop that traveled from city to city with the equestrian events.

It was on the road, Burns said, that he discovered his true talent: that of an accomplished thief.

Killing horses was only a sideline, he bragged to Cullen. He also was so successful as a thief that he didn't really need the horse-assassination fees to survive.

The abundantly rich who frequented the horse shows were incredibly neglectful about taking care of their property, Burns claimed, commonly leaving expensive saddles and other costly gear lying around for someone just to come along and take. He happened to be that someone. He frequently left one horse show with a trunkful of saddles, which he easily peddled, no questions asked, at the next show for one thousand dollars or more each. The kicker, he said, was that everyone knew the saddles were hot, but nobody seemed to care.

It was only later that he got involved in horse killing, and when that happened, it was not for money, but as a favor to his employer, Jim Druck, an attorney who specialized in insurance law.

Druck owned a champion show jumper named Henry the Hawk, which he was very proud of. But Druck also was deeply in debt and he needed the money more than he needed a horse that happened to be insured for $150,000.

"He set me down," Burns said, "and he told me in detail how to make a rig for electrocuting a horse. That's what he wanted me to do to Henry the Hawk."

When Burns said he understood and got up to leave, Druck called him back. "One more thing," he said solemnly.

"What's that?" Burns asked.

"When you plug in the cord, make sure you're out of the way, because that horse is going to drop like a ton of bricks. You don't want him to fall on you."

Between the salary from his day job as a horse transporter and his various other illicit activities, Burns told Cullen that he cleared several hundred thousand dollars, only a portion of which came from his fees for killing horses.

But killing horses was what he became infamous for. It earned him "the Sandman" nickname and it spread his reputation far and wide.

"In the last eight years," he told Cullen, "I've killed fifteen horses. My best streak ever was five within ten weeks in the summer of 1989."

Not entirely to Miller's surprise, some of the names that Burns was spieling were at least vaguely familiar; he and his investigators had already run across them during the Bailey probe. But Burns's information broadened and complicated the original investigation, moving it beyond Chicago to areas considerably distant from the Windy City, spreading, in fact, across much of the eastern part of the country.

One thing it helped prove, however, was that Silas Jayne was not necessarily an aberration in the equine industry. It showed that violence played a major role in the culture's illegal activities both inside and outside Chicago.

Once Burns began to talk and investigators were able to gather corroborating evidence, Miller shoehorned this new material into his plans. While it was important to his case to be able to prove that Bailey had merrily cheated more than a dozen women, he wanted to tighten the noose around the con man's neck by bringing in the violence and tying that, in turn, to Helen Brach. What Miller wanted to be able to document was that it was not a very big step from nonviolent swindles to very violent action against those who threatened to rock the boat. Carole Karstenson was a good example. When it looked as if she was going to be troublesome, she was seriously hurt in a mysterious horseback accident and her barn was burned. If that was the response to a threat from a relative nobody, Miller figured, what would the reaction be against a woman like Helen Brach who could use her money and social position to wreck the whole scam operation?

The problem was, Miller could not yet prove this. He thought he and his investigators were making good progress in that direction when

Burns popped up. Now he had no choice: He had to ride the Burns tangent through to the end.

The prosecutor made an analogy between his position and trains running down parallel tracks. On one track was the Scam Express, and its passengers included Bailey and his cohorts. On the other track was the Assassination Limited with a still not clearly defined passenger list, although Burns was the custodian who cleaned up what the others considered trash.

Miller was unsure if stumbling across Burns had been good or bad. It was going to sidetrack the Bailey investigation; of that, he was certain. But it might be beneficial in the long run, because whatever he could learn about illegalities in the horse industry could not help but end up benefiting the Bailey probe.

What he was unprepared for was the amount of time it would take to follow through on the Burns data. Before it was over, he and his three investigators, along with agents from a half a dozen other agencies, would spend 80 percent of their time for the next two years following the horse killer's leads.

22

Horror in the Horse World

Tommy Burns, the hard-hearted hit man who readily confessed to executing fifteen horses, was having trouble controlling his emotions.

Tears built in the corners of his eyes, then slid slowly down his cheeks. Sniffling and in a cracking voice totally out of character for the boastful, self-proclaimed bad boy of the show-horse circuit, Burns whispered a name: Barney Ward.

Over a period of many months, Burns had been feeding particulars of his horse-killing escapades to Cullen, sometimes in gory detail, spelling out which animal he killed when, for whom, and for how much.

Other names had rattled off his tongue—a virtual Who's Who of the Eastern U.S. horse world—but Ward's had to be dragged out of him.

"Why don't you want to tell me about him?" Cullen asked.

"Ward's my dad," the tearful Burns replied. "He's been like a father to me."

"Well, now that you've brought him up," the FBI agent urged, "tell me about his connections to the horse killings."

Slowly, gradually, with many changes, corrections, and retractions, Burns elaborated upon the Ward connection.

All told, Burns would later testify, he had killed four horses at Ward's request, although Ward has denied any role in the killings. The first had been a horse named Condino, which Burns killed on March 24, 1987.

The next incident involving Ward, Burns claimed, began in March 1989, when Ward was having coffee with a thirty-six-year-old Virginia housewife and former rated equestrian named Nancy Marder Banefield. As they sipped their cappuccinos, Ward began pressing her to pay off

$16,500 she still owed him toward the earlier purchase of a horse named Ginko.

She would be delighted to pay him, Banefield replied, but she did not have the money. She had been trying to sell another of her horses, Rub the Lamp, to get some ready cash, but so far she had not been able to find a buyer.

Was Rub the Lamp insured? Ward asked.

Yes, she said. She had a fifty-thousand-dollar policy on the animal.

"Why don't you have him killed for the insurance money?" Ward asked.

"Why not?" Banefield replied.

On March 5, she sent Burns a $2,500 check as down payment for assassinating Rub the Lamp and asked him to come get the horse. She said Rub the Lamp should be taken to Illinois and killed there.

On June 2, Burns and a stable hand named Scott Thompson went to a stable in Oregon, Illinois, where Rub the Lamp was being boarded, and electrocuted the animal.

Banefield then filed for the insurance and received a check for the fifty thousand dollars three and a half months later. She cashed the check and gave Ward the $16,500 she still owed on Ginko.

The third incident occurred just weeks later. About the middle of the summer, the owner of a facility called Acres Wild Farm in North Smithfield, Rhode Island, Paul Valliere, complained to Ward that he was unhappy with the performance of one of his horses, an animal named Roseau Platiere. According to Burns, Ward told Valliere, one of the show circuit's leading trainers, that he could solve his problem by contacting the Sandman.

Predictably, Burns said, Valliere called. After they chatted, the stable owner agreed to pay Burns five thousand dollars to have Roseau Platiere killed in a manner that mimicked a natural death.

A few days later, on August 3, Burns flew to Sugarbush, Vermont, where Roseau Platiere was performing in a show. Earlier, Valliere had told Burns which tent and which stall the horse was in. "You'll know you have the right one because I'll leave a red halter hanging on the door," Valliere said.

After waiting in the woods for everything to settle down, Burns slipped into the tent where Roseau Platiere was being stalled. It was about 1:00 A.M. and totally quiet.

Burns electrocuted the animal, picked up a $3,500 down payment

Valliere had left for him hidden under the seat of a golf cart that was used as a transportation vehicle around the stables, called a friend for a ride, and went back to the airport to return to Illinois.

Valliere filed an insurance claim for $75,000 on the horse and it was paid in full on September 18.

The next and last job he did that was connected with Ward, Burns said, started in December 1990, when Ward telephoned him in Illinois and left a message saying it was urgent that Burns call him back.

When he reached him a few hours later, Burns said, Ward told him that multimillionaire horse owner George Lindemann, Jr., a then twenty-six-year-old champion rider with Olympic ambitions, wanted to talk to him about arranging the assassination of a champion hunter named Charisma. Ward had reason to keep Lindemann happy. His father, George senior, a pioneer in the manufacture of cellular phones, was chief executive of the Southern Union Company in Austin and one of the country's four hundred richest men. Besides, George junior was a good customer. Just eighteen months previously, he had paid Ward $500,000 for a horse named Lari Three Two Six.

Ward then casually added, Burns said, that the younger Lindemann was willing to pay $25,000 to have Charisma executed, five times Burns's normal fee. The reason: Charisma had not been performing as expected on the circuit.

On December 15, Burns flew to New York. He met with Lindemann's barn manager, Marion Hulick, who showed him the horse to be killed and how to get onto the farm property without being seen.

That night, while Hulick created an alibi for herself by having dinner with a coworker well away from the Cellular Farms complex, Burns slipped onto the grounds and electrocuted the horse.

Six months later, on June 14, 1991, the company that carried the policy on Charisma's life sent Lindemann a check for $250,000 to pay off the claim. The apparent reason the settlement took so long was that the insurance company was suspicious about the incident. Both Hulick and Lindemann lied under oath to attorneys representing the company when they inquired about the circumstances surrounding Charisma's demise.

Besides the horses he killed at Ward's request, Burns told Cullen, there were other executions that he had negotiated independently.

In the summer of 1989, an equestrian named Donna Hunter, a former girlfriend of Jerry Farmer, contacted him about killing a horse named Emili's Choice.

Hunter, along with her husband, Michael, a well-known rider in his own right, owned a stable called Hunter Hill Farms in Mundelein, Illinois. Donna Hunter taught riding at the facility and also served as a horse broker. One of her clients, the woman who had purchased Emili's Choice for her daughter, went to Donna Hunter and said she wanted to get rid of the horse and buy her daughter a different one.

Eager to land a large commission by brokering the sale of the replacement animal, Donna Hunter, without telling her client what she planned for her horse, went to Burns, who electrocuted Emili's Choice.

After the assassination, Donna Hunter guided the woman through the filing of a claim for $45,000 in insurance.

A few weeks later, a Highland Park, Illinois, businessman named Allen Levinson began getting anxious about a horse he had purchased for *his* daughter. The animal, Rainman, had suffered an injury to its back that made it unsuitable to be ridden in competition. As a result, Levinson could see his investment money going down the drain.

The businessman went to the man from whom he had purchased the animal, Donna Hunter's husband, Michael, and asked his advice. Hunter suggested he try to sell the horse.

When no buyer stepped forward, Levinson and Hunter agreed to a plan whereby Hunter would make sure that the horse "disappeared" so Levinson could claim the fifty thousand dollars for which Rainman was insured.

Hunter went to Burns, who agreed to kill Rainman and split the five-thousand-dollar assassination fee with Hunter. In August, Burns took Rainman to Missouri, ostensibly to enter him in a show there. The real reason, though, was to electrocute the animal. The Missouri city was chosen as the execution site because Burns had recently killed Emili's Choice at Hunter's stable and he was worried that another death there so soon after the other might seem suspicious.

In the spring of 1989, Tammie Bylenga Glaspie, of Walker, Michigan, decided to have her horse, Belgium Waffle, killed after the animal suffered a stroke that left him worthless as a show animal. If the horse were dead, she could collect forty thousand dollars in insurance.

Glaspie went with her idea to James Hutson, a stable owner in

Oregon, Illinois. Hutson told her he could arrange for the horse's murder but that she would have to pay the killer, Burns. She also would have to pay him a commission for arranging the assassination.

Burns electrocuted the horse on July 30, 1989; on September 29, 1989, the insurance company sent Glaspie a check for $39,076.

In turn, Glaspie gave Burns his $5,000 fee and paid Hutson a $4,900 fee for serving as the middleman.

In the summer of 1990, Johnnie Youngblood of Naperville, Illinois, and stable hand Steve Williamson stood lookout while Burns electrocuted a horse named Empire.

Youngblood and her business partner, Jerry Farmer—the same Jerry Farmer who helped Richard Bailey swindle lonely women—had sold Empire for $68,000. Soon after the sale, Empire came up lame and the new owner complained to Farmer.

Rather than return the money, Farmer began arrangements for the horse's murder. According to Burns, Farmer went first to Williamson. After initially agreeing to take care of the horse's demise, Williamson changed his mind. So Farmer then went to Burns.

On July 16, 1990, Farmer called Youngblood to tell her that Burns was on his way to dispatch Empire. In the meantime, she said, Farmer told her to race Empire around the track enough to get the horse to work up a sweat and to clean out his stall so there would be no manure there. The object was to make it look as though the horse had died of colic.

"That was one big horse," Burns said. "I had to get a stepladder to attach the wire to his ear."

On July 21, five days after Empire's assassination, Youngblood filed a claim for $68,000 on behalf of the owner.

Armed with the wealth of detail that Burns had furnished, Miller and his investigators began rounding up the suspects. One by one, they talked to everyone whom Burns had mentioned, asking them to help nab others and offering them the chance to be given consideration at sentencing in return for agreeing to help testify at the spate of trials that were expected to follow. One of those who agreed to cooperate was Dr. Ross Hugi.

In the spring of 1991, after Burns had provided Miller with a list of alleged lawbreakers, a Chicagoan named Phil Sudakoff contacted Herbert Kroninger, a trainer from nearby Bolingbrook, Illinois, about killing his horse, a trotter named Instant Little Man, which was insured for eighty thousand dollars. Sudakoff asked Kroninger if he could find a veterinarian to do the job and make it look like a natural death.

Both Kroninger and Sudakoff approached Hugi. They promised him seven thousand dollars if he would dispatch Instant Little Man. Hugi said okay, so Kroninger took the horse to his stable and gave Hugi a $2,500 down payment. What the two did not know, however, was that by this time Hugi was working with Miller.

When Hugi reported the contact with Kroninger and Sudakoff, Cullen told the veterinarian to tell the two that the horse had been killed.

Then, on May 23, 1991, Sudakoff, believing Instant Little Man was dead, filed a claim to collect on his policy.

Even that, though, was not the end of the Burns investigation.

Operating with material obtained from other sources, investigators became aware of a man named Ronald Mueller of Harvard, Illinois, a tall and rangy modern cowboy who looked like an extra from a John Wayne movie. Like Burns, Mueller was reputed to be a man who had killed horses so the owners could collect the insurance. Although Miller had not believed it possible, the tales investigators heard about Mueller indicated he was even more cold-blooded than the Sandman.

In July 1973, Mueller reputedly had killed three horses being transported to Clinton, Iowa, by burning them alive. Asked in advance to make sure that the animals met with an "accident" on the trip, Mueller pulled his horse trailer off the side of the road, doused the hay inside the trailer with accelerant, and tossed a lighted cigarette into the vehicle.

Eleven years later, in January 1984, he was said to have killed a horse named Jatomic Streaker by hitting it in the head with a crowbar. The horse was insured for fifty thousand dollars.

About a year after that, Mueller allegedly dispatched another horse, Prospect Hill, which was insured for seventy thousand dollars, by bludgeoning the animal to death with a sledgehammer.

And in February 1987, he supposedly killed a horse named Pet of the Year by shorting a heater in the horse's watering trough so the animal, which was insured for forty thousand dollars, was electrocuted when it went to drink.

To collect on an insurance policy, owners have to report a horse's death as either accidental or due to natural causes. Apparently, the insurers, who are flooded with claims of horse deaths, take many of the reports at face value.

23

The Missing Piece
Sacramento, 1992

J OE EDWARD PLEMMONS swung his brown eyes calmly from Pete Cullen to Jim Delorto to Steve Miller. "So help me," he said guilelessly in his high-pitched, con man–sincere voice, "I'll tell you the truth. You can take it to the bank."

Over a period of several months, Plemmons had been dribbling details of his connections to the Chicago scammers drop by drop. In jail awaiting trial for selling a horse that didn't exist, Plemmons was facing a stiff prison sentence unless he could work out a deal with Miller: information in exchange for his freedom.

"So you want to bargain?" Miller asked, his skepticism evident in his voice.

"Yes, sir," Plemmons replied, grinning broadly.

"Okay," Miller said after a brief pause. "You tell us what you know and I'll see what we can work out."

After his interview with Cathy Jayne Olsen, Miller asked his investigators to redouble their efforts to try to find someone who could corroborate Olsen's claims that Brach represented a danger to the scam operation. When Olsen told him about her father, Frank Jayne, Jr., and his alleged conversations with Bailey and a rogue cop about having Helen "shut up," the pieces to the puzzle slid into place.

Although he lacked documentation to prove it, Miller felt certain that Olsen had been correct when she told him that Helen had bought a string of broodmares from Bailey. He *knew* she had bought three racehorses from P. J. Bailey and that they had been disasters. From what he knew about Bailey, he was certain the con man could not have resisted the temptation to try to sell her some more horses. It would have been impossible for him *not* to have tried.

Knowing how Bailey operated, any horses he sold her would also have been overpriced and of poor quality. Then he asked himself, What if she had found out that she had been cheated? What would she likely have done? He knew she had not filed a civil suit against Bailey or any members of his group. He was about 99 percent positive that Helen had never talked to an attorney about it or the lawyer would have come forward after she disappeared. But the chances were she had not done anything before she was abducted.

The Brach name and the Brach money would have spoken loudly. If she had been contemplating filing a suit, Miller knew that it would have been all over the newspapers as soon as it was registered with the clerk of court. The publicity would have shattered the con scheme and Bailey *et al.* would never have been able to gull another unsuspecting woman.

Then he had an even more exciting thought. What if Helen had been planning to go to the state's attorney's office and file a criminal complaint against Bailey, as Barbara Morris had tried to do? Prosecutors undoubtedly would have treated Helen differently; they probably would have been only too happy to act on *her* complaint. If she *had* been thinking about doing that and if Bailey *had* found out about it, that could have been the motive for having her disposed of. Otherwise, it was simply too big a risk for him to take. If she'd been successful, Bailey and his group would not only have lost their income, but the chances were good they would have had to serve some prison time, as well.

What Miller had trouble understanding was how Bailey and the others were arrogant enough to think they could get away with their frauds. It all went back, he felt, to Silas Jayne and the iron grip he'd had over the whole industry—how everyone was afraid to talk because they knew Silas or his goons would get them. The Chicago PD probably had a whole drawerful of files about unsolved crimes connected to stables and horses, from theft and extortion to arson and murder.

Then he realized how unwittingly perfect his timing had been. Hamm had made the suggestion to reopen the Brach case at the very end of 1989. By then, Silas Jayne had been dead two years or so and the fear of retaliation had begun to dissipate. If he had tried to initiate a similar investigation five years earlier, he probably would have run into a brick wall as well. After all, Bailey and his buddies *had* gotten away with fraud for fifteen years. If it hadn't been for Hamm's suggestion they might have gotten away with it forever. But not now. He knew he was close.

After his conversation with Olsen, he called Cullen, Delorto, and Ivancich into his office and gave them strict orders. "Spread the word," he told them. "Get the news out to every law-enforcement agency in the country. Anytime anyone anywhere is arrested on charges having to do with illegal activity in the horse industry, I want to know about it."

The process was just getting cranked up when the Burns case blew up. In the months immediately following that, Miller and the investigators had been too busy chasing leads on horse killers to do any more sustained work on Brach.

Then, about a year after Burns decided to tell what he knew, Cullen had gotten a call from an FBI agent in Sacramento. "We've got somebody here you may want to talk to," the agent said. "It's a guy who was arrested in a horse swindle. And he's from Chicago."

"Oh, yeah?" Cullen replied, his interest rising. "What's his name?"

"Hang on," the California FBI said. "Let me get his folder."

Cullen drummed his fingers, waiting for the agent to come back on the line.

"Okay," the California agent said a minute later. "His name is Joe Edward Plemmons."

"Damn!" Cullen ejaculated. "We've been looking for him for months. We heard he knew most of the people in the local horse group and we've been trying to find him to see what he may know about Helen Brach and Richard Bailey."

"Well, he's here," the California agent replied laconically.

"Hold on to him," Cullen urged. "We'll fly out tonight."

"Don't hurry." The agent laughed. "He's not going anywhere."

Plemmons was born in the hills of North Carolina in 1948. Soon after he turned twenty-one, he left the South and migrated to Chicago, where he went to work at a local stable. Finding he liked the Windy City much better than the farm at home, he stuck around, gradually insinuating himself among the men who ran the business.

Barely five-seven and slim, with dark blond hair and a winning grin, Plemmons discovered that he, not unlike Bailey, had a gift for winning the confidence of others. Using that trait to his advantage, Plemmons realized it was easier to cheat people out of money than it was to earn it himself.

Over the years, he cheerfully admitted to Miller, he had participated in a vast number of shady deals, ranging from writing bad checks to dealing with forged pedigree papers on horses. One time, running low on cash, he took thirty thousand dollars from a man who thought he had connections in the drug trade and was paying him for a shipment of narcotics. When the man began pressing him for his drugs, Plemmons lied to him and told him he had been busted and the cops had confiscated both the drugs and the money. "The guy was furious," Plemmons said, "absolutely furious." Then he laughed. "But what the hell could he do?"

One of Plemmons's best friends in Chicago was a horseman named Kenneth Hansen. At one time, he and three other horse-world hangers-on had lived with Hansen and his wife. Although Hansen was almost old enough to be his father, he took a special liking to Plemmons and helped him out of more than one scrape with the police. Hansen even arranged it so Plemmons could get a false ID by using a birth certificate belonging to one of Hansen's sons.

Hansen, Plemmons carefully explained to Miller and the investigators, was a really mean bastard, starting his career in the horse world working as a stable hand for Silas Jayne and eventually bought his own stable. Hansen's brother, Curt, was a hit man for the mob, and Kenny himself had a violent temper that even he respected.

"What does this have to do with Richard Bailey and Helen Brach?" Miller asked impatiently.

"I'm getting to that," Plemmons said softly. "It just takes me awhile."

Miller glanced at Cullen and raised his eyebrows, giving him a "this is what I flew to California for?" look.

"One day early in 1977," Plemmons continued, "Kenny called me and asked me if I wanted to go to lunch with him and Richard Bailey. I said sure."

"Do you remember when that was?" interrupted Cullen.

Plemmons shrugged. "Early 1977. After Christmas. I don't remember the date, I just remember it was unseasonably warm."

Again Miller's eyebrows shot up. Warm? In Chicago in the middle of winter?

"Anyway," Plemmons went on. "We went to Bailey's stable and he gave us a quick tour, then we went to lunch in a restaurant not too far away."

"Do you remember the name of it?"

"No, but that's not the important thing."

"Sorry," said Miller. "Go ahead."

"After lunch, we were chatting a little, just small talk, and then Bailey said—and I'm quoting as best as I can remember—'Something has come up. The Candy Lady isn't so sweet anymore.'"

Miller opened his mouth to say something, then closed it.

"Yes?" Plemmons asked expectantly.

"Nothing," Miller replied. "Go ahead. I'll ask you later."

Plemmons nodded. "Bailey said he was looking for someone to, quote, 'take care of the situation,' end quote."

"Do you know what he meant by that?" Cullen asked.

"Sure," said Plemmons. "He wanted her done away with. But he just didn't want her dead; he wanted to make sure no one ever found her."

"Did he mention why he was asking you two?" Miller asked, trying to control his excitement.

"He said he would pay five thousand dollars to have the job done."

"And what did *you* say?"

"I didn't say anything at first. Kenny and I looked at each other and Kenny said he wasn't interested, that he wouldn't kill an old lady. Then he got up and went to the men's room."

"And what did Bailey do?"

"Bailey looked at me and asked, 'What would it take to get this done?' and I told him I wasn't into killing people."

"And what happened then?" Miller asked.

"Nothing," Plemmons said, putting his hands palm down on the table. "Bailey went back to his stable and Kenny dropped me off. But I'll tell you, Kenny was pissed off. He said that first Bailey had cut us out of the profit on the Brach scam, then insulted us by offering only five thousand dollars to have her murdered."

"Are you sure you don't remember exactly when that was?" Miller asked.

"No," Plemmons replied. "But it wasn't long before Helen Brach disappeared."

"Do you think Hansen would cooperate? Do you think he'd tell us the same thing you just said?"

Plemmons shook his head vigorously. "No way! He'd never do it. Ken Hansen," he added, "is the worst human being on this planet."

The vehemence with which he made that statement caused Miller to look at him in surprise.

"What do you mean by that?"

"Nothing," Plemmons said hurriedly. "Forget it."

It would be a long time before Miller would understand what he was referring to. And when he found out, he would be inclined to agree.

For most of the flight back to Chicago, Miller, Cullen, and Delorto debated how to handle the new information. If Plemmons's story checked out, it was the corroboration they had been looking for to confirm Olsen's story. There was one other benefit, as well. While Plemmons was far from being an angel, he was much more believable than Olsen, who had told several different stories. Also, Plemmons was likely to hold up better under cross-examination.

"I'm a little leery," Miller confessed to his investigators, "but that's part of my job. I need you guys to go out and talk to people and see if you can back up Plemmons's claims. If his story's going to fall apart, I want to know about it before we get him on the witness stand."

Six months later, Delorto called Miller. "I have good news and bad news about Plemmons," he said, sounding tired.

"What's the good news?"

"Plemmons's story about the Bailey offer looks solid. It's going to hold up just fine."

"That's great!" Miller said excitedly. "I guess that gives us Bailey on a platter."

"Yeah," agreed Delorto unenthusiastically.

"What's the matter? What's the bad news?"

"Don't worry about the defense calling Ken Hansen as a witness," he said bitterly.

"What do you mean?" the prosecutor asked, disturbed by Delorto's tone. "What do you have?"

"The murder of three children."

"Three children!" Miller replied, shocked. "What three children?"

"It was back in 1955," Delorto explained. "Almost forty years ago.

You were still in diapers. Three kids, all young boys. One boy was sexually assaulted, and they were all killed and dumped in a forest preserve."

Miller was shaken. "Plemmons told you this?"

"Eventually," Delorto said, "after a couple more interviews. But it isn't just from him. I got it from some other guys, as well. They say Hansen admitted it to them a long time ago."

"God," Miller said. "What else is this investigation going to turn up?"

Over the next few days, Delorto met several times with Miller, begging the prosecutor to find a way to charge Hansen in federal court.

"I'd like to do it as much as you, Jimmy," Miller said. "But I can't. There's no way this can be turned into a RICO. There's no predicate; it isn't part of any enterprise."

Delorto continued to argue, but Miller was adamant.

"We can't do it, Jimmy, and that's that," Miller said, running out of patience. "Tell the state's attorney's office we'll help in any way we can. They'll get him. Wait and see."

"I sure hope we can do it," Delorto replied. "I don't want to see that bastard get away."

24

Nearing the End
Summer 1994

S TEVE MILLER paced slowly back and forth, collecting his thoughts. After four and a half years of living with a multitude of characters who inhabited a world totally foreign to his own, he was finding it difficult to explain his experiences to a group that was just as unenlightened about the horse world as he had been when he started the investigation.

About six months before, shortly after the turn of the year, the prosecutor suddenly realized that he had to quit investigating and get down to grand jurying, otherwise, he was going to lose major portions of the case that had been so painstakingly compiled.

Since almost all of the accusations he wanted to make against the Chicago scammers stemmed from the single criminal complaint filed by Barbara Morris, Miller had used that as a foundation from which he built steadily upward. When the other fraud accusations began accumulating, he spurred his investigators to dig deeper so he could try to prosecute under RICO. If he could convict Bailey on a RICO count, the penalty would be considerably more severe than simple fraud. But to get to the point where he could utilize RICO, he had to go back and re-create what had been going on in the Chicago horse world almost twenty years previously. Plus, there were the fifteen horse killings to which Burns had confessed, each of which had to be investigated individually.

Miller's success in being able to bring everything together depended in large part on getting the cooperation of those who had been involved, not just the victims but also the parties to the scams themselves. Hugi was one of his early flips. By getting the veterinarian not only to tell what he knew but to help him tighten the noose around the others was an important step.

Another occurred when Tom Burns told him that one of the people he had killed a horse for was Donna Hunter. When Miller's men began investigating her, they discovered that at one time she had been romantically involved with Jerry Farmer. In return for leniency, Hunter agreed to give Miller's investigators more information about her former beau. Vital to Hunter's decision was the fact that when she ordered the assassination of the horse Emili's Choice, both she and her husband, Michael, were on federal probation. Both Hunters had been convicted earlier, along with Frank Jayne, Jr., on drug charges. Miller, using an almost guaranteed stiff prison sentence as leverage, convinced her to flip on Farmer.

However, Farmer himself, Miller discovered, was proving exceedingly tough. For almost four years, the prosecutor had been haggling with Farmer's lawyer in an attempt to get Farmer to flip on Bailey and others involved in the scam. The initial force that pushed Farmer over the top and made him realize that a guilty plea was in his own best interest was the arrest of Tom Burns and Burns's assertion that Farmer arranged the murder of a horse named Empire. Also playing roles in that horse killing were Steve Williamson, a stable hand, and Johnnie Youngblood, a horse trainer in partnership with Farmer.

After Burns's confession, Miller realized that his best chance of getting Farmer was to put pressure on Youngblood and Williamson. If he could get them to flip on Farmer, then he could use that information to get Farmer to flip on Bailey. It was a tedious, time-consuming process and it took as long as two years for Miller to work from Point A to Point C. But in the end, it paid off.

In addition to being a trainer, Farmer also operated a horse-brokering business out of a facility called Round About Farms. As a broker, Farmer made money by selling horses directly and by collecting commissions on horses he sold for others. If one of Farmer's customers collected on an insurance claim on a horse purchased from Farmer and then bought a replacement animal, Farmer could make money twice. Such a situation had revolved around Empire.

Farmer originally sold the horse to a customer who has not been identified for $68,000. The customer then took out a $68,000 policy on the horse with Bankers Standard Insurance Company.

Unfortunately, Empire suffered from chronic lameness, which only got worse after its sale. The new owner, therefore, would not have been able to resell the horse without losing money.

The solution, Farmer said, was to have Empire killed, let the owner collect on the insurance, and then use that money to buy another horse.

It had been a long, winding road, but now Miller was under deadline pressure. If he did not act quickly, the statute of limitations on the Morris fraud was going to expire and he would be left with nothing. He had, to his immense regret, already lost Frank Jayne, Jr., because his investigators had not been able to uncover any violations committed by Jayne that fell within the required time period. As far as Miller and his investigators could determine, Jayne had not participated in the Morris swindle. Therefore, any other crimes committed by Jayne were beyond the pale; the statute of limitations had run out. The prosecutor wanted to make sure the same thing did not happen with Bailey and the others.

Miller went before the grand jury and told them about a series of crimes that occurred within the equine industry, some of them going back twenty-two years, and included the murder of Helen Vorhees Brach. He explained the RICO statute and how it pertained to the current situation. He assured them that they would see how it all fit together and became part of a package, how a series of relatively minor crimes becomes part of a much more serious whole. He called it murder by mail fraud.

After the Burns revelations, Miller realized that he would not be able to carry the entire prosecutorial role alone, so he had enlisted help from two fellow assistants: Ronald Safer, who became an overnight expert on Bailey *et al.* and Susan Cox, who immersed herself in details on the horse killings. For a long series of seemingly endless days, the group listened while Cox, Safer, and Miller, backed up by Cullen, Delorto, Ivancich, and almost two dozen witnesses, went into sometimes excruciating detail about the series of crimes allegedly committed by the people Miller had targeted for grand jury consideration.

On July 27, 1994, four and a half years after the almost whimsical beginning of the probe, the grand jury handed up indictments against twenty-three people.

Standing before a battery of microphones and a cluster of TV lights that were hotter than the midsummer sun, Miller read off the names of those who had been indicted, adding their then-current ages, addresses, and the charges.

Richard Bailey, sixty-five, of Chicago, faced twenty-nine counts including racketeering, mail and wire fraud, and money laundering. But the more sensational charges against him were those relating to Helen Brach's disappearance. Miller had not been able to make a murder charge against the con man, but he did convince the grand jury to charge him with conspiring to kill Helen, soliciting her death, and having caused her murder.

Charged along with Bailey in connection with the swindles of the Chicago women but *not* in connection with Helen's disappearance were Robert Lee Brown, fifty-nine, who was accused of racketeering and mail and wire fraud; Jerry Farmer, sixty-one, of Augusta, Georgia, for racketeering and obstructing the IRS; and Dr. Ross Hugi, fifty, of Mundelein, Illinois, for wire fraud.

The other nineteen—all members of the equestrian industry, including two of the top ten performers on the Grand Prix jumping tour, as well as several nationally known trainers and two veterinarians—were charged with defrauding companies who wrote policies on their murdered horses.

Leading the list was Barney Ward, fifty, of Brewster, New York, accused of mail and wire fraud, obstruction of justice by threatening a witness (Burns), and conspiracy. Others were:

- George Lindemann, Jr., thirty, of Greenwich, Connecticut, for wire fraud
- Marion Hulick, sixty, of Greenwich, Connecticut, for wire fraud
- Paul Valliere, forty-three, of North Smithfield, Rhode Island, for conspiracy to commit wire fraud and mail fraud
- Nancy Banefield, thirty-six, of Mathews, Virginia, for conspiracy to commit mail fraud
- Donna Migliore Brown, thirty-seven, of Palm Beach, Florida, for wire fraud
- Tom Burns (aka Tim Ray), thirty-three, of Grayslake, Illinois, for conspiracy to commit mail and wire fraud
- Dr. Dana Tripp, thirty-four, of Valencia, Pennsylvania, for conspiracy to defraud by falsifying Coggins papers, failure to file tax returns, and concealing a felony

- Johnnie Youngblood, thirty-two, of Naperville, Illinois, for mail fraud
- Steve Williamson, fifty-one, of Plainfield, Illinois, for mail fraud
- Tammie Glaspie, thirty-six, of Walker, Michigan, for mail fraud
- James Hutson, fifty-three, of Oregon, Illinois, for mail fraud
- Allen Levinson, fifty-two, of Highland Park, Illinois, for mail fraud
- Michael Hunter, forty-five, of Mundelein, Illinois, for mail fraud
- Donna Hunter, forty-three, of Mundelein, Illinois, for mail fraud
- Phil Sudakoff, seventy-six, of Chicago, for mail fraud
- Herb Kroninger, fifty-three, of Bolingbrook, Illinois, for mail fraud
- Scott Thompson, forty-one, Chicago, for conspiracy to commit mail fraud
- Ron Mueller, sixty-two, of Harvard, Illinois, for lying to a federal law-enforcement officer

Among those observing developments with keen interest were the insurance companies that had paid claims on the horses listed in the indictments as having been murdered. If the allegations proved correct, these companies had been swindled out of hundreds of thousands of dollars.

Considering the many things that can happen to show horses and thoroughbreds, it is not surprising that almost all of the more expensive animals are heavily insured. Horses die every day of colic or some other disease. In such cases, insurance is a godsend for the owners, a way to protect a costly investment. But in the wrong hands, an insurance policy can be an invitation to commit fraud. This was particularly true in the eighties, when financial change was sweeping the equestrian industry. It began when the bottom dropped out of the thoroughbred market; people simply quit buying horses, mainly because the Tax Reform Act of 1986 removed many of the deductions that had been linked to horse ownership. After that, it became a great temptation for owners who had thousands of dollars tied up in horseflesh to start looking through their insurance policies to see if there was not some way of turning the animals into hard cash. One way, of course, was to have them killed.

In a normal year, horse owners around the country submit claims totaling some $30 million. Experts say some 95 percent of those claims are legitimate. But that means that about 5 percent are fraudulent.

If the charges leveled by the Chicago grand jury were proven, it would mean that the U.S. branch of General Insurance Company of Trieste and Venice had claims filed against it for $275,000 (Charisma, $250,000; Streetwise, $25,000); that the American Bankers Insurance Company of Florida lost $40,000 on Belgium Waffle; that the Bankers Standard Insurance Company, a subsidiary of the Cigna Corporations, was out $238,000 (Empire, $68,000; Roseau Platiere, $75,000; Rainman, $50,000; Emili's Choice, $45,000); and that the American Live Stock Insurance Company lost $200,000 on its policy on Condino.

Much to Miller's satisfaction, the guilty pleas began flowing in. Figuring that their best chance of dodging lengthy prison terms was in cooperating with federal prosecutors, the majority of those who had been charged worked out plea agreements with Miller, in many cases promising to testify against their colleagues in return for lighter sentences. In some instances, the indictments already reflected reduced charges, since the accused had indicated a willingness to cooperate before the charges were filed.

Tom Burns, the notorious Sandman, was charged only with conspiracy to commit wire and mail fraud (punishable by a maximum of five years in prison) in connection with the murder of Streetwise, although he had admitted to killing fourteen other horses.

In the plea bargain his lawyer worked out with Miller, it was agreed that Miller would recommend that he be sentenced to six months in a federal labor camp provided he testified against his former friends and employers. It also was part of the agreement that he would not be prosecuted in Florida for his role in Streetwise's death.

On the other hand, Burns's companion, Harlow Arlie, who was not considered crucial to Miller's case, was charged with insurance fraud and cruelty to animals in a Florida state court in connection with the fatal injury to Streetwise. He was sentenced to eighteen months and served six months before being paroled.

Another who was quick to accept Miller's offer was Dr. Ross Hugi. In return for his cooperation and because he was considered to be a major potential witness, he was indicted only on a single count of wire fraud.

Jerry Farmer, another member of the alleged con team, also was treated relatively lightly. While the charges against him carried a maximum possible prison time of twenty-five years, the chances were the judge would be lenient when it came time for Farmer to be sentenced if Farmer took the stand—or was willing to take the stand—against his former partners.

By early 1995, eighteen of the twenty-three persons indicted had pleaded guilty. Robert Lee Brown would later join the group. The only ones electing to be tried were Richard Bailey, Barney Ward, George Lindemann, Jr., and Marion Hulick. Eventually, Ward, too, pleaded guilty to a single charge.

As their lawyers pointed out to all of them, there was a definite risk involved in rejecting the prosecution's offer to plea. If convicted on all the counts against them, Lindemann and Hulick could end up serving as much as fifteen years in prison and Ward could be sentenced to thirty-five years. But Miller's main target, as he had made clear to his investigators from the first, was Richard Bailey. If convicted on all of the counts listed in the sixty-seven-page indictment, the smooth-talking con man, whom Miller playfully tagged the "Galloping Gigolo," could be sentenced to as many as 245 years in prison. In the world of criminal courts, however, a case isn't over until the judge pronounces sentence or sets the defendant free, and there were still some surprises left from Bailey.

25

Married . . . Not Married . . . Married

RICHARD BAILEY, literally, got caught with his pants down.
On the same day the indictments were announced, a team of
federal officers led by FBI agent Bob Buchan, who had been teamed with
Miller on the Hartmann case, stormed into Bailey's Lake Shore Drive
apartment, cuffed him, and took him off to jail. But first, Bailey had to
put his trousers on. He was lounging in his underwear when the officers made their unannounced appearance.

A few hours later, when brought before a magistrate to be arraigned,
Bailey was denied bond. But being behind bars did not remove him from
public view. Less than a week later, he was in the headlines again.

Not surprisingly, the reason behind the flare of publicity had to do
with a woman. But it was not Helen Brach or the other women he allegedly cheated out of considerable sums of money. This time, the name
linked to Bailey's was that of a high-profile member of Chicago's medical profession, Dr. Annette Hoffman, a South African–born plastic surgeon with a prosperous Gold Coast practice and a million-dollar home
in affluent Lincoln Park. In the end, of all the publicized incidents involving Bailey and various women, this relationship was perhaps the
strangest of them all.

Although the Bailey-Hoffman relationship did not become public
until August of 1994, it had actually begun the previous March, when
the two met in a trendy restaurant frequented by Chicago's affluent professionals.

Operating true to form, Bailey turned on all his charm and put a
tremendous rush on the raven-haired physician, a petite fiftyish woman
with a penchant for designer clothes and ostentatious jewelry. Their
first date, the next day, was dinner at the Ritz-Carlton Hotel. The next
day, Bailey took her dancing at one of his favorite places, the Pump

Room. A few days later, she agreed to fly with him to Las Vegas, where they were met by a Bailey-arranged limousine stuffed with fresh flowers. Within an hour, they were wed in one of the city's small chapels.

Ironically, unknown to Hoffman, the Las Vegas elopement was one of Bailey's shopworn scenarios. He had proposed just such a plan with at least one of his previous victims, Jean Robinson, back in 1975.

Whatever expectations Hoffman had when she agreed to become the second Mrs. Richard Bailey (Bailey had been divorced from his first wife, Eunice, in 1988), they were immediately dashed.

The ink had barely had time to dry on the marriage certificate before Hoffman became suspicious that her new spouse was not who or what he claimed to be. Her first tip-off: When they checked into their honeymoon hotel, Bailey paid in cash. When she asked him why, he confessed he did not own a credit card. Hoffman was shocked. What kind of person in today's society, she asked herself, does not have at least one piece of plastic?

This discovery nagged at her so persistently that she decided to hire a private investigator to look into her new husband's past. The next day, while Bailey was asleep in the bedroom of their honeymoon suite, she sneaked his Social Security number out of his wallet. While he snored away, she telephoned a private investigator in Chicago and gave him the number. "Check him out," she ordered.

Soon after the newlyweds returned to Chicago, the PI's startling report arrived. According to the investigator, Bailey had a terrible credit history and had been sued repeatedly by women who claimed he had cheated them out of considerable sums of money. He also had lied about his age, telling her he was considerably younger than his actual age of sixty-five.

Angry and disillusioned, Hoffman hired a lawyer and filed for an annulment, claiming that Bailey had been unable to consummate the marriage. On April 22, thirteen days after the Nevada wedding, a judge signed an order legally dissolving the union.

"He didn't have too much intelligence," she told *Chicago Tribune* columnist Irv Kupcinet, "but he was a fun guy to party with."

But that was not the end of the story. Three months later, Hoffman reappeared in Bailey's life, and in newspaper headlines.

On August 1, four days after he had been arrested, Bailey again asked to be released on bond. Although he didn't have much cash himself, he told the magistrate, his former wife, Dr. Annette Hoffman, was willing to help. She would let him live in her spacious home for at least a month until he could make other arrangements.

Hoffman herself appeared in court to verify his claim. In a newsworthy postscript, Hoffman added that she was even considering marrying Bailey a second time, "depending on the outcome of his legal problems."

U.S. Magistrate Ronald Guzman peeked over his glasses at Hoffman and then at Bailey. "Mr. Bailey is a chronic and habitual liar," Guzman said, "and the Court would be foolish indeed to trust him. No bond."

The saga continued.

On October 27, almost three months after Magistrate Guzman had quashed Bailey's latest effort to be released pending trial, the former stable owner tried again to win his freedom.

This time, Bailey had a new lawyer. Jo-Anne Wolfson, who had represented him at the deposition hearing in 1979, had disappeared from the scene soon after that. Reportedly, she was retired and living in Florida. His new counsel was a well-known and respected defender named Patrick Tuite (who as an assistant state's attorney years before had unsuccessfully prosecuted Silas Jayne). He asked senior U.S. District Judge Milton Shadur—who had the authority to overrule Magistrate Guzman—to let Bailey go and live with one his brothers, William, and his sister-in-law Shirley. He could work in his brother's real estate management business, Tuite said. Furthermore, he would be willing to wear an electronic monitor to ensure that he stayed put.

For the second time, Hoffman also appeared in the courtroom, this time claiming that she did indeed plan to remarry Bailey. To back up the assertion, she produced a prenuptial agreement signed both by her and Bailey.

The courtroom grew unnaturally silent while Shadur, regarded by members of the local legal community as possibly the city's most intelligent and thoughtful sitting federal judge, read the document. While he did not disclose the terms of the agreement, the judge obviously was impressed. "Let me think about it," he said.

Bailey turned to Hoffman and winked. It looks like it's in the bag, the look said.

* * *

In late November, with Bailey's trial set for the following May, Shadur said he had decided to agree to Bailey's request to be freed on bond, provided that Bailey and Hoffman were remarried. It might be seen as "a bizarre resumption of their relationship," he said, but if they wanted to get remarried, that was okay with him.

But the judge also laid down some ground rules. If he did release him, Shadur told Bailey, he was going to have to wear an electronic monitor, he could not leave the house, and Dr. Hoffman could not practice her profession on him. In other words, *no plastic surgery.*

Both Bailey and Hoffman nodded their agreement.

However, Miller and Ronald Safer, who was going to act as coprosecutor when Bailey's case came to court, vociferously objected. Waving a cassette tape, Safer said it proved that if Bailey was released, he might never be seen again.

"What's on the tape, Mr. Safer?" Shadur asked.

It was, the prosecutor said, a recording of a telephone conversation between Bailey and Hoffman in which Hoffman suggested that there would be a better chance of Hollywood becoming interested in a movie of Bailey's life if he managed to escape.

Shadur shook his head, declining to reverse his earlier decision. He thought it was "a bizarre suggestion" that Hoffman would risk her bond on a speculative movie deal. "Let's see what develops in their marriage plans," he said.

On Saturday, December 3, Bailey and Hoffman were married for a second time. This time, there was no flower-filled limousine or pretentious Las Vegas wedding parlor; the locale was a glum, no-frills government office in a lower floor of the jail in which Bailey was being held. There was no honeymoon suite in an expensive hotel. After the ceremony, Bailey went back to his cell. There was no opportunity to consummate that union, either.

On Monday, December 5, the first court day after the wedding, Shadur, with evidence in hand that the marriage had been performed, announced that he planned to order Bailey's release on bond, pending trial.

Miller, obviously upset by the turn of events, quickly cobbled together a formal protest and hurried with it to the 7th U.S. Circuit Court of Appeals, pleading with the judges to consider it an emergency and examine the issue immediately. Within hours, before Bailey could be released, the appeals court put a hold on Shadur's order and issued a counter order saying that Bailey would have to remain behind bars until the group had time to consider the issue thoroughly.

The following Monday, five days later, the appeals court formalized its emergency ruling, declaring there would be no bond for Bailey. He would, the court said, have to remain in the Metropolitan Correctional Facility until his trial, which was then scheduled for May 9, 1995.

After the flurry of activity surrounding the Hoffman-Bailey melodrama, Miller and Safer began digging in for Bailey's trial. In expectation of an expected eight-to-ten-week marathon, the prosecutors began the huge amount of preparation needed before they could begin presenting a complicated case to a jury: lining up witnesses, rethumbing for the umpteenth time huge stacks of reports and interviews, huddling yet again with investigators, cataloging the monstrous stack of documents they would need to have fingertip-ready, and, finally, hammering out their final courtroom strategy.

Toward the end of February 1996, virtually on the eve of the trial, from the prosecutor's point of view, developments took another unexpected turn: Bailey, who had adamantly and vociferously proclaimed his innocence, announced his intention to plead guilty.

The decision stunned prosecutors, who were hoping for a trial so they could present all of the evidence they had compiled against the con man. They feared that if he pleaded guilty, much of the material they had gathered during the long, painstaking investigation might never be revealed and the full extent of his culpability might never be known.

In the end, Miller and Safer did not have to worry. Bailey's decision was far from a blanket confession; he would *not*, Patrick Tuite explained (by then, Bailey had a second lawyer, as well, Ronald Menaker), be pleading to *all* the charges against him. Specifically, Tuite emphasized, Bailey would *not* be admitting to *any* of the accusations relating to the disappearance of Helen Brach.

Well, Miller asked, quite reasonably, what *was* Bailey admitting to?

The answer was not a simple one. It took a confusing two-day session before Judge Shadur to bring it into focus.

With his lawyers acting as his spokesmen—and occasionally personally answering questions from the judge—Bailey admitted the following:

- Acting in concert with Robert Lee Brown to defraud Carole Karstenson
- Taking money under false pretenses from Jean Robinson
- Perpetrating a fraud against Linda Holmwood
- Inflating the prices of horses he sold to two students of a trainer
- Acting with Hugi to defraud Barbara Morris of fifty thousand dollars
- Taking fifty-five thousand dollars from *Joyce Carruthers* as part of a phony partnership deal on the purchase of a horse that actually was worth less than ten thousand dollars
- Acting with Jerry Farmer to defraud *Marilyn Jameson* of fifty-five thousand dollars

Considering the heavy legal implications, Shadur questioned Bailey specifically about his *intent* in his dealings with his victims—that is, had he *planned* to scam them?

"I was trying to get as much money as I could," Bailey acknowledged. "I was charging them too much money, that's for sure."

"And when you were charging them, as you put it, 'too much money,' was it your purpose to get more than you knew that the things were worth at the time?" Shadur asked.

"Yes," said Bailey, nodding.

What Bailey did *not* concede, in addition to the charges involving Helen Brach, was proposing marriage to his victims to help facilitate his fraud. The issue came up specifically in the case of Linda Holmwood, the alcoholic who bought a whole string of virtually worthless horses from Bailey after he plied her with champagne.

"Is it accurate, as the government sets out here, that you made some false promises to her as part of this [plan to defraud]?" Shadur asked.

"No!" Bailey said. "Not as far as saying that I would marry her, if that's what you are referring to. I might have told her that she was a classy lady or something like that, certainly."

He also denied that he ever threatened anyone in connection with any of his frauds.

"So you're saying that's something that did not happen?" Shadur asked.

"I never threatened anyone in my life," he replied.

One thing that was never definitively settled was his intention in placing ads in the "Lonely Hearts" section of a local newspaper. Did he place the ads strictly as part of his con? Or did he have other motives in mind?

"Mr. Bailey is willing to admit that he may have defrauded [the women who responded] if the opportunity came up, but he may not have," Tuite explained.

Turning to Bailey, Shadur—who bears a remarkable resemblance to the actor Vincent Price—glared at him under his bushy brows. "Why *were* you placing those ads?" he asked.

"Judge," Bailey said earnestly, "I was really looking for a woman to marry. I was looking for the right woman."

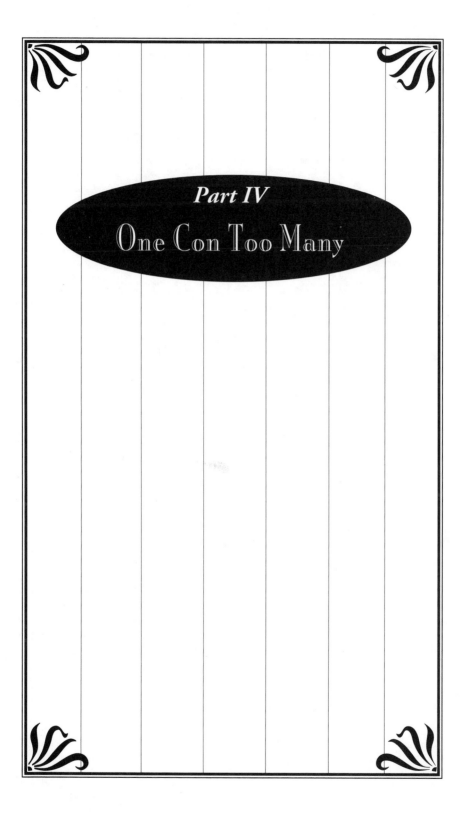

Part IV

One Con Too Many

26

Richard Bailey Goes to Court
May 1995

S TEVE MILLER turned to Ron Safer and grinned. "This isn't going to end the proceedings," he said gleefully. "It's just going to help us focus our case."

For Bailey, the decision to plead guilty to some of the charges against him had been a tremendous gamble. If he had stuck with his original decision to bring his entire case before a jury, the prosecution would have been required to prove he was guilty beyond a reasonable doubt in order to win a conviction.

Instead, by pleading guilty, Bailey would have to go before Judge Shadur at a sentencing hearing. Shadur would listen to the government's evidence and then decide what Bailey's punishment should be.

In effect, it would be a trial with the judge, rather than a jury, making the final decision on Bailey's fate. Whereas the jury would have needed reasonable doubt, the law was such that Shadur could rule simply by a *preponderance* of the evidence. In other words, a jury would have had to find him absolutely, positively, unconditionally guilty to convict him. But Shadur, operating under a precept almost identical to the one that prevails in civil cases, would only have to determine that it was *more likely than not* that Bailey was guilty; the evidence had to be only 51 percent against the con man instead of 100 percent.

There was another factor peculiar to federal courts that also would play a role in what happened to Bailey. The fact that he had pleaded guilty to some of the charges virtually guaranteed that he would do prison time. In this regard, the federal system is much more stringent than the systems in most states. In U.S. courts, there are specific and, for all practical purposes, unvarying rules called "sentencing guidelines" that judges are obliged to follow. If someone is convicted (or pleads guilty) in a federal court to a certain crime, the guidelines lay out the specific penalty. This is contrary to the provisions in many state courts, where individual judges have considerable leeway in deciding sentences. In federal court, a judge has almost no freedom to stray from the guidelines. A federal judge is an equal-opportunity sentencer.

Another important difference between state and federal courts is the not commonly known fact that there is no parole in the federal system. Although sentences can be shortened by "good behavior" provisions, such reductions are minimal compared with the large chunks of prison time lopped off the sentences of those convicted in state courts.

These factors figured into Bailey's decision, especially since he was sixty-five at the time and even a minimal sentence could easily mean that he would spend the rest of his life behind bars. But there were other issues to consider, as well. One was finances. By pleading guilty, Bailey not only had reduced the time *he* would have to spend in court; he also had chipped away at the time his *lawyers* would have to spend in court. It would cost him less in legal fees for lawyers for a sentencing hearing than for a full-blown trial. Considering the fact that Bailey claimed to be essentially broke (most of his assets disappeared, he said, into his former wife's pocket after his divorce), this was not an inconsequential consideration. Even if his new wife, Annette Hoffman, had a substantial bank account, which was not unlikely, considering her profession and the type of jewelry she was prone to display, it was not Bailey's money to spend. The terms of the prenuptial agreement had not been disclosed, but it almost certainly covered this contingency.

Also in his favor was the fact that he had admitted at least a certain degree of guilt, a factor that a judge was allowed to consider under the sentencing guidelines. There was also the possibility that the prosecution's evidence allegedly tying Bailey to Helen Brach's disappearance was less substantial than Miller and Safer had indicated, and this would be more quickly perceived by an experienced jurist like Shadur than by a panel of laypersons.

The flip side of that coin, of course, was that Shadur would be more likely to zero in on the issues and be less swayed by emotion. Defense lawyers want jurors to feel empathy for their client and perhaps treat them more kindly. They do not want them to be so outraged that they are more inclined to convict out of anger over the heartlessness of the crime. Tuite and Menaker apparently were worried that a jury might be so outraged by Bailey's outlandish scams against vulnerable women that they would convict him on the Brach charges just for spite. Shadur, they figured, might more easily be able to separate the issues.

Going into the final stage of the Bailey drama, Tuite and Menaker estimated that Bailey might emerge with a sentence as mild as twenty-seven months.

If this was truly their thinking, an alarm bell should have rung when Shadur made his pronouncement at the end of the guilty-plea session. He was accepting Bailey's plea, the judge said. But at the same time, he was serving notice that his decision on how long Bailey would have to serve would be based not only on the charges Bailey was confessing to but on the "totality" of his conduct. In other words, if Bailey thought he was going to get away with a light sentence by pleading guilty to a handful of relatively minor charges, that was not necessarily going to be the case.

In a deep, resonant voice pregnant with authority, Shadur reminded Bailey that prosecutors would have the opportunity to ask for the stiffest-possible sentence. And all they had to do was prove to the judge's satisfaction that Bailey was also *probably* guilty of other, more serious charges than the ones the con man had admitted.

For Miller and Safer, it was a win-win situation. It meant that at the sentencing hearing—in actuality a minitrial that was likely to last two weeks or longer—they could concentrate on trying to show that Bailey had been instrumental in Helen Brach's disappearance and pretty much let the other charges go, except to the degree they wanted the crimes emphasized as a reminder to Shadur to consider totality.

Bailey's only realistic chance of not spending at least most of the rest of his life in prison lay in his and his lawyers' ability to persuade Judge Shadur that he had had absolutely nothing to do with Helen Brach's fate and that although he had indeed taken money from a number of women, he was not a hard-core criminal who thought nothing of seeking someone's murder.

Because he had to allow time for a federal probation officer to draw up a presentence report—essentially a judge's eyes–only document outlining Bailey's personal history, incorporating both favorable as well as unfavorable material—Shadur set the hearing date for two and a half months in the future.

This time, there was no serious debate on whether Bailey should be released on bond.

*   *   *

While Miller and Safer were denied a jury trial during which they'd hoped they could display their carefully accumulated voluminous evidence, they still would have the opportunity to present much of it while zeroing in on the con man's alleged role in Helen Brach's disappearance—a fact they brought home with resounding clarity during the opening statements.

In his ten-minute oration formally opening the sentencing hearing, Miller went immediately to the Helen Brach issue, giving notice that it would be the thrust of the prosecution's case.

"Helen Brach had everything to live for," said Miller, who was plagued throughout the hearing by a hacking cough. She was a "forward-looking person" who, in February 1977, inexplicably "dropped off the face of the earth, never to be seen again. But," he added, turning to look at Bailey, "people do not suddenly vanish without reason."

In the next few days, he promised Shadur, he and Safer would prove to the judge's satisfaction that the reason for Helen Brach's disappearance had to do in general with activities in Chicago's horse world and specifically with Bailey's manipulations.

"Richard Bailey came from nowhere. He had no formal education, and suddenly the world of the equestrian industry opened up to him," said Miller. Miller went on to say that it was through his role in this industry that he had met Helen Brach, the woman he decided was "the perfect victim."

She was rich, she loved animals, and she fell under Bailey's spell. "Richard Bailey," Miller said, "confided to one of his employees that he had sold her several worthless animals and he told another that Helen Brach was his biggest pigeon ever. He even bragged about how he got her to buy the same horse twice." At the same time, Miller said, Bailey was contemptuous of her, referring to her as "the Golden Goose" and "a lousy biff."

Bailey's plans to continue bleeding Helen Brach went astray late in 1976 or early in 1977, the prosecutor said, when she found out that she was one of his victims. "Helen Brach went into a rage, a fury." She threatened to go to the Cook County state's attorney's office and expose him as a con man. It was then, Miller added, that Bailey took steps to have her killed.

"There is no rational explanation for Helen Brach's disappearance other than she was murdered," he concluded.

Ron Menaker, who presented the opening statement for the defense, categorically denied that Bailey "ever solicited any person to cause the murder of Helen Brach" and said that he did not "conspire or join any group" having anything to do with her disappearance or murder.

In a rambling fifty-five-minute presentation, Menaker traced the history of the Brach-Bailey relationship, claiming it was cordial, platonic, and filled with mutual respect. "Mr. Bailey *never* sold Helen Brach any horses," Menaker said, although the heiress bought three animals from his brother P.J. "None of those horses had any disabilities when she bought them. The accusation that Richard Bailey sold Helen worthless horses is not true."

In mid-1976, Helen Brach, apparently unhappy with her horses' lack of success, changed trainers, firing Bailey's brother and hiring a man named Peter DiVito. Still, according to Menaker, she did not hold Richard Bailey responsible for the horses' lackluster performance. "She was not angry at Richard Bailey. Helen Brach never accused him of ripping her off in relation to these three horses. Helen Brach," he declared, *"was not taken advantage of."*

Although Brach bought seven additional horses, they were purchased by DiVito at public auctions and not through Richard Bailey. At the time she disappeared, Helen Brach was still in the "throes of the relationship" with Bailey, Menaker said. "She knew he had a line of baloney, but she told friends, 'I enjoy being with him.'"

As proof that she held no animosity toward Bailey, she asked him to accompany her to New York on New Year's Eve, 1976, six weeks before she disappeared, so they could dance to Guy Lombardo. And, a few weeks later, after Helen confided to Bailey that she was not feeling well and wanted to go have a checkup, he suggested the Mayo Clinic.

"She said she could not get in there because she had no doctor to refer her. But Bailey said he and members of his family had been going there for years and he could arrange it, which he did."

When Helen went to Rochester, Bailey went to West Palm Beach, Florida, where he arranged to be joined by a female real-estate agent he wanted to thank for handling a property sale for him. "After they had been there a few days, Bailey sent her back to Chicago, explaining that he was expecting a friend to arrive. He later called the real-estate agent and told her, 'My friend never showed up.'"

In short, Menaker said, Bailey had had nothing to do with the disappearance and probable murder of Helen Brach. On their way to trying to solve the mystery, Menaker argued, government investigators took a wrong turn and ended up at Richard Bailey's front door, when they should have been in Pittsburgh.

"The person who could help us in finding Helen Brach is Jack Matlick. He was the last person to see her alive and the first to see her dead."

Although Menaker raised the Matlick issue in his opening statement, it played a very minor role in the defense case. Instead, Menaker and Tuite hammered at two other themes.

One was an attempt to destroy the prosecution's arguments that Bailey had the motive, the opportunity, and the desire to get rid of Helen Brach. Thanks to the legal process known as discovery, under which the government was required to provide the defense with the names of its witnesses and copies of statements they had made, Menaker and Tuite knew who would be taking the stand to speak against Bailey and basically what they would say in response to prosecution questions. The two they viewed as most dangerous to Bailey's defense were Joe Edward Plemmons and Cathy Jayne Olsen.

Knowing that Plemmons was going to be questioned about an alleged offer from Bailey to have Brach killed and that Olsen was going to testify that she had overheard Bailey and her father talking about Helen Brach's murder, Menaker tried to defuse the prosecution bomb before it could be lit.

"For sixteen years, Joe Plemmons never related this," Menaker told Judge Shadur. "You're going to hear about the wheeling, dealing, and maneuvering that resulted in his statement."

Plemmons, Menaker added, was a career criminal who, among other things, took horses that did not belong to him. "Years ago," he said in an impassioned tone, "if you were a horse thief, you were hung. Now you become a government witness."

Cathy Olsen, on the other hand, was a pathetic figure who "has been in and out of mental hospitals for years." She not only had severe mental problems, Menaker added, but she had a personal grudge against her father that colored her perception of the facts. "She is willing," Menaker said, "to sell out anyone else if it will help her."

Since the government case, in effect, was two-pronged—one pointing toward Brach's disappearance and the other toward Bailey's con games—Menaker and Tuite also needed a second line of defense.

In an attempt to answer government accusations about how Bailey gulled vulnerable middle-aged women, the defense lawyers would argue that what Bailey had done should have been decided in a civil court rather than in a criminal one. The victims, the defense claimed, had other remedies available to them for their complaints. Criminal charges should never have been filed, Tuite contended.

The government's response was that while some of the complaints had been heard in civil courts, they were not recognized as the egregious violations they were because Bailey had purposely lied under oath about their gravity. Also, since there were numerous complaints of almost identical behavior, that on its own demonstrated a pattern of activity that threw the case into the criminal realm.

In an attempt to show how ruthless and determined Bailey had been in his quest for money, Miller and Safer called a string of victims and former colleagues who testified about the con man's coldhearted tactics and hidden propensity for violence.

John Staren, a balding, gray-haired commodities broker, said he entered into a brief partnership with Bailey years ago because he thought he was a friendly, charming fellow. But it wasn't long before he got a different picture. "I saw him physically accost a vendor at a horse show and take money from him."

Once he got to know Bailey, Staren testified, he saw that he preyed on elderly women, romancing them and trying to talk them into giving him money. However, behind their backs, he called them "pigeons" and laughed about how he could "put them in his trick bag."

"Did he ever say anything about Helen Brach?" Miller asked.

Staren nodded. "He said she was one of his 'best pigeons' and claimed that he had made a couple of hundred thousand dollars from her."

What bothered him the most at the time, Staren said, was what he took to be Bailey's potentially violent nature. When he told Bailey that he was dissolving the partnership, Bailey got angry.

"His last words to me," said Staren, "were, 'I'd play it cool, because I know where your children and wife live.' "

Miller and Safer called two of Bailey's early victims, Carole Karstenson and Jean Robinson, both matronly women in the late sixties or early seventies, and they essentially repeated the allegations they had made in their civil suits, the documents that helped start Miller on the hunt. Linda Holmwood had died long ago, but the prosecutors called her daughter, Gail Holmwood Jawblonski. The thirty-three-year-old Pennsylvanian told how Bailey had talked her mother into buying five horses in a six-week period. When he thought her money had run out, he dropped her. "She lost all her self-respect, her children; she lost everything."

Lance Williamson, a thirty-nine-year-old friend of Jerry Farmer and a would-be Bailey protégé, said he first met Bailey when he was working for Frank Jayne, Jr.

It was common, he said, for Jayne to order him to drug certain horses in order to camouflage behavioral problems and prepare them for the arrival of Bailey, who would show up with women he wanted to sell the horses to. "He would lie about the value of the horses and their pedigrees," Williamson said. "And sometimes he would switch a horse he had sold with a less valuable animal."

Cecelia Burke, a veterinarian who as a student worked as an intern for Dr. Ross Hugi, testified about how one day she and Hugi were asked by Bailey to perform a prepurchase examination on a horse that Bailey planned to sell to a middle-aged woman and her teenaged daughter. Hugi looked at the horse and said he didn't want to get involved. Bailey's response, she said, was that "it didn't matter if he refused to pass the horse, because he had sold it twice to Mrs. Brach."

27

A Question of Motive

J OE EDWARD PLEMMONS, his dark blond hair parted down the middle, leaned forward in the witness chair and stared at Richard Bailey, who was sitting twenty yards away, his legs nonchalantly crossed, chin in hand.

They had just finished lunch, Plemmons said, he, Bailey, and Kenneth Hansen. Then Bailey said that he wanted them to "take care of a situation" for him. He offered them five thousand dollars to kill Helen Brach.

"Hansen and I looked at each other," Plemmons related, repeating the tale he had told Miller and his investigators during their session in the Sacramento jail. "Hansen said he wasn't interested; he wouldn't kill an old lady." Having said that, he got up and went to the rest room, leaving Plemmons alone with Bailey, who then asked, "What would it take to get this done?"

"I told him I wasn't into killing people. He didn't just want her dead," Plemmons added ominously. "He wanted to make sure no one ever found her."

He didn't know what had happened after that meeting, Plemmons said quietly, recalling the incident eighteen years later in the most dramatic and damaging testimony so far in the hearing. He didn't know whether Bailey had made other arrangements or not. What he did know, though, was that shortly afterward, Helen Brach disappeared.

Speaking in his reedy voice, all trace of his North Carolina drawl long since obliterated, Plemmons wove a credible tale of how Bailey would routinely request that a horse be drugged to cover up physical disabilities or behavioral problems, how he provided falsified papers on request, and how he facilely lied about a horse's ability, all in an attempt to jack up the price.

Speaking in rapid bursts that often overrode Miller's questions, Plemmons admitted his life had largely been devoted to crime.

"I participated in fraud on a regular basis," he cheerfully confessed. "The money was good, and once I got into the Chicago horse world, I had never seen people with so much money."

Under questioning from Miller, Plemmons conceded that at first he had not been readily forthcoming with investigators about the information concerning the Bailey offer. For one thing, he said, he was worried about involving Hansen. Although he was a good friend, he knew that Hansen was hotheaded and he was afraid of what he might do in a fit of temper. "I knew he'd kill someone," Plemmons said, implying that he would just as soon it not be him.

Plemmons said he finally decided to divulge the details of the alleged meeting only after he was convinced it was the only way to save himself from a long prison sentence, as well.

Under cross-examination by Tuite, Plemmons proved just as effusive, readily, almost jollily, confessing to accusations Bailey's lawyer tossed at him.

"Yes, I did that. . . . Sure, that's true. . . . That's probable. . . . That's likely. . . . I probably did. . . . It could have happened," he responded disarmingly when Tuite accused him of stealing money, writing bad checks, or participating in a variety of scams.

Attacking his testimony about the alleged lunch he and Hansen had had with Bailey, Tuite aggressively questioned Plemmons's contention that it took place on a "warm" day.

"It was February," Tuite insisted. "And that winter was one of the coldest on record in the city. How could you possibly claim it was 'warm'?"

"I don't know how it happened," Plemmons said, shrugging, "but it was."

Although the defense lawyer tried vigorously to get Plemmons to admit that his story about the meeting with Bailey was a fabrication prompted by a desire to promote his own self-interests—either to get out of going to prison or to facilitate a possible book deal—Tuite was unable to shake Plemmons's story.

Alternating between victims and characters from the horse world, Miller and Safer presented a parade of witnesses who painted an unflattering portrait of Bailey and peeled back the facade of gentility that hid the corrupt inner workings of the Chicago equestrian industry.

Victor Escalle, a hulking fifty-year-old now working as a chef in North Carolina, told, in a rapid mumble that made him hard to understand, about his days with Frank Jayne, Jr., at Northwestern Stables.

The prevailing philosophy at the facility, Escalle said, was to make as much money as possible.

It was while he was working for Jayne, who was later convicted of selling cocaine, that he himself became addicted to the drug and to gambling. "We used to play backgammon for big money," he said. "In one game, I lost eleven thousand dollars."

To finance his habits, Escalle turned to robbery. One of his victims was the mother of a woman he was dating. He looted her safe and turned the money over to Jayne to help pay his gambling debts.

One day, Escalle recalled, he walked into Jayne's office and found the stable owner in a rare good mood. "He threw me a vial of coke and told me to enjoy myself."

Puzzled, Escalle asked Jayne why he was so happy.

Jayne replied that he and Bailey had just sold a string of broodmares to "the Candy Lady."

Smiling, Jayne broke out the backgammon set and invited Escalle to sit down.

"And what happened?" asked Miller.

"I lost another five thousand," Escalle said dryly.

Under cross-examination, however, Escalle was unaware of the details about the alleged sale of the broodmares.

"Did you ever see any of these horses being delivered to Northwestern?" Tuite asked.

"No," Escalle admitted.

"I used to tease Bailey about Helen Brach," said Richard Faila, a self-employed retailer who was in the horse business for six years and met Bailey through his wife, who had a horse stabled at Bailey's facility. "I asked him how he could sleep with a woman of that age."

"And what did he say to that?" Miller asked.

"He said, 'You just close your eyes and think about the money.' "

After Helen Brach disappeared, Faila continued to prod Bailey. "I asked him, 'Where's the body?' "

"And his response?" Miller prompted.

"He said, 'I'd never kill her. Why would I kill the goose that laid the golden egg?' "

Barbara Mulvihill, a self-employed interior designer, was not a Bailey victim, but she was an on-scene observer during the crucial period just before and just after Helen Brach disappeared. A petite, slim woman who wore her gray-blond hair in a pageboy, Mulvihill replied confidently and precisely to questions from Safer.

In the late seventies, she said, her husband had been a horseman at Oak Brook Stables, another facility owned by Bailey, and Helen Brach had several horses boarded there. One Monday—she knew it was a Monday because the stable was closed to the public—she was at the facility to pick up her husband and was surprised by the frenetic activity.

"What's going on?" she asked.

Helen Brach was coming, she was told, to look over some broodmares for possible purchase. There were five to seven horses involved and the asking price had already been set at $150,000.

"I was in the office when Helen arrived with Bailey," Mulvihill recalled. "She pulled up in a yellow convertible with the top down, although it was cold. She was wearing a scarf over her head, but I could see her blond hair underneath."

Because the office had been emptied, since everyone had gone to the ring to watch the presentation, Mulvihill answered the telephone when it rang. It was Frank Jayne asking if the presentation had been successful. "It rang twice more within a matter of minutes," Mulvihill said, "and each time it was Jayne asking, 'Are they finished?' "

Although such presentations normally took a respectable amount of time, this one was over very quickly. "They didn't get the sale," she said.

John Keefe, a wheelchair-bound former horseman now living in Arizona, read a story about developments in the Brach case in the Phoenix newspapers after Bailey was indicted. He then called federal officials to offer information.

Before Helen's disappearance, he said, in response to questions from Miller, he had been working at another Chicago-area stable and was asked by his boss to evaluate a horse for Helen Brach. She wanted to know if she should spend an additional fifty thousand dollars on a particular horse she owned.

Keefe did not remember the name of the horse, he said, somewhat embarrassed, but he recalled that his examination showed the animal was suffering from a bowed tendon, a defect in the leg structure, perhaps aggravated by an injury, that made the horse virtually worthless as a performer.

He wrote a report saying that in view of the horse's physical condition, he would not spend *any* additional money on the animal.

Although he never talked to Helen face-to-face, she wrote him a thank-you note and enclosed a check for fifty or one hundred dollars.

William C. Corwin, a retailer and former horse-show judge, said his first contact with Bailey was when Bailey tried to bribe him to "send a horse up the line"—that is, give the animal a better rating and advance the animal in the competition.

Despite that experience, Corwin later went to work for Bailey.

One day early in 1977, he could see that Bailey was disturbed about something. When he asked the stable owner what was troubling him, Bailey replied that Helen Brach was considering moving her horses from his stable. "Even worse, she had asked for an independent appraiser to examine them.

"She felt she had been conned by Bailey," Corwin said.

Early in 1977, Ann McGroder, now the thirty-seven-year-old owner of a retail business, had been a teenager fascinated with horses. While taking riding lessons at Bailey's stable, she began spending more time at the facility and eventually got a job there exercising horses.

One day, she was riding a horse named Potenciado, which was owned by Helen Brach, when the animal fell while attempting to jump a rail. What struck her as odd was that the horse remained on the ground and made no immediate attempt to get up. She had to coax him to rise. Usually, she said, horses try to get to their feet as quickly as they can if they fall. In her mind, it was very disturbing that Potenciado did not respond as most horses do. "Horses just don't do that," she explained, at least not healthy ones.

She also became emotionally attached to another of Brach's horses,

Vorhees's Luv. While in good physical condition, the animal apparently had mental problems. "She was squirrelly," McGroder said. "I don't think she had the brain or the scope to be a jumper."

Also disturbing to McGroder was the business climate that prevailed at the stable. "Mr. Bailey told me to let potential male customers believe they could sleep with me if they bought a horse."

Speaking softly and in a heavy accent more reminiscent of Brooklyn than the Midwest, Arthur Katz explained that he and his father, William, had owned a business that produced memorials for cemeteries and crypts. One day in 1966, he said, a woman came in and introduced herself. Her name was Helen Brach and she wanted the Katzes to design for her a memorial for an elaborate family crypt she was building in Ohio.

"She reached into her purse and pulled out a stack of bills that she handed to my father," recalled Katz, a flashily dressed, stern-faced man. "I hope this will do as a retainer," Katz remembered her saying. "It's some pin money I had around the house."

He vividly remembered the incident, he said, because it was extremely rare for a potential customer to drop that much cash in their hands.

"As soon as she left, we locked the doors and counted the money," Katz said. "It totaled six thousand dollars."

Since the job Helen Brach wanted done was complex, it took a lot of preparation and work, putting her into close contact with the Katzes. Over the months, Katz said, Helen Brach and his father became very good friends. Eventually, William Katz assumed a role of confidant to the heiress.

Some ten years after they first met, either in late 1976 or early in 1977, Helen visited the Katzes' small office to discuss a personal problem with William.

"She was very upset," Katz recalled. "She said she was being taken in a horse deal and didn't know what to do about it."

After listening to her story, Katz's father told her that he had some friends at the state's attorney's office. "He suggested that the two of them go to the prosecutors to see about filing charges against the person she thought was cheating her." Brach was receptive to the proposal but said it would have to wait until she returned from a forthcoming visit to the Mayo Clinic.

"What happened then?" Miller asked.

Katz shook his head. "We never saw her again," he whispered.

On cross-examination, Menaker unsuccessfully tried to get Katz to admit that he had offered his information only after he learned there was a reward for information.

"Were you afraid of losing that reward?"

"Oh, no," Katz replied. "I was afraid of losing my life."

28

More Damning Testimony

I N THE Southwest, they have an expression for someone who appears dissipated and bedraggled. Such a person, the saying goes, looks like "a horse that's been rode hard and put up wet." Cathy Olsen had that look.

The forty-one-year-old, blond-haired daughter of Frank Jayne, Jr., looked nervously around the courtroom, almost as if she feared someone would come storming through the door and drag her into a back room for a thorough thrashing.

Speaking fitfully in a voice slurred by ill-fitting dentures, Olsen related how, many years before, she had been befriended by Helen Brach. They had begun to get close, she said, soon after Helen purchased eight or ten broodmares.

Under questioning by Safer, Olsen repeated for Judge Shadur's benefit the story she had told earlier to Miller: that she had heard some men in her father's office commenting about how Helen "knows too much" and how, not long afterward, she overheard another conversation in which one of the men said that Helen "had been shut up."

Olsen's testimony, like Plemmons's, was crucial because it substantiated prosecution claims of a plot to have Helen Brach abducted.

In view of such damning testimony, it was important that Bailey's lawyers discredit Olsen.

As soon as Safer finished his direct examination, Tuite sprang to his feet. Ever since he had learned that Olsen would be one of the major witnesses against his client, he and Menaker had been collecting information designed to disparage what she said. Even more than Plemmons, who freely admitted to leading a less-than-exemplary life, Olsen carried a lot of baggage.

Striding briskly to the lectern that stood at the base of the judge's bench, Tuite launched what would turn out to be a three-hour cross-examination.

During the process, Olsen admitted that she was a check forger as well as a recovering crack addict who also had problems with marijuana and alcohol. At least once, she had tried to kill herself.

When confronted with statements made before a grand jury that partially contradicted her testimony before Judge Shadur, Olsen readily acknowledged that she had not told the "whole story" to the grand jury because she was deathly afraid of her father.

"Did you ever tell anyone that you were 'hearing things'?" Tuite asked.

"Yes," she replied in a subdued voice. Once, when she sought to self-admit herself to a mental hospital in what she called a "desperate plea for help," she told officials that she was hallucinating. "But it wasn't true," she added.

She also admitted that she was given money by the government, allegedly to help her meet her expenses while waiting to testify. She confessed that she had used some of the money to buy drugs.

In response to Tuite's questions, she said she did not remember a 1989 interview with an investigator from the Glenview Police Department in which she did not mention Bailey being present during the alleged conversation about Helen Brach.

"Did you make things up if it was to your advantage to do so?" Tuite asked.

"In the hospital, yes."

"Isn't it a fact," Tuite said sharply, "that for the purposes of this hearing you made up those conversations eighteen years ago?"

"No!" Olsen replied emphatically. "I did not."

"You expanded upon them," he said accusingly.

"No, I did not," she replied.

She admitted she did not tell the grand jury as many details as she did during her testimony before Judge Shadur because "I didn't trust cops."

Why, Tuite asked, had she been reluctant to admit warning Helen Brach that she was being fleeced?

"I was afraid for my own life," she said.

And whom were you afraid of? he asked.

"My dad."

On redirect, Olsen contended that she would have to leave the Chicago area in order to escape the possibility of retaliation from her father.

"Will the ATF pay for this?" Safer asked.

"Yes," she replied.

Miller and Safer were inwardly jubilant about Olsen's testimony. They had feared she would be a weak link in their case, a witness who was much more likely than Plemmons to crack under pressure from Tuite, but she stood up to the defense better than expected.

After exchanging nods with Safer, Miller called his next witness: septuagenarian Mary Herbold, who used to run a tack shop at Northwestern Stables and was friendly with Helen Brach.

In her brief appearance on the stand, she testified that one day shortly before Helen disappeared, she had gone to Bailey's stables to pick up her daughter, who worked there. While she was looking for her daughter, she walked in on a conversation in which Helen was exclaiming that she felt she had been sold "garbage" horses. "She said she knew she had been cheated and was going to the state's attorney's office.

"What did you do?" Miller asked.

"I got my daughter and got out of there."

"Did you ever see Helen Brach again?"

"No."

Miller, in a move designed to keep the defense off balance, switched abruptly from a Brach witness to a Bailey witness, calling Charles Joyce III, an entrepreneur from San Francisco.

Joyce said he had met Bailey at a convention in Southern California and that Bailey had been intensely interested in getting the client list from his home-repair business after Joyce mentioned that he did considerable work for wealthy women.

"He was looking to sell them horses," Joyce said, adding that Bailey wanted his list so badly, he invited Joyce to visit him in Chicago.

While staying at Bailey's apartment, Joyce said, Bailey opened up to him about his philosophy on women. He had three criteria as far as women were concerned, Joyce said: They had to be unattractive, if not ugly; they had to be single; they had to be wealthy.

"And what did Bailey offer you in return for helping him meet wealthy women?" Miller asked.

"He promised me fifty percent of whatever he made. He told me I'd make thousands of dollars."

Knowing that Tuite was going to pick up on Plemmons's comment about it being warm the day Plemmons said he and Hansen met with Bailey—Tuite had, in fact, done that, scoffingly claiming that was proof that it had never happened—the prosecutors had laid a trap for the defense. Now it was time, Miller felt, to spring the ambush. "I call Peter Cullen," he said.

Speaking clearly and distinctly in a tone that did little to mask a quiet swagger, the dark-haired, nattily dressed agent confessed that Plemmons's insistence that it had been a warm day had puzzled him, as well. But when he checked weather bureau records, he found two days that month during which unseasonably warm temperatures were recorded. On February 10, a week before Helen checked out of the Mayo Clinic, the thermometer shot up to 47°F, which was practically balmy for a mid-winter day in Chicago. The next day, February 11, was even warmer, with a high of 52°F.

That still wouldn't work, Tuite smirkingly insisted on cross-examination. "Do you know where Richard Bailey was on February eleventh?" he asked.

"I believe he *said* he was in Florida," replied Cullen.

"Do you have any evidence to the contrary?"

"No," Cullen admitted.

Tuite pointed out that Bailey had a receipt showing he checked into a Florida hotel on February 16.

"But that doesn't tell you he was in Florida on February eleventh," Cullen argued.

Two days later, during the rebuttal phase of the prosecution's case, ATF agent Daniel Ivancich presented telephone records showing that Bailey, despite his insistence that he had been in Florida beginning on February 9, had, in fact, been in Chicago until February 15, which meant he could have met with Hansen and Plemmons on either of the "warm" days, February 10 or 11.

*   *   *

In dramatic Perry Mason–style, Miller left one of his most dramatic witnesses for last, not because he planned it that way but because she did not come forward until the last minute. Later, the fact that the unexpected appearance of Pamela Milner, a shy, frightened-looking special-education teacher in an inner-city school, was so abrupt that he did not have time to check her documents fully, would come back to haunt the prosecution. But at the time, Milner's testimony hit the court like a jolt of electricity.

The thirtyish Milner, the hearing's first and only surprise witness, walked quickly to the stand, her head down. Tugging at the hem of her short green skirt, she seated herself in the witness chair and demurely crossed her legs, which were encased in sparkling bright white hose. A thin woman devoid of makeup, with long, straight dark hair, Milner looked nearsightedly around the courtroom.

In a fragile voice little more than a whisper, Milner said she met Bailey in 1988 when she expressed an interest in a horse she had seen while driving past his stable. "It was a gorgeous, gorgeous gray, with a champagne silver mane and tail, eighteen hands [six feet] high," she gushed.

Bailey took her into his office, she related, poured her a glass of sparkling wine, and told her the horse's name was Mango and that he was asking $14,500 for the animal. She desperately wanted to buy Mango but could not afford him on her thirty-thousand-dollar-a-year teacher's salary. When she asked for time to see if she could swing the purchase, Bailey asked her for a deposit. She offered one hundred dollars, but Bailey asked for five hundred. "While I was trying to make up my mind, he cashed my check," she said.

She never bought Mango, but soon after her meeting with Bailey, he called and asked her out. For the next year, she said, they dated off and on. He took her, she said, to a number of fine restaurants, to the theater, and dancing.

In March of 1989, for some reason not clear to her, he took her to a local bar, which definitely was not up to the standards of the other places she had been with him. "It was a real dump," she said, wrinkling her nose.

While they were sitting in the bar drinking, a man she had never seen before came up to their table and offered to buy them drinks. Bailey, she said, obviously saw this as a challenge to his masculinity, because he got very angry. After the man left, Bailey "became very belligerent" and "he began muttering things that were not clear to me; he proceeded to say things that were very frightening."

According to Milner, Bailey angrily insisted that *he* was "in charge" and he "didn't need this." Extending his hands, he asked her to take them. She quoted him as saying, "Look at these," "Feel these." She added, "They were rough and calloused; he made reference to how strong they were."

Then he said something that puzzled her at first. "He said he had taken care of the Candy Lady. I said, 'Who?' He said a swear word— *bitch* or *shit* or something—then 'that Brach bitch.' "

After that, she said, Bailey gulped down his drink and ordered another, which he quickly polished off, as well. Then he took her back to her car and she drove back to her apartment.

"I was hysterically frightened," she said, speaking almost inaudibly and making nervous jerks, looking down at her hands or at the judge. "He told me things I had no business knowing but," she added emphatically, *"I heard what I heard."*

Locking her apartment door, she testified, she grabbed a slip of paper from her purse, a paycheck stub it turned out, and wrote down what had occurred that evening. Dating it March 17, 1989, she wrote details in case something might happen to her. She said Bailey had frightened her and told her about "the Candy Lady." He had said that he "took care" of Brach. She feared if he remembered telling her her own life might be in danger. She added: "If anything happens to me, tell the police that Richard Bailey took care of the Candy Lady." She put the piece of paper in an envelope and addressed it to her brother, Kevin, then an assistant U.S. attorney in northern Indiana. "Kevin, protect this note with your life." She did not tell her brother about it in person, she said, because she didn't want to put him in danger, as well.

"I was scared to death," she told the hushed courtroom. She said she hid the envelope and later rented a safe-deposit box in which to keep it. And that, she said, is where it had been for almost six years.

"Are you uncomfortable in being here?" Miller asked.

"I am very, *very* uncomfortable," she agreed. "I'm here because you subpoenaed me." When she had appeared in Miller's office to tell her story, she told the prosecutor she was reluctant to testify, so he issued a document ordering her to appear.

"Why are you telling this?" Miller wanted to know.

"I just don't want to be afraid anymore," she said. "I feel I'm doing the right thing. Enough is enough is enough."

Because Tuite and Menaker were caught by surprise, Shadur agreed to give them time to prepare for cross-examination. When the defense's turn came three days later, it was all over very quickly.

Wearing a purple dress with a short skirt, a gold necklace, and dangly earrings, Milner looked just as nervous in anticipation of questioning by Tuite as she had by Miller. As it turned out, she had good reason.

The defense attorney immediately zoomed in on the date she had written on the paycheck stub the night she claimed that Bailey had confessed.

"I wrote March 17, 1989, but I may not have dated it until later," she said. "I wasn't thinking about dates; I was thinking about protecting myself."

"And when did you rent the safe-deposit box to put the note in?" Tuite asked.

"August," she replied, adding that she had rented the box specifically to hold the note and that the note was all that was in it. In response to other questions, she said that she had not told anyone about the note before securing it in the bank vault, not Bailey and not even her brother.

Holding the note up to the light, Tuite struggled to read the numbers that were printed on the stub as it came from the school board. "There's something written over the serial number," Tuite explained. "It says, 'Read this, Kev, do not throw away.'" However, it was not the handwriting that interested him, but the number. "It looks like," he said, slowly listing the numbers, "seven . . . seven . . . five . . . eight . . . nine . . . seven . . . nine. According to the stub, this was for pay period number twenty and the amount of the check was four thousand eight hundred and fifteen dollars and eight-four cents."

Pausing dramatically, Tuite added, "That pay check wasn't issued until October 6, 1989, almost seven months after you claimed to have written on it and two months after you rented the safe-deposit box. This stub did not even exist in March of 1989."

There was a gasp in the courtroom when Tuite made his revelation. Even Judge Shadur was surprised, leaning forward and staring at Milner through his heavy brows.

"In order to become a witness, you attempted to obliterate the paycheck number, didn't you?" Tuite said accusingly.

"That's ridiculous," Milner mumbled.

There was another number, Tuite pointed out, that would have helped pin down when the check was issued, but it was torn off.

"It must have been by accident," said Milner.

As Tuite pressed the issue, Milner tried to explain it away by saying that she had made two other copies of the original note, which she sent to friends for safekeeping. But rather than photocopying the original, she wrote each out in longhand on paycheck stubs, just as she had the night that Bailey allegedly confessed.

"I'd like to see the lawyers over here," Shadur said gruffly, walking to the end of the bench for an unusual sidebar. A few minutes later, Milner was asked to join the conference and they all went into Shadur's chamber.

Twenty minutes later, Shadur and the lawyers returned to the courtroom, but Milner was absent.

"It should have been apparent that the writer was extraordinarily tense," Shadur explained for the record. "When the issue of timing arose, particularly about the handwritten copies . . . it developed that in order for us to obtain the information, it would require we have access to those other copies." She claimed she had sent those copies to others, Shadur said, but she refused to divulge their names. "Mr. Tuite proposed to strike the testimony by reason of his being unable to conduct a proper cross-examination. I granted that motion. It is as though she never came into the courtroom."

If the incident had occurred before a jury, it could have wrecked the prosecution's case. But luckily for Safer and Miller, it occurred only before a judge, who was able to compartmentalize the details and strike it from his calculations about Bailey's guilt. A jury may have had considerably more trouble with the facts, conceivably blaming the prosecution.

29

Bailey Has His Say

A FTER THE lunch break on the last day of May, six working days after the hearing started, Richard Bailey strutted cockily to the witness stand, treading somewhat gingerly in shiny black loafers so new they still had the price tag affixed to the sole.

A short, compact man with wavy collar-length gray hair combed straight back to cover a large bald spot, the sixty-five-year-old Bailey wore a muted plaid sport coat and puce tie with small white figures: go-to-court apparel delivered on the opening day of the proceeding by his new wife, Dr. Annette Hoffman.

Plopping casually into the witness chair and lazily crossing his legs, he carefully placed within easy reach a yellow plastic cup filled with water, from which he frequently sipped.

Ten months in jail apparently had done little to dampen his spirits or dull his self-confidence. Looking as relaxed as if he were sitting in his living room watching the races on ESPN, Bailey began his lengthy testimony by explaining in a clear, deep voice without hint of remorse that he got involved in the horse business three decades previously, when he was in his thirties, after buying a horse from Frank Jayne, Jr., and boarding it at Jayne's Northwestern Stables.

Fiddling with his dark-framed glasses, which he occasionally swapped with reading glasses when asked to peruse a document, Bailey said that hanging around the stable "kind of opened my mind." After selling horses to several wealthy women, he became acutely aware of the moneymaking potential in the field. "I would buy a horse from Jayne, then resell it at a much higher price, giving Jayne fifty percent of anything above the price I paid for it."

"Did you have a special term for this?" Tuite asked.

"Yeah," Bailey said disdainfully. "We called it 'chopping up the watermelon.' "

Relying on his experience in gulling older women, a technique he began honing when he was a dance instructor at Arthur Murray's and perfected during his days operating a driving school, Bailey slipped easily into a pattern of wooing potential customers and then talking them into buying overpriced horses.

"I'd take them out for lunch or dinner and they would get confidence in me," Bailey said almost proudly. "I'd get to know them and see how much they could afford to spend. I'd take them to the best restaurants, first-cabin places, and the first thing you know, they'd start telling me all about their finances, how much they were worth. I'd compliment them, tell them how nice they looked or what a nice outfit they were wearing. I'd tell them they were classy ladies. I'd treat them like no one else had treated them before, buying them little gifts like expensive perfume and send them white roses. I'd always attach a card saying: 'To my classy, beautiful lady. Love, Richard.' "

"Would you sometimes get romantically involved?" Tuite interrupted.

"Yeah," Bailey replied matter-of-factly. "Sometimes."

But did he succeed in selling them horses? Tuite asked.

"Most of the time," he added with a grin.

Occasionally glancing at his wife, who had sat stiffly on the first row of the hard courtroom benches at least part of every day during the hearing, Bailey acknowledged that he often borrowed money from his victims. "But I always intended to pay them back," he added, admitting he didn't always live up to his intentions. "When I told them about putting up their portion [of the purchase price of a horse] and how they would get their funds back, it was never a true story."

As Tuite, anxious to beat prosecutors to the punch, began leading Bailey through a series of questions about his victims and his methods, Bailey grew even more relaxed, slumping in the witness chair, salting his replies with little asides and willful witticisms.

"I used to get a lot of activity from my TV commercials," Bailey said easily, pointing out that Linda Holmwood was a good example. "She saw my ad at three A.M. and called me later in the morning to make an appointment about possibly buying a horse."

"Did you sell her anything?" Tuite asked.

Bailey shrugged. "I sold her a few horses." Apparently anxious to contradict earlier testimony from Holmwood's daughter, who swore that her mother had thought Bailey was going to marry her, he added, "But I never got romantically involved with her; I never promised to marry her. I was already married," he added, referring to his first wife, Eunice.

Did he think Holmwood was rich?

"Sure." Bailey smiled. "I thought she had a half a million dollars in stocks and bonds. That's what she told me."

Did he have a sexual relationship with her?

"Never!" he said emphatically.

Carole Karstenson, however, was another story. Did he have a sexual relationship with Karstenson? Tuite asked.

"Very much so," Bailey replied, laughing. "I couldn't stop her. She wanted sex eight or ten times a night, every night."

Bailey admitted that he sold Karstenson horses, including a string of broodmares. "As best I can remember," he said, "I got the horses from Jayne. At first, Jayne told me he would sell me the twenty horses for fifteen hundred dollars each, but then he said he had made a mistake and the horses should have been thirty-five hundred each. As a result, I had to pay seventy thousand for the animals and I sold them to Karstenson for one hundred thousand."

The fact that Karstenson got taken so badly, Bailey implied, was Jayne's fault, not his. "He had me boxed in. What could I do?"

He was not so reticent, however, in acknowledging the huge profit he and Jayne made on the horse named Elmadge they sold to Karstenson, presumably as a stud to replace Bull Lea's Whirl, which died under mysterious circumstances. Bailey said he and Jayne paid nine hundred dollars for Elmadge and sold him to Karstenson for twenty-five thousand.

"And what did you do with the profit?" Tuite asked disingenuously.

Bailey looked at his lawyer as if the man were slightly retarded. "We split it down the middle."

Did he have anything to do with Bull Lea's Whirl's demise?

"No!" Bailey emphasized. "I did not cause the death of that horse."

With the preliminaries out of the way, Tuite turned to the most important issue: Bailey's relationship with Helen Brach.

He met the heiress, he confirmed, through a woman with whom he had struck up a conversation at a car wash. Although that woman turned down his request for a dinner date, she told him she had a friend who might be interested in meeting him. The friend was Helen.

"We made arrangements to be at a certain restaurant at about seven P.M. on a Friday," Bailey said, adding that he went to the eatery and happened to pass by the table where the woman from the car wash was dining with her husband and Helen. "She called me over and introduced me," he said. "During the conversation, Helen mentioned that she was going to Florida and I said I might meet her there." After that, he said, the relationship bloomed.

"We went dancing a lot," he said. "She was a real good dancer."

One day in 1974, he continued, they were attending the races at Gulfstream Park in Florida when Helen mentioned that she might like to own some racehorses. "She said she would be willing to spend one hundred thousand dollars for a few nice horses."

A few months later, early in 1975, Bailey said he called his brother P.J. and told him he'd like to pick up three nice racehorses.

"Who decided on the price?" Tuite asked.

"My brother," said Bailey.

"Did you receive any of the money?"

Bailey hesitated. "About forty or forty-five thousand dollars," he said slowly.

"Did you sell her any other horses?" Tuite asked, eager to get this on the record, since the government's theory of Helen's disappearance was based on the fact that the heiress was upset over being cheated on a sale involving a string of broodmares, not the original three racehorses she had bought through Bailey's brother.

"Never!" Bailey barked, leaning forward to speak directly in the microphone.

"Did you sell her any broodmares?"

"Never!"

"Did you sell her two or three show horses for one hundred thousand to two hundred thousand dollars?"

"No!" he replied emphatically, adding, "She was not interested in show horses at all. She wanted no part of them."

He admitted, nevertheless, that in 1976, about a year after she bought the three racehorses—about a year before she disappeared—Jerry Farmer wanted to sell her some shoe horses and arranged a showing at his Oak Brook Stables.

"She was there long enough to look at about three horses," Bailey said. "When one of the riders took a crop and just lightly tapped the horse a little bit, Helen looked at me and said, 'Let's go.' So we left. She said she didn't like to see horses get cropped."

By late 1976, Bailey said, he and Helen were still seeing each other "periodically," but there was no romantic attachment. "She wasn't angry at me or anything. In fact, in December, she got tickets for the New Year's Eve bash at the Waldorf-Astoria, featuring Guy Lombardo, and I met her there. We had separate rooms," he added hurriedly. "We spent the evening dancing."

"Who paid for it?" Tuite asked.

"She paid for everything," Bailey replied. "When we called it a night at about three A.M. and I got back to my room, I found a gift from Helen. It was a brown cashmere sweater and a card telling me I was a nice guy, the nicest one she'd ever met."

Turning to the issue of Helen's trip to the Mayo Clinic, Bailey acknowledged arranging her admission but denied taking her there or seeing her after she checked in.

"I went to Florida," Bailey said, explaining that he was subsequently met there by Christina Kubot and the two of them visited Arnold Wennick's farm. "I wanted to see what kind of stock he had and to see if we could cut a deal. Maybe when Helen came in, I could bring her back."

"Were you hoping to get anything on a potential horse sale to Helen Brach?" Tuite asked.

"Maybe ten percent," he said, waving his hand as if it wasn't important. "I told Wennick I had a customer in mind who was gung ho."

Tuite asked Bailey if he had talked to Helen by phone while he was in Florida.

"One time," Bailey said promptly, expecting the question. "It was on the sixteenth. She told me she really liked the clinic but couldn't wait to get to Florida. It was a very friendly phone call."

He tried to call her the next day at her home in Glenview, he said, but was unable to reach her. "Matlick gave me the runaround. He told me she was either in the shower or had just stepped out."

He said he called her again on Saturday, the day she was scheduled to arrive in Florida, but again he was deflected by Matlick. "He acted very nervous. I asked him to have her call me when she returned."

By Sunday, he said, he still had not heard from her, so he called the Glenview number again. "I got the same story. Matlick said she wasn't in . . . she just left . . . she was in the shower . . . whatever. I got the runaround."

Three days later, on Wednesday, February 23, Bailey said he grew tired of waiting for Helen to show up and so he flew back to Chicago.

"Did you call her again?" Tuite asked.

"I think I did," Bailey said. "But I got the runaround again. I figured she had some other guy."

In an attempt to preempt the prosecution, Tuite led Bailey through a string of quick queries touching on various points in the government's theory, questions that he knew would be asked of his client as soon as the prosecutors got the opportunity to cross-examine.

"Did you ever learn that Helen was angry with you over the sale of horses?"

"No," Bailey shot back.

"Did you ever learn that she was going to go to the authorities?"

"No."

"Did you have a sexual relationship with Helen?"

"No," Bailey said. "She couldn't have sex. She had a tipped uterus." His response was a non sequitur. A "tipped" uterus is a gynecological condition that, except in perhaps rare cases, has nothing to do with a woman's ability to have or enjoy sex.

Why, then, did he want to maintain a relationship?

That question required a more thought-out response from Bailey than any the defense attorney had asked so far.

"I was planning on being with Helen for many years," Bailey said, speaking slowly and carefully. "She had a long bankroll, about thirty million."

Then how did he plan to get his hands on some of that money if it wasn't through horses? Tuite asked.

"I was going to sell her home and develop her estate," Bailey replied.

"Did you have any plans to kill Helen Brach?" Tuite asked abruptly.

"Definitely not!" Bailey said emphatically.

Did he take part in any conversations having to do with her death, including meeting with Kenneth Hansen and Joe Edward Plemmons?

"No," Bailey said.

Did he have *anything* to do with the death or disappearance of Helen Brach?

"Definitely not!" Bailey replied forcefully. "I had no motive for getting rid of Helen. When you dump a woman, that's when you have problems. I had no plans whatsoever to dump Helen Brach."

Tuite, looking satisfied, turned and strode back to his chair. His direct examination had taken one hour and thirty-five minutes.

30

Zeroing In

DURING TUITE'S questioning, prosecutor Ron Safer had been furiously scribbling notes on his yellow legal pad. From time to time, he looked up at Bailey and nervously bobbed his head, impatient to take his swings at the smooth-talking con man.

A tall, thin, dark-haired man, as intense as his fellow prosecutor was laid-back, Safer jumped to the attack before Tuite even had a chance to settle into his chair.

"How many people did you cheat?" he asked Bailey.

Bailey shrewdly eyed his adversary, knowing that his responses to Safer's questions would go a long way toward determining his fate.

"Maybe a few hundred," he said placidly.

"Did you lie about prices you paid for horses?" Safer asked in an aggressive tone.

"Yes," Bailey admitted.

"Did you con women?"

Bailey rolled his eyes. "Yes."

"Bull Lea's Whirl was worthless as a sire, wasn't he?" Safer asked, referring to the horse that Bailey had sold Karstenson, claiming he was a valuable stud. "You got one hundred thousand dollars from Karstenson for a stud horse that wouldn't breed and a bunch of worthless broodmares, didn't you?"

"Yes," Bailey said.

And then, Safer said, he had charged Karstenson twenty-five thousand dollars for Elmadge, Bull Lea's Whirl supposed replacement, a horse he and Jayne had bought for nine hundred dollars.

Bailey conceded that was correct.

"Did you know," Safer asked, switching subjects abruptly, "that perjury is a crime?"

Bailey hesitated. "I'm not sure," he said.

"Yeah, you know," Safer snarled. "Do you remember the deposition in the Karstenson case?" he asked, referring to Bailey's denials that he had tried to cheat the woman.

"It's so far back, no," Bailey said.

"You lied repeatedly during that deposition, didn't you?" Safer asked.

Bailey nodded slowly. "Sometimes I lied," he agreed.

"You lied to women, women you knew to be seriously ill?"

On guard, Bailey answered carefully. "I'm not a doctor. How would I know if someone is seriously ill?"

"Carole Karstenson was in the hospital!" Safer pointed out. "Her weight was down to seventy-eight pounds!"

"Yes." Bailey nodded. "She *had* lost a little weight. But when we went to Florida, she was the picture of health, as far as I was concerned."

"You took her money and you didn't care what happened to her, did you?"

As evidenced during Tuite's direct examination, Bailey promptly answered questions he anticipated were going to be asked, but when there was one he didn't want to answer, he hesitated before responding.

"I . . . I . . ." he stuttered. "I was just interested in selling her horses and getting her money."

And what about Linda Holmwood? Safer wanted to know. "You knew she was ill, too, didn't you?"

"I think she told me she might have a problem," Bailey replied smoothly. "I think she told me she might have cancer."

"Didn't you keep champagne in your office?" Safer asked.

Bailey threw his shoulders back. "Dom Pérignon," he said proudly.

Knowing that Holmwood was an alcoholic did not stop Bailey from offering her a glass of champagne every time she went to his office, Safer pointed out. She had, the prosecutor said, originally gone to Bailey to see about purchasing a single horse and he had sold her five, all at inflated prices, by deceiving her and plying her with alcohol.

"Did you tell Linda Holmwood that she was attractive?" Safer asked.

"She was mediocre," Bailey replied dispassionately.

Had he hinted that he wanted to marry her?

Bailey shook his head. "I was very selective to the choice of words I used with her. I didn't want to mislead her. I just wanted to sell her the horses."

"And you didn't care what happened to her as long as you could get the money?"

"That's right," Bailey conceded.

"Once you got some money, you tried to get more money, right?"

Bailey admitted that he had.

Safer stared at him, shaking his head. "Didn't you know what you were doing was illegal?"

No, Bailey said. The women who thought they had been cheated had filed civil suits against him and the courts had ruled on the issue, ordering him to pay specified amounts. Once he had complied, that should have been the end of it. "The entire matter would be settled," he contended. In his view, he had not done anything to result in criminal charges being filed against him.

"At the beginning of 1977," Safer said, "you had a number of lawsuits pending against you, didn't you?"

"Yes," Bailey said slowly.

"Was a lot of money involved?"

Bailey waved his hand. "A few hundred thousand dollars," he said dismissively.

"It was at this time," the prosecutor said accusingly, "that you learned that Helen Brach was angry with you, wasn't it?"

"No such thing," Bailey replied.

"You learned that she was going to the authorities, didn't you?"

"Definitely not," Bailey insisted.

"In that case," Safer asked, digging out a copy of a Glenview PD report on a 1977 interview with Bailey, "why didn't you tell the investigator that you had business dealings with Helen Brach instead of saying that it was only your brother who was involved in the horse deal with her? You didn't tell the Glenview police that you were in Florida when Helen disappeared and were trying to set up a showing to sell her horses, did you?"

"No," Bailey admitted.

"You told Helen Brach you wanted to marry her, didn't you?" Safer asked.

"No way!" Bailey said fervently. "Helen knew I went out with other women and she went out with other men. We weren't going steady."

Deciding to put the Brach issue temporarily aside, Safer questioned Bailey about his purpose in placing the personal ads in local newspapers. "Why did you do that?" he asked earnestly.

"I was looking to get married," Bailey said with a straight face. "I was looking for a long-term personal relationship and I kept running into these women with money."

"You mean you didn't intend to swindle anyone?" Safer asked sarcastically.

"Definitely not," contended Bailey. Although he had pleaded guilty to charges of cheating women in horse deals, he was trying to convince Judge Shadur that he had published classified ads only because he was looking for a straightforward relationship with a woman.

"You did this with older women because they were easier to impress with a rush of attention and affection, didn't you?"

Bailey looked at the prosecutor intently, then shook his head and waved a finger in front of his nose. "No," he said. "It's just that they had more money."

Bailey should have been tired, what with the strain of the hearing, the pressure of being on the stand, and the fact that he was being required to expose all his dirty little secrets in front of the world and, perhaps worse, his new, wealthy wife.

Strangely, though, the hearing seemed to be producing the opposite effect. The longer it went on, the more spirited Bailey seemed to get; the more he should have been depressed and disheartened, the more confident he seemed to become. As the cross-examination dragged on, he seemed more animated rather than more languid, and at times it appeared as if he was actually enjoying the repartee with Safer. The harder the prosecutor tried to zing him, the more aggressively Bailey seemed to respond.

Thursday, June 1, had ended with Bailey still on the stand. Overnight, Safer and Miller reviewed their strategy and determined that they would dig harder at Bailey's financial relationship with Brach, since that was necessary to prove their theory that Bailey had the heiress abducted to keep her from reporting his monetary shenanigans to the state's attorney's office.

"Tell me again," Safer urged, "about that day you and Brach were at Gulfstream and how it developed that she decided she wanted to buy some horses."

Bailey looked bored. "She told me," he drawled, "that she wanted to invest one hundred thousand dollars in racehorses."

"And what did you do then?" Safer prompted.

"I just kind of listened at that point," Bailey said. "But when we got back to Chicago—it was early 1975—I called P.J. and he started looking for some suitable animals." It took his brother awhile, Bailey added, because P.J. normally dealt with show horses, not racehorses. Finally, though, P.J. found two horses and Bailey carried the news to Helen, adding that the animals—which would be named Vorhees's Luv and Brach's Sweet Talk—would cost fifty thousand dollars.

Safer paused, seeming to mull over that figure. "How much," he asked, "had P.J. actually paid for Brach's Sweet Talk?"

"About four thousand," Bailey replied jauntily.

"And how much did P.J. pay for Vorhees's Luv?"

"In the ballpark of five thousand dollars," Bailey responded easily.

"But you didn't tell Mrs. Brach that, did you?" Safer said accusingly.

"No," Bailey admitted.

"Did you tell her you were getting a *commission* on the sale? Did you tell her that you were making four hundred percent profit?"

"No," Bailey conceded, apparently unfazed.

"Well," Safer asked, determined to pursue the issue, "did you tell her that Potenciado cost fifty thousand dollars?"

"That's how much it cost *her,*" Bailey replied, not precisely answering the question.

Safer shook his head in feigned puzzlement. "But P.J. paid about eighty-five hundred for the horse, right?"

"I guess that must be the figure."

"You didn't tell her about your profit?"

Bailey waved the question away. "That's the horse business."

"No!" Safer said angrily. "That's *your* horse business."

"If she would have asked me, I would have told her," Bailey retorted.

Safer shot him a disgusted look. "You made a living for twenty years lying to people about horses, didn't you?"

"Yes," Bailey granted, "but not to Helen Brach."

Safer reached into a stack of papers sitting on the lectern. "On March 27, 1976," he said, lifting a sheet and reading from it, "you specifically told Glenview PD about her coming to Florida but not about her looking at horses. Helen Brach didn't *know* she was going to be looking at horses, did she?"

"No," Bailey said, adding that he had not mentioned it to her in their telephone conversations, either the ones he made from his hotel or the times he tried to call her from a pay phone.

Safer was so surprised, he almost dropped his notes. "Pay phone?" he asked. "How many times did you call her from a pay phone?"

Bailey shrugged. "A couple of times, I guess."

"Have you *ever,*" Safer asked excitedly, "told *anyone* that you called Helen Brach's residence from a pay phone?" The implication was ominous. Bailey's lawyers had made an issue of the fact that the phone records from Bailey's hotel, the Colony, showed no calls to any coconspirators, using that fact as evidence to help disprove a conspiracy theory. But if Bailey had called Helen from a pay phone in an attempt to hide the calls, he could have used a pay phone as well to call his cohorts and there would be no record of the communications.

Bailey looked flustered. Afraid he had said too much, he tried to recover. "I could have," he mumbled. "I don't remember."

Chasing the unexpected opening, Safer asked Bailey to review the phone calls he had made to Brach.

One, Bailey said, was on Saturday, February 19, 1977, two days after Helen checked out of the Mayo Clinic—the day Bailey claimed she was scheduled to arrive in Florida. He had not talked directly to Helen, Bailey admitted, but to Matlick, who said she had just "stepped out."

Safer rummaged through his papers, looking for the records of Bailey's telephone calls from the hotel, which he had been able to get from the Glenview PD. The prosecutor looked up, smiling tightly. " 'Stepped out,' you say? Did you ask Mr. Matlick where she had 'stepped out' to at eleven forty-six P.M.?"

"That does sound sort of suspicious," Bailey conceded.

Bailey said he made another call from his hotel the next day, the twentieth. "I got the same story. I was concerned because she wasn't there. I couldn't *believe* this woman was not down in Florida. It was mind-boggling."

"Then why didn't you try harder to reach her?" Safer asked.

Bailey looked at him contemptuously. "*I* don't pursue a woman," he said. "I don't keep calling and calling. I called her house from a pay phone and Matlick answered. He always had the same BS. I gathered she had found someone else."

"You didn't try to find her?" Safer asked incredulously.

"No," Bailey replied smoothly. "I assumed she must be seeing someone else."

Despite the surprise admission about the calls from a pay phone, Safer was running out of questions. However, he was unwilling to let Bailey off the stand without one more crack at trying to break his alibi.

When *exactly,* he asked Bailey, had he gone to Florida in February 1977?

"February ninth," Bailey replied promptly.

That was strange, said Safer. If he had gone on the ninth, why were there no records to confirm it? The first receipt from a hotel was dated the sixteenth.

Between the ninth and the sixteenth, Bailey contended, he had been staying somewhere other than the Colony.

Okay, said Safer. Where?

Bailey shook his head. "Somewhere else," he said equivocally. "Maybe near Miami."

"You're sure you weren't in Chicago between the tenth and the sixteenth?" Safer asked carefully.

"I could have been," Bailey replied, "but I think I stayed somewhere in Florida."

"Your whereabouts are important," Safer said, "since we believe you met with Kenneth Hansen and Joe Edward Plemmons in Chicago on February eleventh."

"To the best of my knowledge," Bailey replied, "I was in Florida."

"What were you doing there?" Safer asked. "Before you checked into the Colony on the sixteenth to meet Christina Kubot?"

"Playing tennis," Bailey said with a shrug. "Golfing . . . having fun . . . relaxing." He smiled, confident that his alibi was strong. Eighteen years had passed since the period in question and hotel records—if Bailey had checked into a facility at all—had probably long since been destroyed. Even the possibility that documents might be found was ruled out because Bailey was so vague about where he had been. Also, since it was not uncommon for Bailey to drive to Florida (as he had with Karstenson), airline records, if they still existed, would have been meaningless.

31

Wrapping It Up

SAFER DECIDED to attack from another direction. With a series of pointed questions, he succeeded in getting Bailey to admit that he had introduced Helen to Jerry Farmer, his partner in other scams. Bailey acknowledged that he had brought them together, but he was vague about where or when. However, he did agree that the purpose had been to get Helen's approval to transfer her two remaining horses, Potenciado and Vorhees's Luv, from Bailey's stable to Farmer's so Farmer could train them as jumpers.

Did that indicate, Safer asked, feeling better that he had at least gotten Bailey to admit *some* connection to Helen Brach's horses, that she was disappointed in their performances on the racetrack?

"She didn't say *that,*" Bailey replied, dancing around the question.

Well, Safer pointed out, there are only three options open to an owner of unsuccessful racehorses. The owner can sell them, which did not apply in Brach's case, because she had refused to part with her horses voluntarily; even Bailey had admitted she felt about them as she would about her pets. The second option was to train them as hunter/jumpers. The third option, which is what Safer wanted to focus on, was to breed them. Since both horses were stallions, Helen would need mares if she was interested in a breeding program.

"And *you,*" Safer said, pointing a verbal finger at Bailey, "have sold many, many broodmares, haven't you?"

"Wrong!" Bailey replied heatedly.

Safer looked at him quizzically. "But you have perpetrated scams involving broodmares," he said.

"Not that I recall," Bailey said.

"And you wanted to sell Helen Brach some horses, didn't you?"

"Not really," Bailey maintained. "It was her idea to buy the race-horses; I didn't push her into anything whatsoever. She wanted no part of buying show horses, so I didn't push it."

"But you were going to show her some show horses in Florida, right?"

"Yes," Bailey agreed.

Judge Milton Shadur is not a man to suffer fools gladly. By Friday, June 2, 1995, he was evidencing impatience at the case's torpid progress. After seven and a half days of sometimes wandering testimony and apparently purposely evasive assertions by Bailey, the judge seemed impatient to bring the proceeding to a close. But before he could hand down his decision, the lawyers were entitled to summarize their points in closing arguments. By tradition, the prosecution went first, then the defense, and, finally, the prosecution would have the last word.

Safer, the first to speak, concentrated on the prosecution's theory that Bailey was directly responsible for Helen Brach's fate. "There is no reasonable explanation for her disappearance other than that she was silenced by Bailey and his coconspirators," he contended.

While their relationship initially may have been cordial, it changed dramatically after Helen found out she had been cheated. When she threatened to go to the state's attorney's office with her complaints, Bailey panicked. "She had the clout to initiate a criminal investigation," Safer said. "She could have put Bailey in jail."

In response, Bailey went to Florida and arranged to have Christina Kubot visit him to corroborate his alibi. While he was there, Helen disappeared. "So what does Bailey do?" Safer posited. "He makes three phone calls to Jack Matlick and gives up. This is the woman he planned to be with for a long, long time? This is implausible," Safer contended. "Bailey is nothing if not persistent."

Although Bailey had pleaded guilty to some of the lesser charges against him, Safer urged Shadur to go beyond that in determining his punishment. Bailey was, Safer argued, still looking for victims up to the time he was arrested. "He said his reason for placing ads in local newspapers was because he was looking for a suitable spouse. After this hearing, Your Honor, if you believe that, he has a horse he wants to sell you. He was not bringing elderly women to the horse stables because he wanted them to have a nice afternoon."

Bailey, Safer said in conclusion, was not deserving of mercy. "His words are false; his crimes are heinous. He is evil and he should be punished severely."

As Safer gathered his notes, Bailey swiveled in his chair. Turning to face the spectator section, he caught his wife's eye and blew her a kiss.

The core of Bailey's defense, as outlined by Tuite, was that his client never sold Helen Brach *any* horses. Since the government never proved otherwise, Tuite argued, their theory about Bailey engineering her murder was baseless. Besides, Tuite said, Helen and Bailey, contrary to the prosecution's contentions, had had a friendly relationship.

"If Helen Brach was upset with Bailey, why did she move her horses to his stable? Why would she allow Bailey to make a phone call to the Mayo Clinic on her behalf? Why would she leave her home and travel to another state on his word? Why would Mr. Bailey send Kubot home if he didn't expect Mrs. Brach to show up?"

As to his client's apparent failure to be more aggressive in finding out why she did *not* arrive on schedule, Tuite had a ready explanation: "Richard Bailey is a man who has never waited for a woman in his life. Therefore, he made no pursuit of her or an attempt to find out what happened to her."

While Shadur had sat silently during Safer's presentation, he frequently interrupted Tuite. "That's just a lie," he said angrily on one occasion, "a set of lies."

"No," Tuite responded. "The proof just isn't there. You can have theories, but you have to have something concrete."

The culprit, Tuite insinuated, was not Bailey, but Jack Matlick. "I'm not here to say there should be prosecution of Jack Matlick, but he could have done this. There's more evidence to point to his knowing Mrs. Brach was not coming back than Mr. Bailey knowing she was not coming back. Mr. Bailey was in Florida. He made a couple of calls from there and he made a couple of calls from Chicago. Then he dropped it. He didn't take anything from her; he continued to board her horses."

Judge Shadur shook his head, seeming to demonstrate to Tuite that he thought the defense lawyer was straying too far afield. "Linda Holmwood and Carole Karstenson," Shadur said, "they're going to be yardsticks by which I measure whether Mr. Bailey has accepted responsibility. It was exceptionally troublesome to hear Mr. Bailey's testimony—"

"It is not black-and-white," Tuite imposed.

"He had knowledge they did not have about horses and he took advantage of it. And then he doesn't acknowledge it."

"He's a con man," Tuite maintained.

Shadur gave him a stern look. "When they should stop being con men," the judge said ominously, "is when they get on the stand. That is when it is supposed to stop, and it didn't."

Tuite looked as if he was going to speak, but Shadur silenced him with a wave. "I'm not referring to what his conduct *was,*" the judge said. "I'm referring to his contemporary attitude."

Tuite bobbed his head in comprehension. "We have here, without a doubt, an unpopular defendant, based on his egregious conduct over a number of years." However, he added, he did not think that justified a harsher sentence. "Mr. Bailey is sixty-five years old and he doesn't have that many years. . . ."

Shadur, also well into middle age, smiled. "Careful . . . careful," he said, almost playfully.

"The point," said the fiftyish Tuite, also smiling, "is I think that should be factored in." Even more important, the defense lawyer argued, was the weakness of the prosecution's case. "We don't think the prosecution has maintained its burden on the Brach matter."

Since it was late on Friday when Tuite finished, the final prosecution presentation—Miller's—was postponed until Monday.

It would be a short session, Shadur warned. Miller would make his argument; then he would briefly go over the presentence report with all the lawyers. He wanted to adjourn in plenty of time, the judge said, to allow himself to draft his decision and have it ready by Tuesday.

Taking the hint, Miller was particularly brief.

"We feel," he said ardently, taking issue with Tuite's contention that the prosecution team had not made its case, "that we have proved that Richard Bailey defrauded Helen Brach. Mrs. Brach learned about it and Bailey became aware of her knowledge. Soon thereafter, Mrs. Brach dropped off the face of the earth."

After that, Miller added, Bailey lied to Glenview police about the financial transactions he had had with Helen Brach because he was trying to shift the focus away from himself. He professed to care about her, but he made only three phone calls to Matlick and he never did anything else. "Why would he drop Brach like a hot potato?" Miller asked. "Because he knows she's dead. There is no logical explanation for Helen Brach's disappearance other than Bailey's involvement in her demise."

If it had been a criminal trial rather than a sentencing hearing, the normal progression would have been for the judge to issue his instructions to the jury and turn it over to the panel for a ruling on guilt or innocence. But in this instance, the decision on Bailey's fate was up to the judge, not a jury, and there was one last convention to be observed. Bailey was entitled to make a final statement—in legal terms, an allocution—before the judge passed sentence. Traditionally, the allocution gives the defendant the opportunity to concede his guilt even further and accept responsibility for his actions.

In this case, Tuite preempted his client. Striding purposefully to the lectern, the defense lawyer launched into a speech. "Mr. Bailey never thought he would end up where he is now," the lawyer began. "When he was indicted, I suspect that he had not thought of Carole Karstenson and Linda Holmwood for a long, long time; he never followed their lives after that. If he had not been involved with the last two people in the eighties and the nineties, he never would have been here. He basically has been fighting for his life. . . ."

"Mr. Tuite," Shadur interjected, "the issue is not *your* acceptance of responsibility, but Mr. Bailey's."

"He admits lying to them and cheating them," Tuite continued. "It may be cold and callous, but that's what he did. He never once shifted his responsibility anyplace but on his own shoulders. I think this whole bit about the alleged meeting on February eleventh was a red herring. The week before may have been the week he was away. Mrs. Brach's horses were at Oak Brook in December and at Bailey's in January, which shows Mrs. Brach wasn't angry. . . ."

"He was *clearly* a fiduciary," Shadur interjected, meaning that he had a special relationship with Helen in which she trusted him and had confidence in what he told her.

"I disagree," said Tuite.

Shadur smiled. "That's what makes horse races, to make a bad pun."

Tuite was not amused. "Mr. Bailey said, 'I'll put up my mares, you put up your money,' but he didn't put up any money. . . .

"*That* is the salient fact."

"Mr. Bailey has served almost year in a difficult place," Tuite persevered, "a maximum-security facility, as opposed to one of the more pleasant facilities of lower security. Where he was doing his time should be considered. He needs to hope there is some light at the end of the tunnel and it isn't a train coming in his direction."

Shadur nodded abruptly. "Mr. Bailey?" he said.

Responding to his cue, Bailey rose.

"Selling horses was my life," he said in a matter-of-fact voice, reading from a scrap of notebook paper covered with his childlike scrawl. "I never thought that criminal charges would result. As for Linda Holmwood, if I had thought for a minute that was all the money she had, I never would have sold her all those horses. And as for Carole Karstenson, I apologize for revealing our sex life, but that's how I remember her." Looking directly at Shadur, he repeated his denial of being involved in Helen Brach's disappearance. "I had nothing to do with it," he insisted. "I know my sentence could be reduced if I furnished information. I wish I could, but I can't."

Before taking his seat, Bailey reminded Shadur about his recent marriage. "I would like some years at least with my wife," he said plaintively.

32

The Judge Speaks

S TEVE MILLER popped to his feet. Red-faced, he furiously protested against Bailey's whining plea for leniency.

"I don't see any of the sincerity the Court should look for," he said loudly, voicing his outrage. "I think the Court should make the finding that he lied repeatedly . . . that he made promises of marriage . . . that he persisted in his efforts to find more victims. He is wallowing in self-pity. He attempts to place himself in a morally superior position, but he has not accepted *any* responsibility. Never before have I stood before a court and described a person as *evil,*" Miller said, "but I don't think there is a more appropriate word to describe Richard Bailey. He singled out the lonely, the rich, the aged, and the vulnerable."

Shadur waited patiently until the prosecutor finished venting his anger. Nodding grimly, he waved to Miller to be seated. Clearing his throat, he looked out over the silent courtroom. In his hand was his written decision. Forty-one pages long, it covered all the facets of the complicated case, ranging from Bailey's scams, through the question of credibility of various witnesses, to Bailey's culpability in what had happened to Helen Brach. Shadur was famous among members of the Chicago Bar for his intellect, and his decision bubbled with eruditeness, rationality, and comprehensiveness.

Months before, when Miller first learned that Bailey's case had been assigned to Judge Shadur, the prosecutor winced. While he had the reputation of being scholarly and fair, Shadur also was reputed to be "soft" on defendants. As it turned out, Miller needn't have worried.

Although Shadur tried hard during the hearing not to telegraph his feelings, his contempt for Bailey occasionally seeped out via the questions he asked. Now that the testimony was finished, he no longer had to hide his loathing, and it rapidly boiled to the surface.

Citing—as he had warned Tuite that he would—the Holmwood and Karstenson cases, Shadur launched into a concerted attack on Bailey: "The record discloses a whole series of Bailey's other frauds—including his extensive use of lonely hearts ads—all of them calculated to locate and take financial advantage of other women who fit the profile of vulnerability that Bailey considered as making for especially easy marks."

Particularly galling to Shadur was Bailey's lack of remorse and his sarcastic comments, especially those about his sex life with the women he was swindling. "One witness described Bailey as responding to the witness's question as to how he could sleep with women as old as Brach—she was nearly eighteen years older than Bailey, at the time she was sixty-five and Bailey was forty-seven—by saying, 'I close my eyes and think about the money.' Indeed, the government's [list of facts] described a whole series of crude—even more crude—statements by Bailey about his engaging in sexual relations with older women—including Brach—as an integral part of his fraudulent activities."

Although Bailey had admitted guilt in some of the cases, that admission alone did not absolve him of responsibility, Shadur said. There also had to be some indication of remorse, a standard that Bailey had failed to meet.

Shadur also dismissed defense arguments that he should be lenient because Bailey had no previous criminal record, claiming he was merely a "first caughter" and not a true "first offender."

For example, Shadur pointed to the scams perpetrated by Bailey when he operated his driving school, long before he got involved with horses. As a result, the judge said, he considered Bailey's "real-world criminal history" to be significant.

So determined to clarify for the record that he thought Bailey was not only a scam artist but a liar as well, it was not until he was halfway into the decision that Shadur broached the Brach charges.

Even though he needed to be guided only by a preponderance of the evidence, Shadur said, he still was hampered somewhat on the Brach charges by several factors, including the time span since Helen Brach disappeared, the lack of details about her "apparent murder," and the fact that most of the evidence against Bailey came in the way of testimony from witnesses whose credibility normally would be suspect. Despite this, Shadur came out unequivocally against Bailey. He "plainly lied" about when he was in Florida, the judge said. "Bailey also lied to, or equally suspiciously withheld facts from, the Glenview police during the investigative period shortly following the Brach disappearance," Shadur added, including a decision not to tell officers about his claimed conversations with Jack Matlick, "conversations that, if they had really occurred as he now says . . . would certainly have been material because of their suspicious nature." In short, Bailey was a liar. "This Court rejects [his] current testimonial version of those alleged conversations as totally false."

But the fact that he was a ready liar, Shadur asserted, does not make Bailey a man who planned a murder and sought a killer. "All the same," the judge added after an ominous pause, "when the process is the present one of placing evidence in the scales to see which side tips downward . . . Bailey's total lack of credibility in key relevant areas begins that weighing process on the wrong side of the balance scales for Bailey."

Joe Edward Plemmons might have credibility problems, Shadur admitted, but that did not mean his testimony was not valid. In the end, what it came down to was believing Plemmons and Olsen or Bailey. "But Bailey's version," Shadur said, "plainly cannot be trusted." Substantiating testimony from Plemmons was the recollection of Arthur Katz, who said that Brach did indeed plan to go to the state's attorney and report Bailey. "Though Bailey's lawyer sought to shake Katz's story on cross-examination, nothing really cast any doubt on its accuracy— and it has strong internal indicia of reliability, as well," said Shadur. "This Court credits it entirely."

As for Cathy Olsen, Shadur described her as a "dubious witness" and reached his conclusions without giving any weight to her testimony.

Regarding Brach's alleged purchase of broodmares, Shadur pointed to testimony from witnesses such as Cathy Olsen, Lance Williamson, John Staren, and Barbara Mulvihill that supported the contention that she had indeed bought additional horses. In this situation, testimony had to be relied upon, rather than documentary evidence, for several reasons. For one thing, Brach's accountant, Everett Moore, was long dead and his records were not intact. Her personal records that still existed gave no clue, but some might have been lost or destroyed. Tax returns could not be relied upon because Helen Brach disappeared before completing the documents covering the year in which the horses were believed to have been purchased. No boarding bills for the horses could be found, but it was not unusual for stable owners to provide such facilities free to valued customers. In the end, the judge had to rely on what others said about this issue; too much time had passed to expect to be able to find supporting documents.

"In summary," Shadur said, "the totality of the relevant evidence confirms that Brach was ready and willing—and, in fact, eager—to 'blow the whistle' on Bailey upon her return from the Mayo Clinic."

In an aside, Shadur also rejected Bailey's claims that he did not sleep with Brach. "Bailey testified, and expects this Court to believe, that he had sexual relationships with a number of his other marks but a purely platonic relationship with Brach—though that latter claim has been contradicted by his own statements to others. Although this point is not necessary to the decision, if—as appears more probable—he *was* involved with Brach sexually, just as he was with a number of his other victims during his sordid career, it would understandably heighten the level of Brach's fury when she had ultimately learned of the swindles that had been perpetrated on her by Bailey."

While the evidence might not withstand beyond-a-reasonable-doubt scrutiny, Shadur said, it "unquestionably demonstrates a powerful motive for Bailey to dispatch Brach before she could carry out her announced intention to go to the prosecuting authorities."

Furthermore, he added, it was consistent with the "kinds of lies" Bailey fed to police investigating Brach's disappearance. "Indeed, Bailey's 'you don't kill the goose that lays the golden egg' argument really backfires: Here the golden eggs were really the major ill-gotten profits that were regularly being obtained by Bailey and his fellow conspirators from their multifaceted frauds, and for that purpose the goose that was laying those eggs was the multifaceted scheme itself. It was Brach—a woman of prominence and means—who was the potential killer of *that* goose. There was a strong incentive on Bailey's part to prevent her from doing that, and a number of Bailey's associates—Frank Jayne, Kenneth Hansen, and others—were known for violence." All of this, Shadur added by way of explanation, "lends credence to what would otherwise be highly suspect testimony from Plemmons and Olsen."

When he got to the Matlick issue, Shadur grew tentative. "Although this Court has not been made privy to the reasons that have prevented the authorities from proceeding with charges against Matlick, the bits of evidence that have been provided to this Court by stipulation certainly portray Matlick in a highly suspicious light." But he was at a disadvantage, Shadur said, because he had seen all of the evidence against

Bailey and none against Matlick, except for snippets that had come in by way of stipulation among the lawyers. He strengthened his stance, however, by adding that it was not necessarily an either-or question, raising the possibility that both were involved in the crime.

"But this Court will not indulge in speculation," he hurriedly interjected, "let alone reach any conclusion—even tentatively—on such thin information. All that can be said is that tossing the limited Matlick evidence into the scales does not shift the evidentiary balance." In any case, Shadur said, Bailey "surely had a strong motive" for wanting Brach dead.

"In summary," Shadur concluded, "in terms of the appropriate preponderance-of-the-evidence test on the record before this Court, it is more probable than not that Bailey did commit the offenses of conspiring to murder and soliciting the murder of Helen Brach."

Looking directly at Bailey, Shadur intoned his sentence: life in prison. Plus, he added, Bailey would be required to pay $1 million in restitution to his victims, a penalty that apparently would come into play only if he received a healthy payment from a book publisher or a moviemaker interested in buying his exclusive story.

The sentence was hardly out of Shadur's mouth before Tuite jumped to his feet, arguing that Shadur could not levy such a strict sentence under the guidelines in effect during the period closest to the time Brach disappeared. In other words, the defense lawyer asserted that Shadur erroneously had used the current set of guidelines, which were more stringent than the earlier ones.

Shadur clearly was peeved. The defense should have raised that issue earlier, he grumbled. But he was trapped and he knew it. He would review the issue, he said, and reconvene a week later with a decision on Tuite's objection. In the meantime, Bailey would remain in jail.

As the courtroom erupted in mild disarray, Bailey turned and blew a kiss to his wife, who was sitting in the first row, clad in her usual assortment of conspicuous jewelry: a half-inch-wide gold necklace with a diamond in the center, gold earrings, two gold rings studded with diamonds, and a gold watch.

Outside the courtroom, Dr. Annette Hoffman indicated she was not mollified by her husband's show of affection. Bailey had many good qualities, she claimed. "He makes you feel like you're the only woman in the world. I've never been treated so well by a man in my life. He is very neat, very domestic. He always picks up after himself." But the future of their relationship was another question. Wearing a grim expression, Hoffman shook her head sadly. "I heard many disturbing things," she admitted. "I don't know anymore now." Did that mean she was considering another annulment? a reporter asked. She ducked her head. "Yes," she whispered.

In the long run, Tuite's objection had little effect on Bailey's ultimate fate. When Shadur reconvened court on June 15, 1995, he announced that he was revising Bailey's sentence, not in response to Tuite's objection, which he considered "entirely without legal merit," but because a review of the guidelines indicated that the racketeering statutes under which Bailey was convicted do not allow for a literal life sentence.

Instead, Shadur said in a separate thirty-two-page decision, he was sentencing Bailey to thirty years. Not without more than a modicum of irony, he pointed out that the effect would be the same: Since there is no parole in the federal system, Bailey would have to serve at least twenty-five and a half years before he could be released, with some time off kicking in as a result of good behavior. By then, Bailey, if he is still alive, will be ninety-one years old.

Bailey accepted the verdict stoically. As he had at other critical times in the proceeding, he turned to his wife, even as he was being led away by two burly marshals, and blew her a kiss.

Barring a possible successful appeal, it was the end of the road for Richard Bailey. Ultimately, his golden tongue had led to his own undoing. When he walked out of the courtroom and returned to his Chicago jail cell pending transfer to a federal prison, his doom was effectively sealed.

In a sense, that was good news, because it showed that the criminal justice system was functioning: A man could still be brought to justice after almost twenty years. On a personal level, Steve Miller justifiably took a huge amount of satisfaction in Bailey's conviction. It not only signified a successful end to a long, tedious investigation but it made the prosecutor happy to know that a man of Bailey's caliber was off the streets. But, while Judge Shadur's decision ended the debate about Richard Bailey's involvement, it did not solve the enigma of what had happened to Helen Brach.

Miller proved that Bailey not only had a motive to have the wealthy widow killed but that he had actually tried to hire someone to murder her and dispose of her body. Still, it was never intimated that he had played an active role in her disappearance, much less that he was her killer.

Despite Miller's long and thorough investigation, the mystery of Helen Brach endures. Her body probably never will be found; it likely will never be determined how or when she was abducted and slain or by whom. Bailey's conviction tied off some of the ends, but many still dangle loosely. What about Jack Matlick, for example? He has never been charged in connection with his employer's disappearance and it remains controversial why he was so eager to burn her papers. His puzzling tale about her alleged last weekend at home continues to haunt students of the case. Similarly, Frank Jayne, Jr., according to his daughter's testimony, at the very least knew that something sinister was going on.

In any case, none of this was Miller's concern. He set out to see if there was a Bailey/Brach connection and he admirably accomplished that goal. Also, Bailey's conviction did not end his responsibility. Still facing him at the end of the Bailey proceedings was the resolution of the situation dealing with the horse killings.

Of the nineteen people who had been indicted at the same time as Bailey, Brown, Farmer, and Hugi in July 1994, all but three pleaded guilty to various charges. Going into the summer of 1995, as a result of those pleas, Miller looked forward only to the trial of Barney Ward, the owner of Castle Hills Farm in upstate New York; George Lindemann, Jr., the son of one of the country's richest men; and Marilyn Hulick, Lindemann's right hand at Cellular Farms. Originally, the three were to be tried at the same time. But as Judge Shadur walked out the exit door, another federal judge, George Marovich, stepped in.

One of Marovich's first actions was to separate formally Ward's case from that of Lindemann and Hulick. That meant that Ward would be tried alone, while Lindemann and Hulick would go into court together. For Miller, he could not yet look forward to spending leisure time with his wife, Jamie, and their three children. The cell door had no sooner slammed on Bailey than Miller and his new cocounsel, Susan Cox, began preparing for the Hulick/Lindemann trial, which, in a way, was even more crucial than Bailey's had been. From a prosecutorial point of view, the case against Bailey, because of the abundance of evidence against him, had been a relative slam dunk. On the other hand, the evidence against Lindemann and Hulick was much more ambiguous. If Miller and Cox could win a conviction against the Olympic hopeful and his top assistant, considering that Lindemann's financial resources were sufficient to secure the services of any criminal defense lawyer in the country, it would be a real coup.

Part V

The Horse Killers

33

With a Whip and a Chair
Chicago, September 1995

U.S. DISTRICT Judge George Marovich, a jolly-looking, slightly rotund man in his sixties, with a sharp sense of humor and a thick head of iron gray hair, leaned far back in his high-backed black leather chair and surveyed his domain.

On the dark-paneled wall to his left was a six-foot-long oar of blond oak, signifying that he was certified to hear admiralty cases. On his right was a rectangular box with enough comfortable padded chairs to hold the jury of eleven women and one man, as well as the two female alternates who had been chosen in three hours to hear the case.

In the right foreground were prosecutors Steve Miller, the dark circles under his eyes even darker as the result of preparing for two trials in less than three months, and Susan Cox, a petite, soft-voiced woman in her mid-thirties who had short red hair and a fiery Irish temper. They were flanked by FBI agents Pete Cullen and Kevin Deery.

Almost at the judge's feet, on his left, were the defendants: George Lindemann, Jr., the preppily dressed, jockey-sized part owner of Cellular Farms, and the tanned, outdoorsy-looking Marion Hulick, his chief aide.

Lindemann and Hulick were the only ones among the twenty-three people indicted by the federal grand jury in July 1994 in connection with the equine industry scandals who chose to face trial. Even Richard Bailey opted to plead guilty, although he gambled that he would get a better deal from Judge Milton Shadur than he would in a plea bargain with Miller. Lindemann and Hulick, on the other hand, decided to put up a full-fledged fight before a jury, confident they could afford to hire the best legal talent available to plead their cause. When Daddy—in this case George Lindemann, Sr.—has a net worth of between $600 million and $800 million, finding funds to hire a top-notch lawyer is not a problem.

George junior's attorney, sitting at his right, was Jay Goldberg, a sixty-one-year-old society lawyer from Manhattan, probably best known for his defense of crime boss Carlo Gambino's son in 1993. His other previous clients have included Carl "Andy" Capasso (in the Bess Myerson case), Donald Trump, multimillionaire Carl Icahn, Willie Nelson (in his fight against the IRS), and the late Miles Davis. In 1994, Goldberg had been designated "the toughest lawyer in town" in a segment of Robin Leach's *Lifestyles of the Rich and Famous.*

Next to Goldberg was Judd Burstein, a boyish-looking, curly-haired lawyer in his mid-forties, another New Yorker, who was representing Hulick. Also at the defense table were Goldberg's wife, Rema, and a Chicago lawyer, former federal prosecutor Thomas A. Durkin, who would act as consultants.

Behind the defense team was a mass of cardboard cartons—twenty-five in all—filled with copies of reports, transcripts, magazine articles, books, videotapes, cassette tapes, charts, and graphs that Goldberg and Burstein felt necessary to their case. The heap was so immense that the trial lawyers' three gofers barely had room to move.

Finally, sitting on the first row of hard wooden benches that made up the spectator section of the nineteenth-floor courtroom, sat George Lindemann, Sr., a portly man with thick-lensed glasses and a graying beard, and his immaculately coiffed blond wife, Frayda. As Marovich let his eyes roam around the room, Frayda Lindemann extended her arm behind her husband's back and gently brushed the dandruff off the collar of his expertly tailored dark suit.

The judge coughed. "This trial will now begin," he said almost jovially, allowing himself a tight smile. After more than twenty years on the federal bench, Marovich had honed his respect for skillful lawyering and the Lindemann/Hulick trial promised a good show. Later in the trial, probably much sooner than he expected, the judge's patience would grow exceedingly short with the lawyerly maneuverings that erupted with surprising regularity. After only a few such incidents, he would angrily rise as quickly as his aching back would allow and hobble out of earshot of the jury for a hastily convened sidebar conference.

New York lawyers, like New York residents, have a peculiar style, and it does not always travel well. In deciding to hire Goldberg to represent his son, Lindemann *père* may not have realized the impact a Manhattan litigator might have on conservative Midwesterners. Federal courtrooms in particular are generally somber places where discourse is low-key and raised voices are commonly accompanied by raised eyebrows. But Goldberg was a screamer.

Tall and slim, with an erect military bearing and rapidly disappearing gray hair, Goldberg would stalk around the room, always on the move, bouncing on his toes and bobbing his head. He pointed his finger, raised his arms, and howled until spittle flew from his lips. At one point, an increasingly agitated Miller interrupted a Goldberg tirade and asked the judge to order Goldberg to move. "I don't mind him shouting," the prosecutor said, "but I don't like him doing it in my ear."

Goldberg—arguably as a good lawyer should—also dealt heavily in sarcasm, ridicule, and hyperbole. Working his mouth into a sneer, he would attack a witness—especially Tom Burns, the anchor of the prosecution's case—until Marovich had to warm him to back off. Sometimes he accepted the censure; sometimes not.

For Marovich, the trial quickly turned into a serious battle for control of the courtroom. By the time the case finally went to the jury, the judge was exhausted from trying to keep things on track and in perspective. "The way that you people put a spin on every word that comes out of my mouth and every ruling that I make has made me stand here in awe of your excellence," he said in frustration near the end of the trial. "If you were jumpers, you would not be *reserve* champions. I came to a conclusion during this proceeding that maybe the gavel is not the appropriate symbol of judicial office; it should be the whip and the chair."

Considering the potential punishment, Lindemann looked surprisingly at ease. While waiting for the judge to open the session, he lazily extracted a novel from his knapsack and bent forward, scanning the book through glasses with lenses as thick as his father's. Hulick, on the other hand, looked sternly around her, occasionally running a hand through dyed blond hair that desperately needed touching up.

For both of them, especially Lindemann, there was a lot at stake. If convicted on each of the three counts of wire fraud with which they were charged, they could be sentenced to years in prison. But to the thirty-one-year-old equestrian, loss of his freedom might be the lesser penalty.

The more serious consequence might be the end of his career.

After graduating from Brown University in 1987 with a bachelor of arts degree, he was given the keys to Cellular Farms, a showcase horse-training facility on fifty prime acres straddling the New York–Connecticut border. His job was to run the operation, although he owned only 20 percent. The other 80 percent ownership was retained by his parents, George senior and Frayda.

Under George junior's supervision, Cellular Farms has operated consistently in the red, losing roughly $1 million a year. Still, it had been extremely useful to him, since it helped advance his ambition toward becoming a world-class rider. Long before he got his Ivy League diploma, Lindemann's goal was clear: to win a spot on the U.S. Olympic team. But in all likelihood, a conviction would doom that ambition. In fact, just being charged with a felony, particularly one related to his profession, had already caused a serious problem.

Soon after the Chicago grand jury indictments were announced in the summer of 1994, the board of directors of the 62,000-member American Horse Show Association, which serves as the regulatory group for the industry, issued an order prohibiting those who had been indicted from competing in AHSA-sponsored events pending disposition of their cases. It was the horse-world equivalent of exile, a move that not only branded the indictees socially but also damaged them monetarily, since most, unlike Lindemann, depended on participation in the industry to pay the mortgage. Yet among all those affected by the ruling, the one who suffered most immediately was Lindemann, who was in the middle of a series of pre-Olympic qualifying events.

Lindemann decided to fight the ruling, quickly winning the first round when a Manhattan judge ruled that the AHSA had acted illegally by suspending the Olympic hopeful.

The U.S. Olympic Committee, still rattled by the Tonya Harding scandal, decided that Lindemann could continue to take part in qualifying events. At the same time, the USOC warned that a conviction would probably put an end to Lindemann's dream of participating in the 1996 spectacle in Atlanta.

With his path temporarily clear, Lindemann entered the 1995 national championships for dressage, an esoteric style of horsemanship in which emphasis is placed on gracefulness during the walk, trot, and canter. Aboard Graf George, his new $500,000 horse, who won a Bronze

Medal for his rider (not Lindemann) in the 1992 Olympics, Lindemann finished sixth, which put him in strong contention to be chosen as one of the four members of the American dressage team. But a guilty verdict would dash his hopes.

Rising and facing the jury, Miller laid out the bare bones of the government's case. There were, the prosecutor contended, numerous factors that pointed toward Hulick's and Lindemann's guilt. The most prominent, of course, was Tom Burns's confession that he killed the Lindemann horse, Charisma, on direct orders from Hulick and with the tacit approval of Lindemann, who was in Asia at the time the incident occurred.

But, Miller continued, to get to the point where the pair's guilt or innocence could be decided, the jury first had to understand the background. And one of the more important things they had to comprehend was how frustrated Lindemann and Hulick were with Charisma.

When they bought the animal—a handsome bay thoroughbred gelding, sixteen hands high, with a faint star on his forehead and a sock on his right hind leg—in November 1989 from Carriage Oaks Farms in Fort Lauderdale, they had high expectations.

On paper, the horse belonged not to George Lindemann, Jr., but to his younger sister, Sloan, an eager but much less skillful rider than her brother. It didn't take long, Miller said, to determine that the horse was too high-spirited for Sloan, so George took him over.

While Lindemann had no trouble controlling the horse, another much more serious problem soon became apparent: Charisma, who should have been a champion, was a wildly inconsistent performer, up one minute, down the next. "They should have named him yo-yo," Miller quipped.

As 1990 wore on, Hulick and Lindemann became ever more disconcerted. In July, after Charisma had a terrible day at the Hampton Classic, an important show on the Eastern circuit, Lindemann decided he had had enough. Ignoring rapidly building storm clouds, he ordered Hulick to release the horse, "turn him out," in the industry idiom, into a paddock and leave him there all night.

"The horse could have been struck by lightning," Miller said. "He could have panicked from the noise of the thunder and broken a leg running in a strange field." In fact, Miller said, that is precisely what Lindemann hoped would happen. "Turning to Marion Hulick, Lindemann asked, 'Is the horse insured?' She said, 'No.' His response was, 'Then insure him.' "

Charisma not only survived that night, Miller added, but he performed magnificently the following day and finished as the show's reserve champion, the second-place horse.

But Charisma's performance continued to fluctuate. "The lightningstorm episode involving George Lindemann, Jr., was his first mistake. But it was Marion Hulick's turn to make the next mistake," Miller said.

Later, at another less-important show, when Charisma was being ridden by a rider hired just for that performance, a "catch rider," in horseshow parlance, Charisma did poorly. "And what did Marion Hulick say? She said, 'I want this horse dead for the insurance.' "

It was only several months later, after Charisma turned in a particularly sour performance at an Indoor Season show in Washington, the Super Bowl of the show-horse world, that the decision was made to hire Burns.

The crime was compounded after Burns killed Charisma, Miller argued, when Lindemann and Hulick ordered other employees to lie about who had ridden the horse, telling them to say that Sloan and George had been the only riders, when in fact there had been two others, Molly Ash and Lyman Whitehead.

Hulick and Lindemann didn't want the insurance investigators to know about Ash and Whitehead because they would have asked them to give statements under oath about their involvement with Charisma. If that had happened, Ash would have had to tell them how she had protested the order to turn Charisma out into a storm, and Whitehead would have had to report Hulick's comment about killing the horse for the insurance.

A few minutes later, when Goldberg and Burstein made their opening statements, both belittled the prosecution's accusations, claiming that Hulick and Lindemann were experienced horse people and that they knew when they bought Charisma that a five-year-old horse would be inconsistent.

Furthermore, Goldberg insisted vehemently, the insurance payoff was inconsequential to Lindemann. To a man of his wealth, Goldberg told the blue-collar jury, $250,000 was of no more value that a postage stamp would be to a person of ordinary means.

"There would be no reason in the world that coming from a family worth close to a billion dollars, that for a postage stamp he would risk his life, his career, his standing, and would kill what wasn't even his horse."

It was, he added, not even proved that Charisma had been electrocuted. As far as he was concerned, Charisma had died a natural death. "The medical experts will tell you that horses die at times unexpectedly and suddenly, and that's what happened to this horse." The alleged electrocution, he said, was invented by Burns.

The person on whose shoulders rests the entire government case, Goldberg said, working himself up to a state of apparent outraged indignation, was Burns. "If you have a reasonable doubt about the credibility of Tommy Burns, you will have a doubt about the entire case. He *is* the government's case. No matter how the government will try to divert you with the side issues, the proof will show that Tommy Burns *is* the government's case."

According to Goldberg, Burns was a thief and a liar who could not be believed under any circumstances. He was, the defense lawyer said, a man so eager to save his own skin that he invented the story about Hulick and Lindemann hiring him to kill Charisma because he thought that would help him win favor with prosecutors and enhance his chances of selling his story to publishers and to Hollywood.

"For Tommy Burns," Goldberg said, raising his right hand and pointing his index finger skyward, "this case is of critical importance not only for freedom for someone who belongs in jail, but it also means money for his lifetime of crime. And," he added, curling his lip, "Mr. Miller says he has only a ninth-grade education.

"You," he told the jury, "are going to find yourselves filled with doubt because of Burns's lifetime of deceptions, the fact that he would say anything to make a deal. And when you add to that the enormous reputation and accomplishment of George Lindemann and the absence of any motive whatsoever to kill his sister's horse, you will find yourselves hesitating to believe the government's version of the case."

Burstein carried Goldberg's hypothesis a step further. If Lindemann lacked motive, he said, Hulick had even less reason to have Charisma killed, since she stood to gain nothing by the horse's death.

"Why is this woman who was a renowned trainer of horses, a renowned trainer of young riders, why is this woman sitting in this courtroom being charged with participation in the supposed killing of a horse that she didn't own, in which she had no financial interest, and from which she did not stand to gain a penny should any insurance monies be recovered? Why," he asked indignantly, "is she here?" It was, he concluded, because Hulick filled a gap in Burns's tale. According to Burstein, Burns never mentioned Hulick when he first told Miller's investigators about killing Charisma. It was only after he discovered that Lindemann was out of the country that he had to invent Hulick as the middleman.

The whole story, Burstein maintained, was a Tom Burns fabrication. "The question is, can you believe Tommy Burns beyond a reasonable doubt? He's a con man," Burstein concluded. "He's trying to make a very important trade. He's hoping to trade his freedom for the freedom of Marion Hulick and George Lindemann."

34

The Sandman Sings

I was a one-man crime wave," Tom Burns confessed in a deep, tense voice, lowering his eyes and vigorously rubbing his left hand against his right as if trying to erase some revealing, immutable stain. "Basically," he added softly, "I was just a piece of garbage."

Decked out in a dark jacket, neatly pressed shirt, and stylish, expertly knotted tie—the garb required in his new life as a successful salesman of used cars—the scrubbed, freshly barbered man sitting in the witness chair hardly looked like the coldhearted hard-core criminal he proclaimed himself to be.

He and Harlow Arlie broke the leg of a horse named Streetwise with a crowbar, he admitted, and he had killed fourteen other horses for owners who wanted to collect the insurance. Besides being a horse killer, he also took part in other crimes designed to defraud insurance companies, such as cleaning out a friend's house so he could file a claim on the "stolen" furniture and jewelry. And, in his spare time, he perpetrated credit-card frauds and became an accomplished thief willing to steal just about anything that wasn't nailed down.

A chunky man a little taller than average, with blond hair parted almost down the middle, Burns had a round face and a ready smile. When his apparent eagerness to paint himself in the worst-possible light and his quick response to Susan Cox's questions were added in, he came across as likable, despite the disclosures about his checkered past. As the prosecution's leadoff witness and the main target-to-be for Goldberg, the man *New York* magazine rated one of the city's top one hundred lawyers, Burns was proving amazingly adept.

How much money, Cox asked him, would he estimate he had received as a result of his life of crime?

Burns tilted his head to the side and looked at the ceiling as if deep in contemplation. "I don't know," he said after a short pause. "A couple of hundred thousand, a few hundred thousand dollars, I guess, over a six- or seven-year spell."

"And have you ever paid any taxes on any of that money?" Cox asked.

Burns grinned. "No, ma'am," he said with a chuckle.

And of that several hundred thousand dollars, how much would he estimate had come from killing horses?

"I've never really counted," Burns said, turning serious. "But it probably isn't that much. I got promised more money than I actually ever got paid."

Anticipating the line Goldberg and Burstein would follow on cross-examination, Cox asked Burns a series of questions about how truthful he had been with the government in his revelations.

It had taken awhile, he admitted, but finally he had told investigators everything. The reason the truth was slow in coming, he added, was because he was interested in protecting Barney Ward, who had been like a father to him. But, after almost two years of question-and-answer sessions with Cullen, Delorto, and David Hamm, maybe as many as one hundred all told, and considerable soul-searching on his own, he finally had decided that he could no longer protect his mentor. But once he made that decision, he was free to tell the entire story about the death of Charisma.

And what was that? Cox asked.

Burns sighed. It began, he said, on December 13, 1990, when Harlow Arlie, who was working as a groom at his in-law's stables, Equestrian Oaks, gave him a message to call Ward.

When he called his mentor back, Ward told him to reschedule his annual trip to New York and come earlier if he wanted "to make a lot of money." He knew that Ward had only one thing in mind: killing a horse.

"And did he tell you who it was you were going to make a lot of money off of?" Cox asked.

"Yes," Burns said. "Lindemann."

After calling the travel agent, Burns flew to New York and went straight to Ward's Castle Hill Farm. When he got there, Ward gave him a slip of paper with Marion Hulick's phone number on it and suggested he call her immediately.

"Did you know Marion Hulick?" Cox wanted to know.

Burns nodded. "Yeah, but she had no reason to like me. I never really got along with her." In the past, they'd had a couple of disagreements, Burns added. Once she had accused him of stealing some saddles from her and another time she had correctly accused him of stealing money from her purse. He gave it back. "Plus," he added gleefully, "I ran over her husband's motorcycle."

"Why did you do that?"

Burns smiled. "I didn't like him."

After talking to Hulick, Burns asked one of Ward's employees to take him to Cellular Farms, a forty-minute drive away, because he was unsure how to get there.

They tracked Hulick down in her apartment/office and Burns poked his head through the door. He was unpleasantly surprised when a man greeted him; the last thing he wanted on this visit was to see someone who knew him. "This guy was looking at me," Burns said. "He called me by my name and then I recognized him. His name was Shep. He had worked for me at one time."

By now, Burns said, he was worried because Hulick had told him the place was practically deserted. Instead, he had seen one person who knew him for sure and there had been six or eight other people bustling about outside, getting ready to take the horses to Florida the next day to begin making preparations for the 1991 horse-show season.

"I got Marion to the side and just basically told her that she was crazy. To me, this didn't make any sense at all. There were too many people around."

But Hulick was not convinced. "She told me, 'It's got to get done tonight.' I asked her why it couldn't wait and she said, 'George wants it done while he's in Asia.' "

Reluctantly, Burns agreed if she would pay him his normal 10 percent fee or twenty-five thousand dollars.

"And what did she say?" Cox asked.

"She said she didn't care. George would pay." However, she added that he couldn't be paid before the insurance claim was settled. Although he normally asked for some money in advance, he did not think it was necessary in this case because Ward was involved. "Barney would make sure I got the money."

Once they had a deal, Burns said, he, Hulick, Shep, and the woman who worked for Ward, *Jean Hastings,* who had driven him to the farm, climbed into Hulick's Cadillac Seville for the short ride to the barn where Charisma was housed.

On the way, he said, she pointed out an area where some construction was under way. On the other side of that, she said, was a side road from which he could get onto the farm without being seen.

When he first entered the barn, he was impressed with its extravagance. "There were cobblestone floors and brass poles that held the stalls up. The stalls were extralarge. It was beautiful."

Again, he said, he was disturbed because there were a number of people in the barn and he was anxious about being recognized. "I thought, This is really stupid. Most of my life I'd been a career criminal and I was pretty good at it. I'd always been able to cover my tracks pretty good, and this just seemed ridiculous."

Before he could mention it to Hulick, she walked into a nearby stall and went straight to the horse that was inside. She straightened the animal's blanket and then started patting his neck and pointing, which to Burns meant that was the horse that she wanted killed.

"What did the horse look like?" Cox asked.

"It was a bay thoroughbred," Burns replied firmly. "I don't know if it was a gelding or a mare."

From the barn, they went back to Hulick's apartment and Burns asked her what time he should come back. "She said probably at ten o'clock. She was going to send everyone out to dinner. I told her to lock up the dogs."

After that, Burns said, he and Hastings left and he checked in at the Hilton Hotel in nearby Danbury, using Hastings's name, since she had one of Ward's credit cards.

He took her back to Ward's, went to a hardware store and an electrical-supply outlet to buy the material to make his executioner's rig, and had a few drinks in the bar. Since he didn't want to leave the car parked along the road while he was in the barn killing Charisma, he made arrangements with Hastings for her to drive him there and then pick him up after he had done his work. He picked her up, then, en route to Cellular Farms, they stopped at another bar for a few more drinks.

"Was that your normal practice before killing a horse?" Cox asked.

"Yes," he nodded solemnly. "Everybody wants to make me out to be a monster and everything else. I mean, it was a lousy thing to do, killing a horse. It was pretty cowardly. I just pretty much got drunk, got in my own mind zone, before I did it."

It was almost exactly 10:00 P.M. when they got to the farm and

Hastings dropped him at the roadside. He crept into the barn, killed Charisma, and went back to the road to be picked up. He and Hastings had a couple of more drinks, then he took her back to Ward's and returned to the hotel.

He returned to Illinois and began making plans to go to Florida to pick up his twenty-five-thousand-dollar fee plus ten thousand dollars in expense money from Hulick. In the meantime, he talked to Donna Brown about killing Streetwise and figured he could do two things at once while in Florida: collect his money on Charisma and execute Streetwise. However, before he could meet with Hulick, he and Arlie were arrested for breaking Streetwise's leg.

Before turning him over to the defense for cross-examination, there was one more issue Cox wanted to go into with Burns: his relationship with Barney Ward.

While you were in jail in Florida for the attack on Streetwise, did you try to raise money for your hundred-thousand-dollar bail?

Yes, Burns replied. He tried unsuccessfully to get the money that was still owed him for killing Charisma and he asked Ward for help. "You know, he'd never let me down before. He was the closest thing I ever had to a father. I knew he had the money or had access to the money and I asked him, 'Are you ever going to . . . you know, are you going to get me out of here or what?' And he said real sarcastically, 'What do you want me to do? Cash in a CD?' "

"And what was your response?" Cox asked.

"I started crying," Burns said softly. "I just couldn't believe that as big as this was, nobody was going to come to my assistance, because turning government witness was the last thing I ever wanted to do."

Not long after that conversation with Ward, Burns added, he was lying on the bunk in his cell when a guard yelled his name. "I got up and there was a man in the lobby, a bail bondsman from Miami. He told me that Barney had put up my bond."

Once he was freed, he went to Palm Beach and met Ward in a restaurant. "He asked me if I had told on everybody and I said that I had. Then he asked me, 'Did you tell on Lindemann?' and I told him I did not. Then he told me when I got back to Chicago to tell on people like Jerry Farmer and Donna Hunter, other people I had killed horses for, but under no circumstances was I to tell on Lindemann."

About three weeks later, Burns said, he saw Ward again in Florida and Ward threatened him. "He said if I implicated him, he wasn't going to hire anybody or anything, that he would just kill me himself. He had threatened me before," Burns added, "but never like that. He usually flies off the handle, but this time he was calm and collected. He just looked at me very serious and he told me that."

Several months later, Burns attended the wedding of Ward's oldest son and Ward again brought up the issue of him talking to investigators. "He told me to lie to them. Just make up stuff. Ruin my credibility." Ward said if he kept Lindemann out of it, Lindemann would set him up in his own business.

Realizing he was in a lot of trouble, Burns said he thought about fleeing the country. It was better than being a government witness, and at that point he had not divulged enough information to have anyone indicted. But his plans fell apart because he was not able to raise enough money.

"During this period," Cox asked, "did you continue to protect Barney Ward? That is, not reveal his role as a middleman in any of these killings?"

"Yes," Burns confirmed. "For a year and a half or two years. I couldn't ever imagine getting up and doing what I'm doing now. Ratting on him. I just never wanted to do it."

Cox finished her direct examination of Burns twenty minutes after the session opened on Friday, September 8, 1995, some two hours total from when it began. Although she would have a chance to question him again later on redirect, it would not be until after Goldberg and Burstein had their opportunity to grill him.

In most trials, there is only one defendant, so there is only one opposing counsel the prosecution has to worry about. In this case, since there were two defendants, attorneys for both Lindemann and Hulick would get to pummel the witness before the prosecutor would have the chance to question him again on redirect.

Cox and Miller knew their fate probably rested on Burns. If the self-admitted career criminal who dropped out of school when he was fourteen could survive the pounding he would have to take from two high-priced New York lawyers, the prosecution would be in excellent position to win a conviction. Although they had other witnesses waiting in the wings, a large part of their testimony would be little more than substantiation of what Burns had already said. After Cox asked her last question and was returning to her seat, she flashed Miller a tight smile. There's nothing we can do but wait, the look said, wait and see if Burns can survive the no-holds-barred attack we both know is coming.

35

A Battle of Wills

JAY GOLDBERG leaned forward at the waist, like a schoolmaster disciplining a misbehaving student. "In July 1992, did you write a letter to Barney Ward?" he asked belligerently. "Yes or no?"

"In 1992?" Burns asked in mild surprise. "Yes. I did."

"Okay," Goldberg replied, satisfaction evident in his voice. "And as you sit here, do you recall what you said?"

Burns looked puzzled. "It was kind of a good-bye letter, you know. I didn't know how to tell him about how I rolled. I just didn't have the guts to tell him basically what I had done and told on your client."

"Did you tell him, sir," Goldberg continued, his voice rising, "that you were under such enormous pressure from the authorities that you reached the point where you didn't know right from wrong?"

For more than an hour, Goldberg had been hammering at Burns, attacking his initial lack of candor with federal authorities and his past criminal behavior. The more he questioned him, the more aggressive Goldberg became. And the more pressure the defense attorney applied, the calmer Burns grew.

"You told him that, didn't you?" he asked accusingly.

"Yes, sir, I did," Burns replied.

"And you told him," Goldberg said, his voice at high volume, "as you described the authorities, you used words like f—ing assholes. Is that correct?"

"Not that I remember," Burns said coolly.

"Oh," Goldberg replied sarcastically, "you wouldn't use those words?"

"Oh, yes I would," Burns said with a smile. "I just don't remember using them in that instance."

The response made even the jury laugh—a bad sign for the defense.

*   *   *

Early on, it became clear that Goldberg's strategy was to adopt the demeanor of the schoolyard bully. Although it was a defense attorney's duty to be aggressive and attack prosecution witnesses, not all defense attorneys went as far as Goldberg. During the O. J. Simpson trial in Los Angeles there was debate in legal circles about whether two of Simpson's lawyers, Barry Scheck and Peter Neufeld, would be detrimental to the defense because of their contentious "New York style." In the Simpson case, Scheck and Neufeld carried it off successfully. But whether it would work for Goldberg and his client, Lindemann, was another question. Chicago wasn't Los Angeles and Jay Goldberg wasn't Barry Scheck.

Undeterred, Goldberg plunged ahead, trying to elicit from Burns confirmation that he was tailoring his testimony to fit the prosecution case because it was in his own self-interest.

"Did you tell somebody from the *Palm Beach Post* that Susan Cox said, 'It's up to you, Tommy, as to whether George Lindemann gets convicted'? Did she say that to you?" Goldberg asked.

"She did not," Burns replied.

"Did you tell that to a reporter from the *Palm Beach Post*?"

"I don't recall saying that," Burns replied.

"You don't recall that?"

"No, sir," said Burns.

"Now do you recall everything that Susan Cox said to you on that day?"

"I don't really recall that day," said Burns.

Again he asked Burns if Cox had said that to him and again Burns replied that he did not remember.

Abruptly switching subjects, Goldberg asked Burns if he had ever been sentenced as a result of his plea of guilty to the single charge of conspiracy to commit wire and mail fraud.

"You still haven't been sentenced, is that right?"

"No," Burns said.

"Did you ever say to either Mr. Miller or Ms. Cox, 'Listen, why don't you schedule the case for sentence. Sentence me. You can trust me. I'll still testify'? Did you ever say that to them?" he asked loudly.

Cox sprang to her feet. "Objection."

"Sustained," Judge Marovich said quickly.

"All right," said Goldberg. Then, ignoring the order, he repeated. "But you haven't been sentenced. Is that right?"

"No."

"You are aware, are you not, that it's up to these people," he said, pointing at the prosecutors, "at this table—"

"Objection," Cox said loudly.

Marovich, grabbing his back, rose with a groan. "Let me indicate something to you at sidebar," he said testily, pointing to the area at the left side of the bench where he met with lawyers to discuss issues that he did not want the jury to hear.

"First of all," the judge said peevishly to Goldberg as soon as the lawyers had gathered, "I really do not have any desire to impede your cross-examination, but I just suggest to you that after a while certain points have been made perfectly clear. I mean if you don't think that this jury understands—"

"I'll move on," Goldberg interrupted.

Marovich continued: ". . . that this guy is in big doo-doo and is out to save his butt, then you are insulting the people in that jury box and taking my time. And as far as making it appear that the prosecutors are the only ones that have any say on his sentence, that is making a potted plant out of the judge, and I resent that. Let's move on."

"Judge . . ." Goldberg began.

Marovich looked at him angrily. "Let's just move on!" he said decisively.

Waving a copy of a March 6, 1992, interview with Cullen, Goldberg asked Burns if it was correct that at that time he had admitted to the FBI agent that for the previous thirteen months he had been providing him false information about the incident involving Lindemann and the murder of Charisma. "And all that information you had given him was false. You told him that?"

"Yes, sir," Burns replied obdurately.

"But now you told Agent Cullen that you wanted to be truthful. Isn't that a fair statement?"

"Yes, sir."

"But even when you were telling Cullen that the past year's statements to him were false and now you wanted to be truthful, you weren't being truthful. Isn't that a fair statement?"

"I was not being truthful at all," Burns admitted.

"You were able to look at him straight in the eye and just lie to him. Is that right?"

"To a point, yes."

"And no pang of conscience, right?"

"Not at that point, no, sir."

Goldberg nodded briskly, content he had made his point. But it was an empty victory. Through his browbeating, he had made Burns admit he had been lying to federal officials. But Burns had long before admitted that himself, explaining during direct examination that he had consistently lied to Cullen and Miller about the Charisma incident because he had been trying to protect Barney Ward. In using such an aggressive style, Goldberg was creating an interesting situation; he was taking a risk that the jury would begin to feel sympathetic toward Burns, a man with a limited education who was trying to correct the mistakes of his past and get on with his life. Goldberg did not improve the situation a few minutes later when he began ridiculing Burns about his job.

"Did you ever say that your one goal in life is to be a used-car salesman?" he asked mockingly.

"Absolutely," Burns replied.

"And that's what happened to you, right?" Goldberg persisted.

"Yes, sir."

"Okay," Goldberg added with a sneer. "I mean, hopefully you don't sell these cars in the Chicago area, do you?"

"Objection!" Cox interjected.

Judge Marovich nodded vigorously. "Counsel," he said sharply to Goldberg, "let's not talk about used-car dealers, because they might want to talk about lawyers next."

"All right," Goldberg replied, unabashed. Soon afterward, he again began berating Burns, ridiculing him for telling a television reporter that Charisma was a mare and that he did not know the difference between a mare and a gelding. Goldberg's point, although he was slow in developing it, was that Burns had *not* killed Charisma and was falsely claiming that he had so he could work a better deal with the government. And, soon afterward, he derided Burns's sartorial choices.

Had he, Goldberg asked, threatened a man because he thought he was giving authorities information about him?

"I never threatened him," Burns said. "If I threatened him, I would tell you. I have no problem with it."

"You've threatened many people. Is that right?"

"Absolutely."

"By the way, just so I understand it, when you ply your trade and commit these crimes, you don't look like you look on the witness stand in terms of your attire, do you?"

"I thought I looked pretty good," Burns replied.

"Did you," Goldberg asked antagonistically, "have any discussions with the FBI agents about the clothes you ought to wear when you appear on the witness stand? *Did you?*"

"I always dress nice," Burns replied evenly.

"You always dress nice?" Goldberg repeated scornfully.

"Yeah."

"Even when you do the horse killings that you claim you did?"

"Yes," said Burns.

"You wear a suit and a tie," he sneered. "All right."

"Objection!" said Cox.

Marovich threw up his hands. "Let's go to lunch."

After the break, a calmer Goldberg tediously worked his way through a stack of documents detailing when and by whom Burns was questioned about various aspects of his claim of having killed Charisma.

According to the documents produced by Goldberg, Burns, not long after he was arrested, gave investigators facts about other horses he had killed but postponed revealing details about Charisma until February 26, more than three weeks after he had been arrested and four days after he had been released from the Alachua County jail under a hundred thousand dollars' bail. The reason, Goldberg asserted, was that during those four days he met with a woman named Ann Madej, who furnished him with information about Charisma's death, information that Burns later repeated to investigators to substantiate his claim about murdering the Lindemann horse.

"In those four days between February 22 and February 26 you met with a certain person and found out the date Charisma died. Isn't that true?"

"I knew when the horse died," Burns replied, shaking his head. "I killed it."

"And you knew, did you not, from speaking to that person the facts and circumstances relating to the death of Charisma? Isn't that true?"

"No, sir," Burns maintained.

Goldberg continued to pursue the issue, contending that Burns not only did not give details about Charisma's death until much later but also never mentioned Marion Hulick or Gerald Shepherd's presence at Cellular Farms until February 26. "Is that correct?" he asked.

"No," said Burns. "I mentioned Shep's name before, but possibly not Marion's."

Perhaps in an attempt to confuse Burns or maybe through disorganization, Goldberg skipped abruptly from day to day, year to year, subject to subject, often being repetitive, dropping one issue and starting unexpectedly on another. The thrust, however, was that he was trying to get Burns to admit that he had made up the story about Hulick and Lindemann so he would have more clout with authorities in working out a favorable plea bargain. To do this, Goldberg implied that Burns collaborated with Ann Madej in order to get details he could use to give more veracity to his story, and with Gerald Shepherd to get him to swear falsely that he had been at Cellular Farms on December 15. To make this theory convincing to the jury, Goldberg would have to demonstrate not only that Burns was a totally disreputable individual but that there was a wide-ranging conspiracy to help Burns frame Hulick and Lindemann. In order to give substance to that hypothesis, Goldberg had to discredit Tommy Burns totally.

Burns, however, refused to cooperate, repeatedly denying that he had, in effect, concocted a master plan, or that he had anything in mind other than protecting Barney Ward when he continued to lie to Cullen, Miller, Delorto, and Hamm.

Despite a warning from Marovich that he was being repetitive and running the risk of alienating the jury, Goldberg continued to thrash at Burns about his inconsistent statements to investigators—statements that Burns had repeatedly admitted making.

Midway through the afternoon, after Burns's cross-examinination had been going on for almost three hours, Marovich began pressuring Goldberg to finish. After a long and involved series of questions relating to his plea-bargain agreement, Goldberg summed it up.

"And the agreement," he said, "is that the government will recommend that the maximum time—it's up to the judge, whatever the judge does," he said, glancing at Marovich, "but the government will recommend that you do no more than six months in a federal prison, and that if you have to do time for the state of Florida, it will be included to run at the same time as the federal sentence. Is that right?"

"Yes, sir," Burns said solemnly. "Yes, sir."

And that same agreement, Goldberg said, bound Burns to tell the truth to investigators.

"That's correct," Burns agreed.

"But despite that agreement," Goldberg yelled, "you will agree with me that for years you lied repeatedly. Correct? Yes or no?"

"Absolutely," Burns replied staunchly.

Attacking Burns's veracity was one thing, but by appearing to try to tyrannize him, by ridiculing him on his career choice, his clothing style, his alleged inability to tell a male from a female horse (given that he was operating in total darkness with a penlight and his interest was not in determining the horse's sex but attaching an alligator clip to the flesh around the rectum), and his intelligence, Goldberg was running the risk of vastly overplaying his hand.

Perhaps along the way, Goldberg had lost sight of the fact that the jurors, predominately blue-collar workers, could much more closely associate with Burns than they could with him, a silk-stocking lawyer to the rich and famous. Despite several admonitions to jurors that they were not to let Lindemann's wealth influence their thinking, Goldberg's strategy and mien may only have perpetuated the belief among the panel members that the rich used money and position to take advantage of the poor.

36

Open Warfare

I N CONTRAST to Jay Goldberg, Judd Burstein was Mr. Nice Guy. While Goldberg favored intimidation, Burstein preferred reason. But, while Goldberg was erratic, jumping from subject to subject, he got where he was going fairly rapidly. Burstein, on the other hand, was a plodder.

Despite warnings from Judge Marovich that his questions seemed irrelevant, Burstein elicited from Burns the admission that he did not tell his used-car customers about his criminal past. "And that," he said, coming to the punch line, "is because you believe that your history of lying and cheating has led you to become a person who has very little credibility. Correct?"

Burns smiled. "That's pretty much right, sir."

Marovich sighed. It had taken Burstein thirty-one questions and more than twenty minutes to get to that meaningless admission. It took him another forty-five minutes and 110 questions, most of which were about matters that had already been covered, before he got to the next significant area.

And was he correct, Burstein wanted to know, when he assumed that Miller and Cullen were angry when they found out that Burns had been lying to them for two years about some of the details regarding Charisma's execution?

"Oh, yes," Burns agreed. "They were furious."

"And you believed at that time it was important for you to say what-ever you could that would convince them that you really were at Cel-lular Farms on December 15, 1990?"

"I didn't lie about the way I killed that horse," Burns corrected him. "Just about the way it was set up."

By that time, Marovich was alternatingly glaring at the defense lawyer and the clock. "Let me ask you something, because I want to make sure that what we're doing is productive," Marovich said to Burstein. "Do you have any reason to believe that if you ask the same questions that Mr. Goldberg asked that you are going to get different answers?"

"Absolutely not, Judge," Burstein said. "But I'm going someplace—"

"Then there's no reason to do it, is there?" Marovich interrupted.

"But I'm going someplace else with it. I need a predicate for it," Burstein insisted.

Marovich shrugged and looked apologetically at the jury.

For the next twenty minutes, Burstein went through a step-by-step list of the horses that Burns had admitted killing, how much he got paid, and then, finally, he got to Ann Madej.

Earlier, Burns had testified that when he flew to Sugarbush, Vermont, to kill the horse Roseau Platiere for Paul Valliere, he had been picked up and later taken back to the airport by a friend. It was Ann Madej, a dark-haired, plain-looking young woman then still in her teens whom he knew from Chicago. At the time, Madej worked for Valliere, although her mother would later buy the horse farm owned by Burns's in-laws and she would take over the operation. It also was Ann Madej who had visited Burns in Illinois after he was released from the Alachua County jail and took him money of her own to help pay for his attorney. To the defense, this was sinister. Madej's Illinois visit to Burns after he was released from the Florida jail, they contended, was not to take Burns money but to bring him information about Charisma so Burns could fabricate his story about killing the horse and make a better bargain with the government by delivering a rich, high-profile horse owner, Lindemann. While the defense would later try to suggest that a sexual relationship existed between Madej and Burns, both vigorously denied it, each claiming that they were simply friends.

Burstein wanted to go into Madej's visit in depth, but Cox objected, claiming it was irrelevant.

"How can it be irrelevant, Judge?" Burstein asked indignantly.

Marovich stared at him. "Well, what is it relevant for?"

"I'll explain it at sidebar, Judge."

Wearily, Marovich summoned the lawyers. Surrounded by the attorneys, Marovich turned to Burstein. "Tell me your intriguing theory," he demanded.

Burstein began a long-winded explanation about how Ann Madej kept cropping up at strategic times and how she could have given Burns information about Charisma.

"Is what you are trying to tell me when I cut through all this crap is she was the one who was telling him how to finger Lindemann?" Marovich asked.

Burstein nodded. "Yes."

"Well, why don't you ask him *that*?" Marovich said peevishly.

"I'm allowed to do it my way," Burstein replied.

Marovich glared at him. "*Maybe* you are," he said. "You are allowed to do it if I allow you to do it. I would just as soon you ask him directly: 'Is she the one who gave you any information about Lindemann?' "

Cox, who had been seething, interrupted. Burstein knew what Ann Madej had talked to Burns about, she said, because Burns had been wearing a wire at one of the meetings and the defense had a transcript of the conversation.

Marovich looked at Burstein. "Don't be jacking around with stuff you know better about," he warned.

"He knows better," Cox said angrily.

"Ask the question," Marovich said, turning and walking away.

Burstein cleared his throat and stared at Burns. "Sir, am I correct that you did not tell the government that Ann Madej was coming because you wanted the chance to meet with her alone so that you could get the details that you weren't able to provide the government about Charisma?"

Burns stared back. "No," he said, cutting off that avenue for Burstein. The defense lawyer moved on to another subject.

Despite Marovich's obvious impatience, Burstein's questions dragged on through the rest of the afternoon and into the next court day, which was Monday.

At first, after a weekend break, it looked as if Burstein was going to break new ground.

"Do you think," he asked Burns, "that you would still get your six months in prison if you told the government that what you had been saying about Marion Hulick and George Lindemann was not true?"

"Sir," replied Burns, "it doesn't matter."

What did he mean, it didn't matter? Burstein asked.

"If they are convicted or not, it doesn't make any difference to my deal. I just got to tell the truth."

"That's the only thing you have to do?" Burstein asked. "It has nothing to do with conviction?"

"I have nothing to gain if they get convicted," Burns said tiredly. "All I have to do is tell the truth."

After that, Burstein strayed back into the same territory that Goldberg had already staked out, droning on until Cox objected to a question about how Burns's stories had been inconsistent.

"This has been gone into," Cox complained.

Burstein looked injured. "This is a new line, Judge."

"Oh, Mr. Burstein, please," Marovich groaned. "It has been covered. It has been re-covered. And it has been re-re-covered. We've heard all about a series of lies that were ongoing. And now if you have more questions in another area, you may inquire. And if you don't, then I suppose your cross-examination is over."

Pledging to plow new ground, Burstein went on for another hour and would have gone longer until he brought up yet again Burns's testimony before the grand jury.

"Are you going to read the same testimony?" Marovich asked testily.

"I'm just going to ask him a question, Judge."

"Don't read the same testimony again," Marovich warned.

When Burstein's question dealt with a matter already covered, Marovich lost his patience. Ordering the jury out of the room, he told the lawyers to take a seat.

"You know, Judge, I was wrong," Burstein said sheepishly.

"I know," Marovich said. "I don't even care. I'm not interested in curbing you people, but I want to take up some other matters." It had been gnawing at him that the defense had refused to stipulate that Barney Ward and Tom Burns had worked together in other incidents of horse killings; it was something he thought the jury should know and he wanted to tell them. "I will instruct the jury," he announced, "that the defendants do not contest Tommy Burns's testimony about killing Condino, Roseau Platiere, and Rub the Lamp." However, he added, he would also tell them that they could not conclude just because Burns told the truth about those incidents he was also telling the truth about the murder of Charisma.

The lawyers nodded, but Marovich wasn't finished.

One other issue, he said, dealt with Helen Brach. Unfortunately, he said, her name had already been mentioned in testimony and he didn't want it to go any further than that. In fact, at an appropriate time, he planned to tell the jury that there was *no* suggestion that Lindemann or Hulick was involved in her disappearance.

A third thing he wanted to discuss was the Lindemann fortune and how that might affect some of the questions that would be raised. "The only question that I want to have asked and answered is whether there are other people of wealth who were involved within the scope of this investigation. Depending upon how much more you want to play with that, I will allow other questions or I will not."

"Your Honor," Goldberg spoke up. "The fact that George Lindemann did not commit the crime because he is a person of wealth does not, with all due respect, open the door to a response that other wealthy people commit crimes."

"And that's not the inference that the question gives," replied Marovich. "The negative side of it is, just because you got a lot of bucks doesn't mean that you don't do."

When Susan Cox got her chance to question Burns again on redirect, she went directly to the issues raised by the defense, with top priority given to the Goldberg/Burstein claim that he had lied about Lindemann and Hulick so he could work a better deal.

"Mr. Burns," Cox said crisply, "are you attempting to buy your way out of jail by falsely implicating these two people?"

"No, ma'am," Burns responded quickly.

Rapidly, she outlined the key provision of the plea agreement: The U.S. attorney's office would recommend a six-month sentence for Burns provided he testified truthfully, with *truthfully* being the operative word.

"Do you understand that if you tell any lies, any lies whatsoever on the stand, the government can revoke your plea agreement and you can go away for a lot longer than six months?"

"Yes, ma'am," he replied.

"How long can you go to jail for?" she asked, eager to make sure the jury understood.

"About twenty years," he said solemnly.

Running down her checklist of questions, she had Burns repeat his claim that Barney Ward summoned him to New York to kill a horse for George Lindemann, that what he bought at a Radio Shack on December 15 was not CB equipment, as the defense insisted, but devices he needed to build his rig to electrocute Charisma, and that he had checked into the Hilton using a credit card supplied by Jean Hastings and that the charge was billed to the Ward account.

Chaffing at Goldberg's claims that Burns could not tell for certain if the horse he claimed to have killed was a mare or a gelding, Cox got Burns to confirm that he had been operating in the dark with only a penlight.

"Did you do a gynecological exam on the horse?" she asked.

"No," Burns replied quickly.

But the major issue she wanted to go over with him was the dispute over when he had first confessed to killing a horse at Cellular Farms.

"Now," she asked, "did you tell those agents in the very first interview that you killed a horse for George Lindemann?"

"Yes, ma'am."

"And you did not give a lot of detail about that. Is that right?"

"No, ma'am."

"Why not?"

"Because," Burns said, "I told them I didn't want to cooperate until I was out of jail."

Was there anyone else, Cox asked, whom he told about killing a horse at Cellular Farms.

Burns nodded. "Barney Ward, my old lawyer Roger Matkowski, and probably Harlow Arlie. That's about it."

After establishing that Burns was not having an affair with Ann Madej and that his wife was present when the two met in a Chicago hotel, Cox asked Burns to reconfirm that the reason he had lied for so long about who set up the Charisma killing—lies he would have to account for when it came time for him to be sentenced—was to protect Barney Ward.

"I basically never lied about how I killed the horse," Burns said, "just who set it up."

Cox nodded and looked at her list. There was one more major area she wanted to cover.

"Is George Lindemann a big part of your cooperation or a small part of your cooperation?"

"They never treated him like he was a big part."

"In fact," Cox added, "you told the government about many, many people whom you killed horses for. To your knowledge, how many people did you discuss with the government? Roughly."

"Thirty," said Burns.

"And how many of those have pleaded guilty?"

"Ninety percent of them."

On cue, Marovich told the jury what he had promised the lawyers he would say—that Lindemann and Hulick had nothing to do with Helen Brach, and the fact that others had pleaded guilty to charges in connection with cases that stemmed from the same investigation did not mean that Hulick and Lindemann were guilty of charges similar to those that others had admitted.

On recross, Goldberg tried to get Burns to refute his statements to Cox and cough up the answers the defense wanted to hear—that Lindemann and Hulick were special targets; that he had indeed purchased CB equipment, not alligator clips; that Ann Madej had given him information, not money. Burns, however, remained firm, sticking by his denials.

An hour later, the Burns examination bogged down terminally when Goldberg loudly protested about Cox getting Burns to say that he reported the Cellular Farms incident at his first interview with government investigators. His quarrel was with the word *first*.

Struggling to control his temper, Marovich sent the jury out of the room.

Turning to the lawyers, he let go.

"I have tried with all of the patience at my command to tell you in big-picture terms what it is we have been dealing with here. I have heard you ask the same questions over and over and over again, and I have watched you trying to get the last drop out of everything. Now what more is it we are going to get?"

"I am somewhat taken aback at having to get up when Ms. Cox says, 'Isn't it true from the *first* time you met a federal agent that you told them that you killed a horse for Lindemann?' She knows that is untrue," Goldberg said loudly, "and I take offense at it." Furthermore, he said, he planned to raise it in his final argument and tell the jury that it was "a piece of deceptive behavior" by a government attorney in an attempt to mislead them.

From his point of view, the first interview took place on February 3, when Cullen and Miller flew to Florida. Burns, he asserted, had not mentioned Charisma at that time. It had been another ten days, he said, before Burns brought up Cellular Farms.

Cox's temper flared. "I respectfully take objection to the absolutely unfounded and, I think, at the very least, unprofessional attack on my credibility as a prosecutor," she fumed. Goldberg, she said, knew that when Steve Miller went to Florida on February 3, it was with one purpose: to ask Burns what he knew about Helen Brach. That interview, she claimed, as far as this jury was concerned, did not count as a meeting on the horse killings.

Marovich waited until the lawyers calmed down. "What the record is," he said, "right or wrong, has to do with my own personal sense of fairness. And it may be wrong, but it is the record. But there is another thing," he added. "I don't like to deal with lawyers impugning one another. I don't want to be resolving debates between officers of the court as to who said what or who is lying or who is fabricating, or whatever."

Telling them to take their seats, he asked them one by one if they had any more questions for Burns. When they all said no, he called the jury in, told them to go home for the day, and declared the Burns examination finished.

But Goldberg had one more thing he wanted to say. He felt that the judge's decision to allow testimony about the guilty pleas of others and about other wealthy persons who had committed crimes "improperly bolstered" Burns's image with the jury. That and the fact that the judge also had allowed Burns to testify that he had told his lawyer immediately after being arrested—either February 2 or February 3—long before Burns could have gotten information from Ann Madej—that he had killed a horse at Cellular Farms were bad decisions, for which there was only one remedy: The judge would have to declare a mistrial.

Marovich did not hesitate. "I think it is in there properly," he said. "It is not the stuff of which mistrials are called for. Denied."

37

Building a Case

S TEVE MILLER struggled unsuccessfully to hide his delight. As soon as the last spectators had cleared the courtroom, he turned to Susan Cox and grinned broadly. "We did it," he whispered triumphantly.

Tom Burns, the prosecution's chief witness, had undergone two days of grilling by the defense's highly skilled legal team and come away virtually unscathed. The most damning information Goldberg and Burstein had been able to pry out of the thief-cum-horse killer was that he had repeatedly lied to investigators over a two-year period. Despite their best efforts, the defense had not been able to get Burns to admit that he had made up a tale about George Lindemann and Marion Hulick in some sort of ill-defined scheme for revenge, or that he was working with the government as part of a plan targeting the Cellular Farms operator and his chief trainer.

Basically, Burns had provided the foundation of the prosecution's case. In what Miller and Cox felt was simple, believable testimony, he had explained who had hired him to kill Charisma as well as when and how it happened. Now it was up to Cox and Miller to supply a string of backup witnesses who would authenticate what Burns had said and give more depth to the case, specifically to contribute a motive for the murder of the $250,000 horse. Leading the list was Harlow Arlie.

A tall, well-built, articulate black man, Arlie described in concise terms how he had answered the phone at Equestrian Oaks, where he was working as a groom, in mid-December 1990. The caller was Barney Ward, who was looking for Tommy Burns. Not long afterward, Arlie said, an excited Burns told him that he was flying to New York to kill a horse for Ward.

Arlie confessed that he was jealous. Burns had told him that he was going to be making twenty-five thousand dollars for killing a horse and he wanted to get in on the deal. "I wanted to make a few hundred dollars myself." However, Burns had nixed the idea. "Maybe next time," he quoted Burns as telling him.

A day or so after that conversation, he saw Burns, suitcase in hand, leaving for the airport. When he returned several days later, he was wearing a big grin. "It was a piece of cake," he told the groom. "Everything went smooth."

When Arlie questioned him further, Burns told him—according to Arlie—that he had been able to bypass the security system at the farm and that he had not had to worry about being disturbed, because everyone had been out to dinner when he slipped into the stall and killed the horse.

A few weeks later, Arlie added, Burns told him he had been asked to kill another horse and he asked if Arlie wanted to help him. The horse, whose name was Streetwise, could not be electrocuted because of a clause in its insurance policy and it would "have to have an accident." Arlie, for an agreed-upon fee of five hundred dollars, broke the horse's leg with a crowbar, but both he and Burns had been caught soon afterward and taken to the Alachua County jail.

Burns was angry because no one was coming to his rescue, Arlie said. He felt he had been abandoned by the people he had killed horses for, particularly Barney Ward.

Since he had nothing to trade with prosecutors, Arlie was convicted on a felony charge of killing Streetwise and had served only six months in a Florida prison.

Under cross-examination, Arlie admitted to Burstein that he had worked out an agreement where he would not be charged in federal court if he testified truthfully in Chicago.

Arlie was followed by Penelope Baumont, a senior vice president for a Chicago-area commercial real estate firm who kept a horse at Equestrian Oaks and had become friendly with Arlie. She had been horrified, she testified, when Arlie explained to her that Burns was a hit man and was going to New York to kill a horse.

"You didn't think it was legal to kill horses, did you?" Burstein asked her during cross-examination.

"No," she replied.

"But you didn't call the authorities, did you?"

"No," she said. "I was dating a criminal defense lawyer and he advised me not to."

Miller and Cox were pleased with the testimony of their first two witnesses; everything was going according to plan. Then, just before lunch, Goldberg reinstated his demand for a mistrial.

"Are we going to get these on a regular basis?" Marovich asked drolly. "Just so I know how to prepare myself."

The basis for the motion, Goldberg repeated, again was Cox's question to Burns about how he had mentioned Cellular Farms in his *first* interview with federal investigators.

"To be charitable," Goldberg insisted, "that is absolutely untrue. In addition, today she stands up here in a plaintive voice, insinuating her own credibility into the case: 'You're not falsifying your testimony, are you?' " he said, raising his voice an octave to mimic Cox.

"A prosecutor," he added, "can strike hard blows but not low blows. I think that today's behavior of asking what any first-year law student would know is an improper question, which Your Honor quickly sustained an objection to, conveys to the jury not only the false impressions she made yesterday but her own credibility being injected into this case. The sum total of it is to deprive the defendants of a fair trial."

Cox, her cheeks redder than her hair, glared at Goldberg. "Am I going to be allowed to respond?" she asked Marovich.

"I am satisfied," Goldberg continued, ignoring her, "that on the basis of the behavior today, there is a studied effort to deprive my client of a fair trial and I would ask you, if you don't declare a mistrial, to admonish the prosecutor."

Marovich looked at Cox and nodded. "I think it's your turn."

"Mr. Goldberg has been a lawyer for a long time," she said evenly, "and apparently he has learned that when you can't do anything else, you attack the prosecutor."

Goldberg grimaced, prompting Marovich to glare at him angrily. "If there is some pain that is inflicting upon you, go out there and take an Alka-Seltzer or do something about it, because it is aggravating to me. I don't know how it is that you think you are having an impact on me, but this is not having a good one. Save it for somebody else."

"Mr. Goldberg knows that my questions," Cox continued, "had to do with the time that Mr. Burns was being questioned about something other than Helen Brach or Richard Bailey, which Your Honor has repeatedly said should not be injected into the case. And for someone who basically does a closing argument every other question he asks the witness, for him to suggest that my question is a basis for a mistrial is truly ludicrous."

Marovich looked sternly at Goldberg. "I do not take the same offense at her conduct that you do," he said, "and it certainly, under no circumstances, would move me for a mistrial." She was, he added, simply doing what he had ordered her to do: to keep Helen Brach and Richard Bailey out of the Lindemann/Hulick trial. "It has been my observation," he continued, "and this is not being critical of any of you—it is what lawyers do. You yell and you scream and you rant and you grimace and you rage and you posture and you do everything else about talking about receiving a fair trial, when in fact that is the last thing you want. It has been said that anybody can get a fair trial; I want one that is prejudiced in favor of me."

Turning to Goldberg, he added, "It certainly isn't going to move me to create a mistrial because the prosecution is following the line of questioning that is tailor-made to prevent what I don't want here. So, most respectfully, nice try, but your motion is denied. And I don't want any more conversation about it. I'm going to lunch."

Gerald "Shep" Shepherd smoothed his thinning carrot-colored hair, ran a quick hand through his beard, and slipped into the witness chair. Cocking his head slightly toward Miller in a manner adopted by many who are hard of hearing, he waited patiently for the questions.

Yes, he said, he had been in Marion Hulick's apartment/office on December 15, 1990, when Tom Burns showed up with a blond-haired woman. He was at Cellular Farms because he was looking for work and he thought Hulick could find him a job.

He was shocked when Burns, whom he probably had not seen for eight years, knocked on the door. He was not surprised, however, when Burns failed to recognize him immediately because he had gained weight and shaved his beard. They exchanged pleasantries and he was getting ready to leave when Hulick invited him to accompany her and Burns on a tour of the farm.

While they were driving around the property, Hulick behind the wheel, Burns in the passenger seat, and Shepherd in the backseat, Hulick pointed toward a forested area and told Burns, "This is a seldom-used road; you can park here and come back."

A few minutes later, she swung into a spot in front of the barn and the three of them went inside. Hulick disappeared into a stall, spent a few minutes with the horse, came out, and they left. The next he knew, he said, he was being telephoned by the FBI and a reporter, both of them asking about Burns.

Satisfied that he had gotten confirmation of Burns's claim that he had been at Cellular Farms when he said he was, Miller turned Shepherd over for cross-examination.

"I didn't know Tommy Burns was a horse killer," Shepherd told Burstein. "I was shocked when I found out."

Under questioning from Goldberg, Shepherd admitted he had never heard Hulick say anything about wanting a horse killed.

Molly Hasbrouck, née Ash, was a college student looking for a summer job in 1990 when she was hired to exercise horses at Cellular Farms. One of the horses she worked with was Charisma, taking him out of his stall so he could stretch his muscles, working him through trots and canters and on a longe line, an exercise rope. She also was a rider, and that summer she had shown Charisma in some of the small classes to get him warmed up for Sloan Lindemann.

She knew, she said, that Hulick and Lindemann had discussed Charisma's inconsistency. "He didn't perform the same every time. There was never really a reason as to whether he was good or bad."

In her experience with Charisma, she said, she discovered that the horse had trouble relaxing. "He would buck on the ends of the rings sometimes, or just get too fast, not take his time to jump the jump properly."

At the time, he was performing in the second-year "green hunter" division, a class for hunters where the jumps were three feet nine inches, as opposed to jumps of three feet six inches for first-year green hunters. "Three inches doesn't sound like much, but it turns out to be a pretty big step up for young horses."

In an attempt to find a cure for Charisma's inconsistency, those who worked with the horse tried different techniques of preparation and varied his daily routine, but nobody had found a solution.

When the crew from Cellular Farms went to Southampton, Long Island, for the Hampton Classic in July 1990, they were getting ready for the show when Charisma "tied up."

"What is that?" asked Cox.

"When a horse ties up," said Hasbrouck, "basically all his muscles from the hip down cramp to the point where they can hardly move."

"And can that be a serious problem for a horse?"

"Yes, it can," replied Hasbrouck, adding that usually when that happens, a horse is given a few days of stall rest and kept from heavy exercise.

In this instance, however, Hulick told her to take Charisma to a paddock and turn him out all night.

Had she agreed with that decision? Cox asked.

"No," said Hasbrouck. "It upset me. I didn't think it was the right thing for the horse. I thought it was potentially very dangerous to his physical well-being. I thought if I rode him down the street for a mile and turned him out in a field where no other horses were, that he was going to run and exercise himself to the point where he would probably just tie up again."

Hulick saw that she was upset, Hasbrouck said, and told her to disregard the order to turn him out but to be sure she was at the stable area before Lindemann arrived the next morning so he would think the horse had been turned out.

That had been the day before the competition began. The following day, the first of competition, Charisma performed well in the first class but "blew up" in the second class. Lindemann had been riding the horse, she said, and he was so frustrated by Charisma's performance in the second class that he again ordered him turned out.

This time, what bothered Hasbrouck was the weather. "It was hurricanelike. There were high winds, thunder and lightning, a torrential downpour." Because of that, she said, she again disagreed with the decision to turn him out. Had it been her horse, she said, she would have been very afraid for his health. The next morning, when she went to retrieve Charisma from the paddock, she had been anxious. "I wondered if the horse was going to be standing when I got there."

Charisma apparently had been unaffected by the storms and performed well in that afternoon's competition. Despite that, he was turned out again that night, although the weather was not as severe as it had been the previous day. Again, she disagreed but said nothing. "I had known George and Marion since the time I was a young junior rider and I always respected George's riding ability and what he had done in the business. Marion was always an authoritative figure to me. I worked for them. I didn't feel like it was my place to say anything. I was nineteen years old. It was a summer job."

On cross-examination, Goldberg tried to defuse Hasbrouck's testimony about the potentially dangerous effects of turning the horse out by pointing out that thoroughbreds, "hot bloods," in horse-world terminology, are by nature tense and excitable and they require different training techniques.

In an effort to counter the claim that Charisma was inconsistent, he showed that the horse had been the reserve champion, number two, at two other important shows, Stoneleigh Burnham and Northampton. Furthermore, Hasbrouck had said that Charisma had come back from his "blowup" on the first day of competition at the Hampton Classic—which was a more important show than the other two—and was named reserve champion there, as well.

In his attempt to show that turning Charisma out had not been a bad decision, Goldberg worked himself into a tight spot.

"Turning out is one of the techniques, much like longeing. Is that right?"

"No," Hasbrouck added forcefully. "It's not right. Holding a horse on the longe line for twenty minutes is nowhere close to the same as turning it out all night."

"Turning a horse out" means setting it loose in a pasture and "longeing" is exercising a horse at the end of a rope.

Goldberg backed away and recovered when he got Hasbrouck to confirm that green hunters such as Charisma were often inconsistent.

Burstein also stumbled when he tried to get Hasbrouck to admit that Charisma's participation as a second-year green hunter, even though he was only five years old, was an indication of the owner's faith in the horse's potential.

"To me," Hasbrouck said, "that's a sign of rushing a horse. I mean, if a horse has that much potential, why wouldn't you give it the time it needs?"

Cox, on the other hand, scored a major point on redirect.

"Did any other horse besides Charisma ever get left out in the middle of the night in a strange field in a lightning storm during a horse competition?" she asked.

Hasbrouck shook her head. "Not to my knowledge."

38

Defining Inconsistency

SUSAN COX studied the stack of documents under her nose: graphs, tables, text, charts, and handwritten notes, a jumble that she would have to put together in some sort of easily understandable form for the government to clarify its case against Hulick and Lindemann.

In criminal cases, it is generally accepted that three factors are all but necessary to achieve a homicide conviction. The prosecutor must prove desire, opportunity, and motive. Basically, the same would apply to get a conviction in a horse murder. If Cox and Miller hoped to convince the jury to return guilty verdicts against Lindemann and Hulick, they were going to have to meet the same standard.

They felt confident they had shown desire through the testimony of Molly Hasbrouck, and they had two more witnesses waiting to substantiate that testimony. Proof of opportunity would come via the testimony of a woman named Colleen Fitzpatrick Reed, former barn manager at Cellular Farms. Tom Burns's testimony fell into both categories. The main problem with him was credibility, which the prosecutors hoped had been successfully supported by Harlow Arlie, Penelope Baumont, and Gerald Shepherd. What they needed to address very quickly was motive; they had to give the jury a plausible reason why Lindemann and Hulick had wanted Charisma dead.

When they picked the panel on September 6, Goldberg and Burstein had thoroughly culled from the group anyone with knowledge about show horses and the equine industry. Since then, the two defense attorneys had, at every opportunity, discharged considerable smoke every time the question of *why* Lindemann and Hulick might have wanted to be rid of Charisma permanently had come up. So there was a $250,000 death policy on Charisma? According to Goldberg, $250,000 was next to nothing to Lindemann. The horse wasn't performing up to expectations? "What do you mean?" asked Goldberg. It had won *rib-bons.* It was a *circuit* champion. It was at the top or near there in a number of very *prestigious* shows. To a jury that did not understand the nuances of the horse world, it could be very confusing, maybe even fatal to the prosecution, if the subtleties of the situation were not elucidated.

So it was Cox's job to try to put the motive aspect in perspective. Her vehicle was a bright, extremely articulate official from the American Horse Show Association named Eric Straus, the group's assistant executive director, a horse owner, rider, and show-horse judge until he joined the staff at the AHSA.

Cox began with the basics. What, she asked, for the edification of the jury, is show hunting?

"Show hunting," he replied, "simulates in a competitive environment, typically in a ring, foxhunting."

Cox nodded. "Okay. So it's foxhunting without the foxes?"

"Yes." Straus smiled, adding that for a rider in hunter competition to get a good score—and points were the *major* object in hunter competition—a rider needed to complete the round as evenly as possible, make the performance as artful as possible, with emphasis on finesse and smoothness. Speed was not important. On the other hand, points would be withheld if the horse jumped poorly or unsafely, if its pace was erratic, or if it had "bad manners"—that is, if it was not well disciplined and, for example, bucked.

To help jurors understand the problem that Charisma was posing for Lindemann and Hulick, Straus explained that Charisma was an uncommonly young horse to be participating in the division in which Lindemann had him entered: second-year green hunter. As a second-year green hunter, Charisma was required to jump over obstacles three feet nine inches high, three inches higher than those he had faced in 1989 as a first-year green hunter, when he had won recognition as an all-around champion. As far as Charisma or *any* horse was concerned, that extra three inches was formidable.

In addition, when Charisma was ridden by George Lindemann, Jr., a professional, and not by his sister, Sloan, an amateur, he performed in the most keenly competitive shows that AHSA sponsored, usually rated A-3. That made it tougher still.

Straus further explained that points in the hunter competition were awarded on a complicated formula that took into consideration not only the individual horse's performance but how many horses were participating in a given event or class and how the horse ended the competition in relation to the other horses. Also, a judge's decision to award or subtract points was totally subjective; it was not like totaling up scores in a baseball or basketball game.

A horse participating in a typical A-rated horse show, he said, would be required to perform in five classes or events: under-saddle (in which the horse walks, trots, and canters but does not jump), jumping in both directions around the ring, and jumping over fences.

Every show had a champion and a reserve champion; in addition, medals commonly were awarded to the top six horses. So just saying that a horse had won medals was virtually meaningless, since it might be beribboned but virtually lacking in points.

Points were important because they accumulated during the year. In the autumn, the number of points recorded by AHSA determined if the horse would be invited to the Indoor Season.

Dragging an easel to the front of the courtroom, Cox pulled forward two large charts, magnified and attached to stiff backing. One showed Charisma's performance in 1989—before he was sold to the Lindemanns—the other in 1990—after he moved to Cellular Farms.

According to AHSA statistics, Charisma, who had been purchased in November 1989, performed well in shows in the Florida circuit, January through March 1990. He was AHSA champion in the amateur, but not professional, division. Nevertheless, he was reserve champion in three professional shows. In mid-May, he was reserve champion at the Old Salem Farm Horse Show in upstate New York.

Surprisingly, for reasons not reflected in the statistics, Charisma apparently did not compete in the Devon Horse Show in May–June, an event Straus called the "crown jewel of the spring season," even though he had qualified. "That's very unusual," Straus mused, "since it's very competitive to be qualified and most people, once they qualify, certainly want to compete there."

Cox pointed out that, since there was a record kept only if the horse scored points, Charisma could have competed and failed to score.

At the Hampton Classic in July—the show during which he was turned out into a paddock despite the fact that lightning storms were sweeping through the area—Charisma finished second among ten in his first class. But in the second class, he was ninth out of ten.

Skipping ahead to the Pennsylvania International, the first of the three shows of the Indoor Season, Straus pointed out that Charisma was fifth among thirty-three in the first class, third out of thirty-three in the second, and seventh out of thirty-three in the third. No points were recorded for him in the remaining two classes.

"And you can't tell from the records whether the horse just dropped out or whether it didn't place at all, is that correct?" Cox asked.

"That's correct," Straus confirmed.

"And what about the Washington International?" Cox asked, referring to the second of the three shows and the Super Bowl of the horse world.

Straus shook his head. "Out of forty-three horses, it did not place in any of the classes."

With the background laid, Cox began to focus on the purpose of Straus's testimony: to try to show a motive for why Lindemann and Hulick would be so disgusted with Charisma that they would be willing to have the horse killed.

"Now, having considered the entire performance history of the horse in 1990, do you have an opinion?"

"Yes," Straus said unhesitantly. "It seems erratic and inconsistent when I compare the 1990 record against the 1989 record. In the first-year green division, jumping three foot six, the horse was never less than third in its classes. And in classes at the second-year level, 1990, it seems very erratic in that it placed well in Florida, but later in the year it had lower records."

Anticipating the question from Goldberg and Burstein on cross-examination, Cox asked Straus how he could say the horse was inconsistent when overall it seemed to have a pretty good year.

"Well, in Florida, it won very good ribbons in classes with large numbers. But as the year went on, it was winning lower-place ribbons in classes with fewer horses, which then culminated in the performance at the Pennsylvania and Washington horse shows."

What about the competition? Cox asked. Were the horses Charisma was competing against in Florida basically the same ones it was competing against all year, ending with the Washington show? Could competition have gotten stiffer as the year went on, which would account for Charisma's poorer showings?

Straus said the competition was basically the same. "I saw many of the same horses and names appearing in the results records. It would seem that a horse that had done so well in Florida should be able, as an equine athlete, to beat these other horses consistently."

The Washington show was the last one in which Charisma competed before he died. How, Cox asked Straus, would he characterize the horse's performance there?

Straus shook his head. "Dismal," he said. "Disappointing. To score nothing would be extremely poor."

On cross-examination, Goldberg attacked the core of the prosecution theory that implied consistency could be expected from a horse as young as Charisma.

"And would you agree with the proposition that green working hunters are at times inconsistent?"

"Yes." Straus nodded.

"And do you know of any horses, be they green or otherwise, that win all the time?"

"No," admitted Straus.

"Particularly green working hunters competing in their second year are not known, on the basis of your experience, to be consistently successful, are they?"

"Yes," Straus said emphatically, disagreeing with the defense lawyer's premise. "I have seen consistent second-year horses."

"But they are the exception rather than the rule, wouldn't you agree?"

"No, I would differ with you on that."

Goldberg tried to get him to change his answer, but Straus remained firm. "They're not expected to be inconsistent when compared to first-year horses," the AHSA official insisted.

"Okay," Goldberg said. "Would you agree that a five-year-old working green hunter is a young horse to be competing in that division?"

"It's among the younger, yes," Straus said.

Trying to show that it may not have been Charisma's fault that he seemed to get progressively worse, Goldberg suggested there might have been other factors: a change in the horse's environment, a new rider, a new trainer, stiffer competition, or even unforgiving judges.

"Judging hunter competition is more akin to judging ice-skating, isn't it?"

Straus conceded that it was, but he and Goldberg differed strongly on two other issues. The first was over Goldberg's insistence that the fact Charisma was crowned champion of the Florida circuit was a spectacular achievement. Straus refused to concur.

"When Charisma was the Florida circuit champion, it was the champion among all other horses entered in that class. Is that correct?"

Straus shook his head. "It's not the show championship that AHSA confers points for. That's a *circuit* title." In other words, Goldberg was talking apples and oranges.

"You're not sitting here and saying that this horse was not the Florida circuit champion in 1990? You're not saying that, are you?" he asked belligerently.

"No," said Straus. "I'm *not* saying that. I'm saying that's not an AHSA title. It's a circuit title." The implication was that a circuit title was much less significant than an AHSA show title, although Goldberg was trying to assign them the same status.

Moving to the chart, Goldberg pointed to the number of points won by Charisma: 50 points, 181 points, 57 points. "But he was still the champion, so I take it that other horses were inconsistent, as well. Is that a fair statement?"

"It's an incomplete statement," Straus said doggedly.

"Well," Goldberg said sarcastically, "tell me how I've missed."

"I don't know that the same pool of horses competed all the time. I don't know what other competitors were involved, what the point totals were, or the margin of difference between first and second."

"But nonetheless you would agree that being crowned the circuit champion is most important to a horse owner. Is that a fair statement?"

Straus shrugged. "It's a personal judgment call."

39

Finishing Touches

COLLEEN REED sat stiffly in the witness chair, staring straight ahead.

A tall, slim red-haired woman who left her managerial job at Cellular Farms to help her husband run a horse-products business in Ohio, Reed, formerly Fitzpatrick, obviously was uncomfortable about being asked to tell tales about her former employers. But Miller had no choice. He had subpoenaed her because he considered her information vital to the case against both Hulick and Lindemann.

Turning first to Hulick, the prosecutor asked Reed about the night of December 15, 1990, the night Charisma had died.

Reluctantly, Reed related how she had been in her apartment at Cellular Farms when Hulick called and asked her to dinner.

"I told her I was on duty," Reed said, adding how she had reminded Hulick of farm policy, which prohibited the duty person from leaving the premises.

According to Reed, Hulick told her not to worry about the policy. "We'll only be gone a couple of hours; it'll be okay," she quoted Hulick as telling her.

Recalling the incident almost five years later, Reed testified she could not remember where they went, what they ate, or exactly how long they were gone, but she did recollect how unusual the suggestion had been.

Switching to Lindemann, whom Miller was anxious to depict as a cost-conscious micromanager to counter the defense's claim that money meant nothing to him, the prosecutor questioned Reed about the Cellular Farms operation. Had Lindemann taken an active part in day-to-day activities?

Yes, Reed replied. Indeed he had. One of her duties, she explained, had been to find the best prices for the supplies they used in the barn.

Once, she recalled, Lindemann demanded she find a better price for the rubbing alcohol that they used to massage the horses' legs. She had been authorizing payment of six dollars a gallon, a price she considered fair, until Lindemann ordered her to see if she couldn't do better. Cost memorandums, she added, were always coming down from him: Use fewer wood shavings on the bedding, because it was getting expensive; call a vet only if necessary, because medical bills were running too high.

Under questioning from Miller, she acknowledged that Lindemann expected a lot from his horses as well as from his employees.

In the fall of 1990, she remembered, she had been at a very important show in Harrisburg, Pennsylvania, the first of the three invitation-only gatherings that make up the prestigious Indoor Season, and Charisma was performing erratically.

"Did you hear George Lindemann say anything about Charisma at that time?" Miller asked.

"Yes," Reed replied. "He told me he hated the horse. He couldn't figure him out."

And what about Marion Hulick?

"She said the horse was not being good, that George was displeased with the horse and we had to make him better."

Miller nodded in satisfaction and flipped through his notes. Returning to her statements about the night she and Hulick went to dinner, the prosecutor asked if she could pin down the time.

Reed frowned. No, she said, but it probably had been between nine and ten.

What had she done when they got back? he asked.

Reed shrugged. "I was tired, so I probably just let my dogs out for ten minutes or so to go to the bathroom; then I called them in and went to bed."

The next morning, she said, she was getting dressed when there was a knock on the door. It was a groom reporting that one of the horses had been found dead in its stall. It was Charisma.

There was some blood in his manure, she recalled, and a tiny bit of blood in one of his nostrils, but otherwise he looked as though he could get up at any minute. There were none of the usual signs present when an animal has been sick: The ground was not pawed up; the stall had not been kicked; there were no wood shavings on his coat or in his mane, which horses usually pick up when they roll around in pain. "It looked like he had just dropped dead," she said.

After Charisma's death, Miller asked, was there anything unusual that occurred in regard to the pending insurance claim?

Yes, she said. She was called into a meeting with Lindemann, Hulick, and two other employees. "George said please do not tell the insurance man that there were other riders for Charisma other than he and his sister." Hulick independently told her the same thing, she added.

Did you understand what you were being asked to do? Miller asked. "Yeah," Reed said. "Not tell the truth."

Lyman Whitehead, a thirty-two-year-old trainer and freelance rider, said he had been hired in October 1990 to ride Charisma because George Lindemann, Jr., had injured his arm. The event was a small show at Overpeck Farm, which Lindemann wanted to use as a preliminary to the important Indoor Season.

Charisma's performance at Overpeck was so-so, not disastrous, but far from spectacular, since he failed to win anything.

Hulick, Whitehead said, was particularly upset about Charisma's lackluster performance, saying she "wished the horse were dead so she could get her money out."

Under cross-examination by Burstein, Whitehead conceded that Hulick sometimes tended to be emotional and that he had paid no particular attention to the remark. However, under redirect, Whitehead admitted he had described Hulick to an FBI agent as "an abrasive, cold individual."

Now a severe-looking woman of twenty-three, Ann Madej walked stiffly to the witness box, obviously the most uncomfortable of all the witnesses called so far by the prosecution. Easing into the chair as if it might shock her, Madej stiffened her back and glared at Susan Cox.

Her occupation, she said in clipped, percise tones, was "selling horses," and her place of business was a facility in Libertyville called Meadow Ridge Farm. Before her wealthy mother bought it for her, it was named Equestrian Oaks and it had been owned by Tom Burns's in-laws and run by his wife, who still worked there.

Yes, she acknowledged, before moving to Libertyville, she had worked for Paul Valliere at his Acres Wild Farm in Rhode Island. Valliere was one of the people for whom Burns had admitted killing a horse.

Yes, she added, she had visited Burns in Chicago in February 1991, after he was released from the Florida jail.

Yes, she gave him $7,500 of her own money to help him pay for an attorney.

No, she said, she had not given him information about Charisma and Cellular Farms so Burns could use it to frame Lindemann and Hulick.

Yes, she had seen Hulick during the annual show in West Palm Beach in the late winter/spring of 1991.

Yes, she gave Hulick Burns's phone number after she had asked for it twice.

She denied that she had ever visited Cellular Farms and was unable to describe the place or the horse Charisma.

Obviously an unfriendly witness, Madej's direct examination was over in less than fifteen minutes.

Under cross-examination by Burstein, Madej admitted she learned of Charisma's death in January 1991, four to six weeks before she went to Chicago to meet with Burns. She also arranged for Valliere to send money to Burns for attorneys separate from the money she had given him.

"You knew," Burstein asked, "that Paul Valliere was sending this money because he had been involved with Tommy Burns and he was trying to pay him off, so to speak, right?"

"Yes," Madej replied tightly.

Although Lindemann and Hulick were codefendants in the trial and Lindemann was paying all of Hulick's legal fees, the relationship between the two, at least according to one former employee, had not always been smooth.

Michael Rooks, a thirty-five-year-old former truck driver at Cellular Farms, testified that Lindemann told him in 1989 that he was considering firing Hulick because of a commission check she had written herself on the sale of a horse. For a time afterward, her check-writing privileges were curtailed.

There was another time, Rooks added, a couple of years later, when the group was in Florida, that Lindemann again came close to discharging his trainer.

"What was the reason?" Cox asked.

"I can't remember exactly," the sleepy-eyed Rooks drawled. "They had a fight over something and—"

"Objection!" Burstein interjected.

"I think you're right," Judge Marovich agreed, ordering Cox to move on to another subject.

Despite some differences they may have had about other things, Hulick and Lindemann apparently agreed on one: Charisma was a baffling horse.

"He was inconsistent," Rooks said. "He'd do very well one day in one class and come right back, say five minutes later, and be a totally different horse. He was somewhat irrational."

They tried several things to see if they could make him more constant, Rooks said, like swapping his rubber bit for a steel one and turning him out all night. But nothing seemed to have any permanent effect.

Going back to the comment about turning him out, Cox asked Rooks if he had been at the Hampton Classic in July 1990.

Rooks nodded. "As I remember, the horse went in the ring and was very good and got a very good ribbon. Then he came out of the ring for a short time, three to five minutes, I would say, and went back in the ring and was totally different. He behaved badly."

Lindemann was puzzled. "I don't understand why he'd do that," Rooks quoted him as saying. "Then he said he wanted the horse turned out that night."

At that point, he said, Hulick reminded Lindemann that the horse wasn't insured.

"And what did George say?" Cox asked.

" 'Insure him!' " Rooks said.

Then what happened? Cox inquired.

"While I was there, she got on the cellular phone and called. I left, but before I did, I know she called the insurance company. From her end of the conversation, I could tell that."

At the time Lindemann ordered the horse turned out, Rooks added, it looked as if a big storm was moving in.

"Did you want to go outside yourself?" she asked, since Rooks would have been the one physically to take Charisma to the paddock.

"No," Rooks said. "It was a bad storm. The clouds were black and it was lightning."

On cross-examination, however, Goldberg took issue with the storm story. "The storm had blown over, agreed?" asked Goldberg.

"Yes," Rooks replied.

Later, prosecutors introduced weather records showing the storminess continued throughout the weekend.

Rooks's testimony completed the prosecution's case. The trial had been going for eight days and lawyers from both sides were starting to show fatigue. Judge Marovich himself also was becoming very touchy.

What had seemed in the beginning to be a very simple trial had grown increasingly complex. Although jurors were not aware of it, there was a large body of complicated legal issues seething below the surface and the lawyers were much more at one another's throats than the jurors suspected.

While they probably surmised from the few scenes of courtroom contention they had witnessed that the competition between the defense and prosecution was fierce, the jurors did not know that out of their presence the conflict was so acrimonious that Marovich was having tremendous difficulty keeping the lid on.

Jurors did not know, for example, that Goldberg had twice asked for a mistrial and that the requests were refused by Marovich. Although such motions were not unusual—a good defense lawyer would be expected to do that in order to help build a record for a possible appeal—the basis for Goldberg's motions were more than commonly technical, basically a matter of semantics about Susan Cox's use of the word *first* in alluding to Burns's interviews with federal investigators. And, in arguing about the issue, debate had been uncommonly bitter, with Cox taking Goldberg's remarks as a personal attack on her integrity.

The fight between the lawyers did not make Marovich at all happy. "I do not want any of this personalized," he said angrily. "I believe that lawyers have a certain obligation and duty to one another, and it is the standard that is going to prevail in this courtroom while I sit on this bench."

Much of the problem stemmed from style, particularly Goldberg's. The New York lawyer liked to obfuscate, gambling that he could exaggerate about some of the more technical issues and not run the risk of being tripped up by a knowledgeable jury. Almost every time he mentioned a horse show that Charisma had participated in, for example, he referred to it as "prestigious," as if every one, indeed, was extremely important. Even Marovich got tired of hearing the reference and urged Goldberg to desist.

At every opportunity, as well, Goldberg pointed out that Charisma had won ribbons, although ribbons were not the important factor in hunter competition. And every chance he had, he praised Charisma for racking up a specific number of points, when the total was meaningless without considering other factors, primarily how many points competing horses had scored in the same show.

What was proving particularly unusual, however, was the way lawyers from both sides worked so hard at developing spin that it made Marovich's job increasingly difficult.

"Infallibility doesn't come with the job description," he grumbled during one heated debate out of the jury's presence, "and I have never claimed it for myself. Part of the problem, very frankly, of making a monumental issue out of every single question and every area that is conceivable to the mind of man is that you run the problem of maybe me missing something along the line that is truly important. My job is to try to give somebody a *fair* trial, but they are not entitled to a *perfect* one."

Some of the tension evaporated after the prosecution announced that it had completed its case in chief, but there was still a lot to anticipate. The defense was expected to call medical experts to argue that Charisma died a natural death. The defense had promised in opening remarks to call Sloan Lindemann and there were broad hints her brother and Hulick would testify, as well.

And once the defense was finished, the prosecution would have rebuttal testimony.

But it was Friday afternoon and everyone was exhausted. "Have a good weekend," Marovich told jurors and the opposing counsel, "and come back Monday ready to hear defense witnesses."

40

The Final Fence

E VEN THOUGH it was Sunday morning, Steve Miller was stuffing his briefcase, preparing to leave for his office in the Loop for some last-minute preparation with Susan Cox, when the phone jangled. Miller grabbed it on the third ring. "This is Jay," the caller said. "I just wanted let you know that we aren't going to be putting on a case. We plan to rest as soon as proceedings begin tomorrow."

Miller thanked him, hung up, and immediately dialed Cox. "I'm not really surprised," he told his cocounsel. "If I were in their shoes, I'd probably be doing the same thing. If they called Hulick and Lindemann, that would shift the focus and only complicate things."

Cox was smiling to herself. All during the trial, Miller had mispronounced Hulick's name, calling her *Huh-lick* rather than *Hugh-lick*, much to Judd Burstein's mounting aggravation. Just because the trial was almost over didn't mean he was going to change his habits.

"Should we scrub today?" she asked. They had spent all day Saturday going over points they wanted to stress on cross-examination of anticipated defense witnesses and they had another all-day session planned.

"No," Miller said without hesitation. "Jay wouldn't lie to me, but we'd better be safe. There's nothing that says they can't change their minds."

From Miller's point of view, the decision by the defense not to present a case simplified things considerably. Instead of testimony from defense witnesses and then a prosecution rebuttal case, the lawyers would move directly to final arguments. Cox would go first, followed by Burstein. Then it would be Goldberg's turn and, since the prosecution always has the last word in criminal cases, Miller's. That meant that by Tuesday afternoon the lawyers' work would be over; everything would be up to the jury.

*   *   *

Susan Cox dismissed the need for histrionics. Final argument, she figured, translated into plain talk, and that was what she was going to serve up to the eleven women and one man in the jury box. Standing relaxed at the end of the prosecution table, her feet slightly apart and her shoulders back, Cox talked to the jurors as if they were sharing a cup of coffee in the second-floor cafeteria.

It wasn't a complicated case, she said chattily; it actually was quite simple. George Lindemann, Jr., and Marion Hulick were stuck with an expensive but mediocre horse that had been bought with high expectations. "No matter what they did," she said, "and they tried all kinds of things, they just couldn't fix the horse.

"You heard a lot of talk about how wealthy the Lindemanns are and you heard Mr. Goldberg say that two hundred and fifty thousand dollars was just a postage stamp to them. Why would they commit a crime for such a paltry sum? Well, I don't care, rich or poor, a quarter of a million dollars is still a quarter of a million dollars."

It was bad enough, she continued, that the horse was getting worse instead of better, but there was another thing that had to be factored in. "This horse did not meet its promotions, and that made George Lindemann and Marion Hulick look bad. Remember, a horse doesn't know when it wins, but the owner does. And everybody else in this small, elite circle knows when it wins, too, and they talk, and they snicker, and they point it out."

The defense had gone to great lengths to make Tom Burns a liar, she added, but there was one thing they needed to ask themselves about his testimony. "Does it ring true in light of all the other evidence in the case?" If he was not telling the truth, all the other witnesses they had called also would be lying. "Ask yourself with respect to each witness: What reason would he or she have to lie from the stand under oath? And if you can't think of a reason, your common sense should tell you that that person is telling the truth."

Burstein began with a promise. "I'm going to offer you a reason why you can decide this case in a minute and a half. Without regard to most of the evidence in this case, you can decide immediately in Marion Hulick's and George Lindemann's favor." The reason they could do that, Burstein told the jurors, was because the prosecution's case was riddled with shortcomings and their key witnesses could not be believed.

Methodically, he went through what he perceived to be holes in the prosecution's case, beginning with "a complete absence of medical proof" that Charisma had been electrocuted.

"They never brought in any medical experts," Burstein said, "and that's just astounding. If this horse was electrocuted, how come there is no medical finding? How come there is not even an explanation from some doctor that what we know about the horse is consistent with the horse having been electrocuted? The fact that there is no answer to that question is enough in itself to create reasonable doubt."

Even more astounding, according to Burstein, was the testimony of the prosecution witnesses. Mike Rooks, he said, was "mistaken" in his testimony about Hulick trying to arrange for insurance. "I'm not sure if Mike Rooks is confusing this with another time, but you can be sure that things did not happen the way he says they did."

Of course, Burstein added, Tom Burns was a liar. "When it came to school, he had a ninth-grade education. But when it came to crime and lying and cheating, this guy had a Ph.D."

Gerald Shepherd also was lying, Burstein said. "I'm not saying he's lying about being at Cellular Farms in December of 1990. Everybody agrees he was there. But he's lying about being there on the only day that matters, December 15, 1990. I didn't say he was a good liar, it's not his life's work. But he did a lousy job of getting his details straight."

But the main reason the prosecution case fell apart, Burstein said, was because the government did not prove motive. "Think about it. Once you realize that the horse really wasn't a disaster, once you realize that they didn't have any money obligations, once you realize that they could have sold the horse, you have only one conclusion: If they did what the government says they did, they committed a completely irrational act. And that's contrary to everything you know about them based upon the witnesses you heard at this trial."

As much as Susan Cox eschewed melodrama, Jay Goldberg embraced it. It was as much a part of him as his briefcase and tailored suit. One of the old school, Goldberg loved words and the way they could be strung together to form long, complex sentences intended more for their supposed harmony than their enlightenment, replete with repetitions, loop-backs, and pauses. A necessary adjunct, of course, was style. Putting together sentences in itself was not sufficient; they had to be accompanied by the dramatic raising and lowering of the voice, and by hand and body gestures designed to cover a range of emotions from shock to anger to indignation. In his closing argument, he used them all.

He began sedately, standing rigidly at the lectern, looking dignified in a dark blue suit, white shirt, subdued red and blue tie, and a crisp white linen handkerchief, its three points up, in his breast pocket. "I have to recall," he began, after thanking the jurors for their dedication, "that a number of issues that I will be dealing with today were first put on your table by the government, which first spoke with you in their opening. They raised issues, did they not, as to performance of the horse, as to training techniques, as to a host of other circumstances?"

As he spoke, his hands slipped into his pockets, and he began pacing. There was a frown that gave way to a scowl. Soon he was raising and lowering himself on his toes and bending at the waist, bobbing like a physical fitness enthusiast in the midst of an exercise regimen. And as he progressed, his voice rose both in timbre and volume.

Contrary to what prosecutors had asserted—that the investigation of George Lindemann, Jr., and Marion Hulick was a by-product of a search for the killer of Helen Brach—it had, in fact, been instigated by federal authorities. *They went to Tom Burns,* he said, and *told him* that they knew that he had killed a horse for Lindemann. In addition, they told him that the Lindemanns were worth $650 million.

"Of what consequence," he proclaimed loudly, "was Lindemann's wealth?" It was only important, Goldberg went on, because authorities wanted a rich target and Lindemann presented himself as a likely victim.

Goldberg was implying that agents fed Lindemann's name to Burns and encouraged him to finger the operator of Cellular Farms because of his money and prestige. The fact that the government claimed that Helen Brach, not Lindemann, had been the reason for the initial questioning of Burns was disingenuous. And the fact that prosecutors wanted the jury to believe that was a diversionary tactic.

For 115 minutes Goldberg orated passionately about Burns, federal investigators, and witnesses who testified against Hulick and Lindemann.

"Let me tell you something," he shouted, pointing at the prosecutors, "you have to get up very early, earlier than they got up, to be able to rest comfortably on the words of Tommy Burns. He's fooled professionals for years. Make no mistake about it. If you have a reasonable doubt, if you find yourself hesitating to believe Tommy Burns because of all the things you know about him, because of his abilities to con, you *will* have a reasonable doubt."

Lindemann, he asserted, was targeted because he was wealthy, because he had gone to Brown University. "You're to draw some inference adverse to him because he did poorly in English and he did well in history? What is this?" he asked indignantly. "What is happening here? George Lindemann has come before this court and he has pleaded not guilty, not guilty by reason of innocence. He would have to be crazy to kill a prizewinning horse with enormous potential, owned and bought by his sister, Sloan, who everybody says liked the horse."

While not repeating his earlier claim that to Lindemann a quarter of a million dollars was like a postage stamp, he still attacked the government contention that the money was important. "And then they're going to show the horse farm lost a million dollars a year. What does that mean? The two fifty would have made a difference? The farm is in existence all these years, a million here, a million four there, a million here. What would the two fifty do? Make it in the black? The two fifty was monumental?"

With his voice dripping sarcasm, Goldberg ravaged the investigators because they seemed slow in starting the investigation. "And they sit. I'm not accusing them of wrongdoing. I'd be the last one to do that. The FBI? And then they make their fatal wrong turn. As dedicated and decent as they are, they make their fatal mistake." That, he said, was letting Burns out of jail so he could gather information and concoct a fabrication against Lindemann and Hulick.

He attacked not only the investigators and Burns's story about the assassination but also Harlow Arlie, Penelope Baumont, and, most violently of all, Gerald Shepherd.

"Shep—after he speaks to the FBI and before he goes to the grand jury—he gets on the telephone and calls this man who is not listed in the telephone book, and he speaks with him for instructions, you may conclude."

Winding down, mindful of the two-hour time limit Judge Marovich has put on each of the attorneys, Goldberg ended on a patriotic note. "Ladies and gentlemen of the jury, a verdict of not guilty does not mean that the government loses. The government never loses when justice is done," he said piously.

Steve Miller, in style, appearance, and attitude, was Goldberg's antithesis. With his coat open and his hand stuffed casually in his left pocket, Miller looked like a college sociology professor addressing an adult-education class. In a quiet, even voice—which would be the last, except for the judge's—that the jurors would hear before they began deliberations, Miller went over the defense's allegations claim by claim, using reason to combat bombast.

"We never alleged that this crime was committed out of financial need," he began. "We said it was committed out of greed."

There were two motives, he declared. One was that George Lindemann did not like Charisma. The second was money. "There was a quarter of a million dollars sitting there should this horse die. And, again, it doesn't matter how wealthy one is, a quarter of a million dollars is a lot of money."

To concur with the defense, he said, jurors would have to believe that Gerald Shepherd, Colleen Reed, Molly Hasbrouck, Michael Rooks, and Penelope Baumont were perjurers. "According to the defense, the government is bringing this case only because George Lindemann is wealthy. Every witness is a criminal, every person sitting at this table," he said, indicating where he and Cox sat, "is a wrongdoer. It's a conspiracy. And the only two people who are innocent are George Lindemann and Marion Hulick. That's the grand theme that their entire defense is structured around."

Urging them to use their reasoning ability, Miller pointed out that it would have been impossible to put together a plot of such immense proportions, studded throughout with details that would have been impossible to fabricate or anticipate, minutiae such as knowing that there was a telephone call from Barney Ward's farm to Cellular Farms early in the afternoon on December 15; that the upstate New York roads were glazed with ice that weekend; or that Tom Burns, a renowned horse killer, happened to be registered in a hotel only a few miles from the place where Charisma inexplicably dropped dead.

"We never said that Charisma had not started out as a good horse, and we never said that Charisma was a horse destined for the glue factory. What we said was that George Lindemann had high expectations for this horse, that they paid more for this horse than for any hunter Cellular Farms had ever bought, that he didn't like the horse, and that Marion Hulick didn't like the horse."

The plan to murder Charisma did not begin with the hiring of Tom Burns, Miller said, but with the decision to turn him out overnight in a strange paddock during a lightning storm. "Do you believe for a moment that leaving a horse out during a violent storm is anything other than an attempt to kill the horse?"

Lindemann and Hulick became disillusioned when the horse failed to perform up to expectations. He was entered in twenty-one shows between May and December, Miller pointed out. "It is the reserve champion four out of twenty-one times. It doesn't win once; it came in second four times. Out of forty-three horses entered in the Washington International, it came in dead last." To add insult to injury, Miller said, two of the four times Charisma was crowned reserve champion, the rider had been Molly Hasbrouck. "George Lindemann was shown up by a college student."

Why, he asked, would Lindemann and Hulick risk their reputations, their standing, and their freedom to commit a crime when they claimed they didn't need the money?

He leaned toward the jury box: "Ladies and gentlemen, irrational crimes are committed every minute of the day in this country. Crime is not rational. It was rational only to the extent that they thought they'd get away with it."

Like Goldberg, Miller consumed almost all of his two hours of allotted time, painstakingly tracking the path of the investigation and expanding upon the labyrinthine path it took. There was, he added, a special reason for why it took so long. Not only were there other trails to follow, but the very nature of Lindemann's and Hulick's crime defied rapid solution as well. "Frauds are complex crimes to investigate," said Miller, who had made a career out of investigating fraud. "They are complex crimes to understand." They don't unravel, like a bank robbery or a drug deal, and sometimes, he added, investigators don't even have enough information on which to base the proper questions.

Miller also explained why he was recommending only a six-month sentence for Burns. At the time he was arrested, he said, the only thing they could accuse him of was killing Streetwise. Then, by confessing to the other crimes, he essentially was making certain he could not be prosecuted for them.

"Do you think it would be fair, and, more important, do you think investigators could ever get anyone to talk again if once, after hearing about a person's life of crime, authorities were to say, Um, we gotcha. We didn't know about those other crimes until you started cooperating and now we do and you're going to jail for a long time?"

Part of the deal with Burns, Miller said, was that if he lied, he could be prosecuted for every crime he had disclosed, even the ones they had not known about until he confessed to them. "If it were to be found out that he made up the crime about Lindemann, everything would blow up, and he will be sentenced on fifteen horse killings. So he has an absolute positive reason to be telling the truth here."

At one point, Miller's statements drew a strenuous objection from Goldberg. "These horses," Miller said, "are tools for people like George Lindemann to make them look good. They spend their lives making these animals perform unnatural acts to make them look good."

"Your Honor," Goldberg screamed, jumping to his feet. "I object to this. Making animals perform unnatural acts. This is offensive. This is not what this case is about."

Marovich looked at him wearily. "It amazes me," the judge said slowly, "what offends somebody. We're talking about making the horses jump over the fence. If that's natural or unnatural, take it or leave it, but that's what we're talking about."

Suppressing a smile, Miller continued: "They employ professional trainers and experts to get the horses to go higher and higher and higher so that they can look good. You decide for yourselves whether those are the acts of someone who loves a horse so much that they would never do this crime."

The case went to the jury late on Tuesday. Just before noon on Thursday, September 21, 1995, the panel returned with a verdict: Both George Lindemann and Marion Hulick were guilty of three counts of wire fraud each. The defendants accepted the verdict without expression or comment.

On January 18, 1996, almost three months after the verdict, Judge George Marovich pronounced sentence. Lindemann was sent to prison for thirty-three months and fined $500,000. In addition, he was ordered to reimburse the insurance company the $250,000 they had paid in the claim on Charisma, and to pay back the government for the cost of his keep while in prison serving his sentence.

Hulick, who had remained stoic during her trial the previous autumn, cried throughout most of the sentencing hearing and begged Marovich to give her probation instead of sending her to prison, claiming she would do anything to avoid spending time behind bars. When pressed by Marovich, however, she refused to testify under oath in more detail about her involvement in the plan to kill Charisma or to cooperate with prosecutors.

But because she had written him a letter accepting responsibility—essentially admitting her guilt—Marovich knocked six months off his intended sentence and reduced her prison time to twenty-one months. "But I have to hold my nose when I do this," he said. Hulick, unlike Lindemann, was not fined.

"I want to indicate how offensive your conduct is to society," Marovich lectured the two as he announced his sentence. "To me, it's reprehensible that two people like yourselves who are apparently accepted by the horse community and aspire to carry America's flag into the Olympics" would do this.

Noting that the base sentences of thirty-three months was the maximum he could levy under federal guidelines, Marovich added: "I want to spread the word throughout the country among the 'horsey set' that this type of conduct will not be tolerated and will be severely punished."

Ironically, after living with the case for almost six years, Steve Miller witnessed the sentencing as a civilian rather than as a government prosecutor. In November, three weeks before the sentencing, Miller resigned from the U.S. attorney's office after seventeen years to go into private practice as a partner in a major Chicago firm, Sachnoff & Weaver. In the future, Miller would wear a different hat, switching from prosecutor to defender for persons accused of white-collar crimes.

As with the Bailey verdict, Miller took enormous personal satisfaction in the conviction of Lindemann and Hulick. As far as he was concerned, Lindemann was one of the "idle rich," a spoiled thirty-one-year-old "without character" who got precisely what he deserved. While others indicted in connection with the horse killings admitted their guilt and accepted the consequences, Lindemann refused to shoulder blame "even when he was guilty." Instead, he launched a campaign of vengeance against the American Horse Show Association for suspending him by filing a $100 million damage suit against AHSA. From Miller's point of view, this represented pure spite. When Charisma didn't do his bidding, Lindemann destroyed him. And that, Miller asserted, was what he was trying to do to AHSA via his legal action.

Given the molasseslike slowness with which the system commonly moves, Lindemann probably will be in and out of court for years to come. In the meantime, the equine industry likely will continue to operate much as it has always done, with scandal seething just below the surface and bubbling to the top only when the next major investigation commences. One of the most disturbing conclusions to be drawn from the Miller investigation is that those who had their horses cold-bloodedly assassinated were not acting aberrantly, that the industry is saturated with horse owners who see nothing illegal or immoral in having animals murdered simply because they do not perform according to expectations. "Tommy Burns isn't the only horse killer out there," Miller commented dourly. "And he isn't even the worst."

Epilogue
Wrapping It Up

THIS STORY has involved a large number of interesting people. Although it is impractical to try to track them all, I can offer a few details about some of the major ones.

On October 21, 1995, forty years and one week after the crime, Kenneth Hansen was sentenced to from two hundred to three hundred years in prison for the murders of Robert Peterson, 14, and the Schuessler brothers, John, 13, and Anton, 11. He has appealed.

In November 1995, Susan Cox took over as lead prosecutor for the cases resulting from the investigation after Steve Miller left the U.S. attorney's office for private practice.

Before finalizing his decision to go into private practice, Miller rejected an offer from the local Democrats to run for the office of state's attorney in Cook County in the 1996 election. "I don't really have any political ambitions," he said somewhat apologetically.

Also in November, a federal grand jury handed up an indictment charging a suburban Chicago horsewoman, Donna Biebrach, 35, of Northbrook, with mail fraud. The charge alleges that Biebrach hired Burns to kill her horse, Gondola, in January 1990 so she could collect twenty thousand dollars in insurance.

Four months later, on the last day of February 1996, a year and a half after the original indictments were announced, the U.S. attorney's office made public federal charges against eight more people involved in the equestrian industry, including owners, riders, trainers, and brokers. The charges brought to thirty-six the total number of people accused by state or federal prosecutors in connection with the Miller investigation. Charged were:

Trainer Wally Holly, 59, of Trabuco Canyon, California, and rider Freddie Vasquez, Jr., 24, of Buffalo Grove, Illinois. They were accused of mail fraud for making a false insurance claim for $15,000 in connection with the death of Vasquez's horse Arlene. Allegedly, they injured the horse with a crowbar in January 1991, at Perfecta Farm, in Streamwood, Illinois, so it would have to be put down.

Trainer Robert Cheska, 40, of Waukesha, Wisconsin—who was convicted on February 1, 1996, in a court in suburban Chicago's Lake County of helping set fire to the home of James Heinsohn—and owner George Nuber, 64, of Inverness, Illinois, were each indicted on two counts of mail fraud in connection with the January 1987 murder of Nuber's horse Valentino. According to the indictments, they hired Tom Burns to kill the horse while he was stabled at the Jumping Jack Farm in Ocala, Florida, to collect on a fifty-thousand-dollar insurance policy.

James Heinsohn—who pleaded guilty to arson charges in Lake County in January 1996—was accused of making false statements to the FBI in connection with the February 1987 death of his horse Pet of the Year. The indictment said he lied to agents when he said he did not know in advance that the horse, which was insured for forty thousand dollars, was going to be murdered. Earlier, Ronald Mueller had pleaded guilty to charges of electrocuting the animal.

Trainer and competitor Laura Stern-Grzebieniak, 34, of North Barrington, Illinois, and former trainer/broker Lisa Brandon, 39, of Sarasota, Florida, were accused of making false statements to investigators in connection with the April 1987 death of the horse Cloud Castle, which was insured for fifty thousand dollars. According to the grand jury, Brandon solicited Stern-Grzebieniak to pose as the insured party on the Cloud Castle policy.

Trainer Dennis Mitchell, 46, of Knoxville, Tennessee, was accused of failing to pay income taxes for several years and of destroying his financial records when he learned he was being investigated by the Internal Revenue Service. Mitchell, formerly of Naperville, Illinois, was a business partner of veterinarian Dana Tripp, who pleaded guilty in October 1995 to a charge of lying to investigators.

On March 19, 1996, Barney Ward, a former Olympic rider and neighbor of George Lindemann, Jr., pleaded guilty to a charge of having helped arrange the murder of Charisma. He also admitted that if he had gone to trial, the government had enough evidence to convict him of helping arrange the murders of three other horses as well.

Not long after Bailey's conviction, a Chicago appeals expert, Allan Ackerman, took over the case from Patrick Tuite and Ronald Menaker, a common practice in criminal law. After accepting the case, Ackerman told reporters he thought Judge Milton Shadur's decision was "mean-spirited, misleading, and incorrect."

George Lindemann, Jr., hired an Illinois attorney to handle the appeal for him and Marilyn Hulick.

Pending at the time this was written was a decision on a request by the American Horse Show Association to dismiss the $100 million suit filed by Lindemann against it.

Tom Burns, who underwent two days of vicious cross-examination by the attorneys for Lindemann and Hulick, had a final word. After Lindemann was convicted, Burns was quoted in the *Chicago Tribune* as saying, "I hope the only time he gets to ride a horse is in the prison rodeo."

Frank Jayne, Jr., as of the time this went to the printer, has never been charged in connection with the plot to murder or defraud Helen Brach, or with any other equestrian-industry crimes.

Cathy Jayne Olsen was absorbed into one of the several federal programs designed to protect witnesses in major cases.

Federal protection was also provided to Joe Edward Plemmons, who testified not only against Bailey but against Kenneth Hansen.

Dr. Annette Hoffman continues to be married to Richard Bailey.

As early as October 1994, more than six months before Richard Bailey's sentencing hearing, Dr. Hoffman was soliciting true-crime writers to tell her husband's story.

In September 1995, Agent Jim Delorto retired from the ATF.

Barbara Morris became engaged to an FBI agent, Clint Rand, whom she met during the Bailey investigation.

John Menk is living in quiet retirement in a northern Chicago suburb.

In 1979, Carole Karstenson, who had spent out of pocket or signed notes for $268,000 worth of horses and their care, collected $30,000 as a result of a civil suit against Richard Bailey. Out of that settlement, however, she had to pay off the balance of the note she had signed for the broodmares, plus interest, after Frank Jayne, Jr., took her to court.

In 1996, the National Horse Show, the third event of the Indoor Season, will return to New York's Madison Square Garden after seven years at the Meadowlands Sports Complex in East Rutherford, New Jersey.

Details on what happened to those charged in the July 1994 indictments can be seen in Appendix C.

Dramatis Personae

BECAUSE OF the many years over which this story evolved, there are a huge number of characters. I have attempted to list here only the major ones. For the reader's convenience, I also have included the names of various horses who play an important role in the tale. Alphabetically:

Harlow Arlie	A groom arrested with Tom Burns after the assault on Streetwise.
Paul "P.J." Bailey	Richard Bailey's brother. In partnership with his brother, he sold three horses to Helen Brach at exorbitant rates.
Richard Bailey	Con man and prominent figure in the Chicago equestrian world.
Frank Brach	Helen Brach's husband. He died in 1970, leaving her the fortune he had accumulated as head of E. J. Brach & Sons, the famous candy company.
Helen Brach	Candy-company heiress who disappeared in 1977. When she vanished, her estate was valued at some $30 million. She was the richest woman ever to disappear in this country.
Brach's Sweet Talk	Along with Vorhees's Luv and Potenciado, these were the three horses Helen Brach bought from P. J. Bailey without the knowledge that Richard Bailey was a silent partner in the transactions.

Vivian Bravos	One of Richard Bailey's earlier victims.
Donna Brown	Wife of Buddy Brown, a Gold Medal winner in the 1976 Olympics and the owner of Streetwise.
Robert Lee Brown	A Chicago horseman involved, along with Richard Bailey and James Farmer, in gulling vulnerable women.
Bull Lea's Whirl	A "shy" stallion owned by Carole Karstenson.
Tom Burns (aka Tim Ray and the Sandman)	A thief and horse killer turned government informant. Has admitted murdering fifteen horses.
Judd Burstein	Marion Hulick's defense attorney.
Joyce Carruthers	A victim of Richard Bailey.
Susan Cox	An assistant U.S. attorney and coprosecutor of Marion Hulick and George Lindemann, Jr.
Peter Cullen	An FBI agent and centerpiece of Miller's investigatory team.
James Delorto	An agent with the federal Bureau of Alcohol, Tobacco and Firearms and a key member of Steven Miller's investigative team.
Elmadge	Bull Lea's Whirl's replacement in the scheme to defraud Carole Karstenson.
Jerry Farmer	A widely known horse trainer and primary member of Richard Bailey's scam team.
Jay Goldberg	Prominent New York lawyer and George Lindemann, Jr.'s defense attorney.
David Hamm	A state police investigator who played a major role in early investigations initiated by Miller.

Kenneth Hansen	Former Silas Jayne employee and Chicago horse-world figure convicted of murdering three young boys in 1955. His connection to the boys was uncovered during the Miller probe.
Dr. Annette Hoffman	A prominent plastic surgeon in Chicago; Richard Bailey's second wife.
Linda Holmwood	Another Bailey victim. She died in 1982.
Dr. Ross Hugi	A Chicago-area veterinarian involved with Richard Bailey's stable.
Marion Hulick	George Lindemann's manager, who set up Charisma's murder by Tom Burns.
Daniel Ivancich	An ATF agent and a permanent member of Steven Miller's team.
Marilyn Jameson	A victim of Richard Bailey.
Frank Jayne, Jr.	Silas Jayne's nephew; he had close ties to Richard Bailey. He was convicted in the eighties on narcotics charges.
George Jayne	Silas Jayne's younger brother; assassinated while playing bridge with his family at their home in 1970.
Silas Jayne	Much-feared godfather of the Chicago horse world. He served six years in prison for setting up the murder of his younger brother. He died in 1987 at age eighty.
Carole Karstenson	Richard Bailey's first significant victim in his horse-world scams.
George Lindemann, Jr.	Millionaire horseman, would-be Olympic rider. He masterminded the execution of his sister's horse Charisma.

George Lindemann, Sr.	One of the richest men in the country; a man who accumulated his fortune through companies as diverse as contact-lens manufacturing, cellular phones, and natural gas.
Ann Madej	Friend of Tom Burns unsuccessfully alleged by the defense to be a coconspirator in an attempt to frame George Lindemann and Marion Hulick.
Jack Matlick	Helen Brach's houseman at the time she disappeared. He was the only person who claimed to have seen her during the four days after she checked out of the Mayo Clinic.
Ronald Menaker	One of Richard Bailey's defense attorneys.
John Cadwalader Menk	Guardian Ad Litem for Helen Brach. He tried to do through civil law what police investigators had not been able to accomplish: find out who had abducted Helen Brach.
Steven Miller	The assistant U.S. attorney who spearheaded the investigations leading to the indictment of, at the time this was writing, twenty-three figures from the equine industry, many of them nationally known.
Everett Moore	Helen Brach's accountant and financial adviser.
Barbara Morris	A Richard Bailey victim; her accusations of fraud by Richard Bailey set off the Miller investigation.
Cathy Jayne Olsen	Daughter of Frank Jayne, Jr.; a major witness against Richard Bailey.
Joe Edward Plemmons	A personable Chicago con man turned government informant; a key witness against Richard Bailey and Kenneth Hansen.
Colleen Reed	Former Cellular Farms barn manager.

Jean Robinson	One of Richard Bailey's early victims.
Ronald Safer	An assistant U.S. attorney and coprosecutor of Richard Bailey.
Gerald Shepherd	An acquaintance of Tom Burns who substantiated Burns's claim that he was at Cellular Farms on the day Charisma was killed.
Streetwise	A seven-year-old chestnut jumper; put down in Florida after Tom Burns and an accomplice, Harlow Arlie, broke his leg with a crowbar.
Dana Tripp	Veterinarian and champion rider.
Patrick Tuite	A lawyer who has seen both sides. As a young man, he prosecuted Silas Jayne. Later, he was Richard Bailey's defense counsel.
Charles Vorhees	Helen Brach's younger brother.
Barney Ward	Former Olympic rider; neighbor of George Lindemann, Jr., and alleged go-between in murders of Charisma and three other horses.

Glossary

AHSA	American Horse Show Association, a national group with 62,000 members; the regulatory group for the industry.
Broodmare	Female horse used for breeding.
Catch rider	A replacement rider hired for a short term or a specific event.
Circuit	A series of horse shows in a particular geographic area.
Class	A single event at a horse show.
Colic	An often-fatal disease among horses.
Dressage	An esoteric equestrian sport in which the emphasis is on style and delicacy of movement.
Fences	In hunter competition, fences are composed of natural material, such as walls, brushes, or rails; in jumper competition, fences are brightly painted man-made obstacles.
Gelding	A castrated male horse.
Green	A young horse; a "green hunter" would be a young horse participating in the hunter competition.
Hand	A way of measuring a horse's height; one hand equals four inches.

Hotblood	A thoroughbred horse.
Indoor Season	A series of three invitation-only competitions held on consecutive weekends each autumn: the Pennsylvania International in Harrisburg; the Washington International in Washington, D.C., generally regarded as the Super Bowl of the horse world; and the National Horse Show at the Meadowlands in New Jersey.
Longeing	Pronounced "lunging"; exercising at the end of a tether, or longe line.
Manners	Deportment; behavior. In hunter competition, points are subtracted for "bad manners," such as bucking.
Pigeon	A target for a swindle.
Points	Awards in hunter competition; given under a complicated formula based mainly on the horse's performance, rather than on the rider's.
Rated shows	Categories for AHSA competition running from A to C. A-rated shows are subdivided in three parts, with A-3 being the highest.
Reserve champion	Second place.
Show hunter	A horse, usually a thoroughbred, trained to participate in events simulating a fox hunt; in competition, show hunters, also called hunters, earn points, as opposed to jumpers, which compete for cash.
Show jumper	A horse trained to complete a jumping course as quickly as possible, as opposed to hunter competition, where style is more important than speed.
Stud	Male horse used for breeding.
Ties (tying) up	A medical problem similar to a cramp, but more severe.

Under-saddle	A class in hunter competition that involves walking, trotting, and cantering, but not jumping.
Warmblood	A part-thoroughbred horse prized for its jumping ability.

An Abbreviated Chronology of Events

1950

Helen Vorhees, then thirty-eight, leaves her native Ohio to move to southern Florida, taking a job at the prestigious Indian Creek Country Club in Miami Beach. There she meets millionaire Frank Brach. A year later, they are married.

1955

October 16: Three young boys disappear on their way home from a movie. The bodies of Robert Peterson, fourteen, John Schuessler, thirteen, and his brother, Anton, eleven, are found two days later in a ditch in a Chicago-area forest preserve.

1970

Nineteen years after Helen and Frank are married, Frank, then seventy-nine, dies after an extended illness. Not long after Frank's death, Helen lets his longtime employee Jack Matlick go. Six months later, however, she rehires him.

1972

Late fall: Frank Jayne, Jr., introduces Carole Karstenson to Richard Bailey.

1973

April 4: Silas Jayne and two others go on trial for the murder of Silas's brother George. One man is convicted of murder, while Silas and the other are found guilty of a lesser charge of conspiracy to commit murder. Silas, then sixty-six, is sent to Illinois's Vienna Correctional Center, where he remains until his parole six years later.

Fall: Helen Brach meets Richard Bailey.

November 5: Karstenson gives Bailey a check for a hundred thousand dollars, allegedly as part of a partnership agreement. A few days later, they drive to Florida and stay until the day before Thanksgiving.

December 7: Karstenson checks into the Mayo Clinic.

1974

Valentine's Day: Bailey and Karstenson are reconciled; he gives her a pearl necklace.

Fall: Helen Brach tells Bailey while they are watching races at Gulfstream Park that she might be interested in spending $100,000 on racehorses.

1975

March 31: Brach pays fifty thousand dollars to P. J. Bailey for Brach's Sweet Talk and Vorhees's Luv. (He had paid four thousand and five thousand dollars, respectively, for the horses.)

Summer: Helen adds Potenciado to her stable, paying P. J. Bailey $45,000 for the horse. (The cost to him had been $8,500.)

1976

December 31: Brach and Bailey, with Brach picking up the tab, attend a gala at the Waldorf-Astoria in New York, dancing the night away to the music of Guy Lombardo and the Royal Canadians.

1977

February 9: Helen Brach, sixty-five, a widow of seven years and estimated to be worth some $30 million, flies to Rochester, Minnesota, from Chicago and checks into the Mayo Clinic for a thorough physical.

February 16: Richard Bailey checks in the Colony Hotel in West Palm Beach. Christina Kubot arrives in town as his guest. Bailey makes an eight-minute call to Brach at the Mayo Clinic.

February 17: Bailey and Kubot visit the Arthur Winnick Farms and Bailey makes arrangements for a showing on February 19 for an "important client."

February 17: Helen Brach disappears.

March 4: Matlick goes to the police in Glenview and asks to file a missing person's report on Helen Brach. After learning that only a close relative could file such a report, Matlick calls Helen's brother, Charles Vorhees, in Hopedale, Ohio, and tells him he fears that Brach never arrived in Florida.

March 6: Vorhees, a railroad-car inspector, flies to Chicago. Met by Matlick, the two return to the estate and systematically search the house. Among the things they find are several collections of Brach's thoughts and descriptions of experiences, as well as papers filled with seemingly nonsensical notes. Matlick, apparently with Charles Vorhees's approval, burns the documents.

1978

More than a year after Brach's disappearance, the nude body of an elderly woman is discovered in a wooded park on Chicago's South Side. Although authorities initially believe the body to be Brach's, the medical examiner declares the body unidentifiable because of decomposition. He rules out the possibility it could have been Helen by pointing out that the dead woman wore dentures, whereas Brach did not. The body was buried in potter's field. A dozen years later, in 1990, because of renewed interest in Brach's disappearance, the body was exhumed for reexamination. However, when examiners opened the casket, they discovered that the head of the woman was missing, so the dental work could not be rechecked.

January 11: Matlick is deposed by John Menk; Matlick mentions Brach's will.

January 27: Judge George Schaller approves Menk's request for a search of the Glenview mansion.

March 1: Charles Vorhees is deposed by Menk.

April 1: A group that includes four lawyers, the Glenview police chief, and the chief investigator meets at Brach's Glenview mansion at 10:00 A.M. for a search. They find a copy of the will and Brach's suitcase.

1979

April 14: Graffiti in red spray paint appears on a road in Glenview. The message: RICHARD BAILEY KNOWS WHERE MRS. BRACH'S BODY IS! STOP HIM! PLEASE!

May 23: Silas Jayne, seventy-two, is paroled after serving six years for conspiring to murder his brother.

June 15: Bailey deposed by Menk.

October 8: Everett Moore's first deposition.

1980

February 18: Everett Moore's second deposition.

June 25: Menk's term as Guardian Ad Litem ends.

1984

February: Probate Judge Henry A. Budzinski declares Helen Brach dead.

1987

Silas Jayne, age eighty, dies of leukemia.

1988

Richard Bailey and his wife of some thirty years, Eunice, are divorced.

Frank Jayne, Jr., Silas's nephew, is convicted of selling cocaine at his stable. Also convicted are two people who were later charged in the horse-killing scheme, Michael and Donna Hunter. After the conviction, federal authorities confiscated the stable and sold it to a man who promised to keep the property drug-free: Richard Bailey.

1989

December: U.S. attorney's office begins an investigation into the disappearance of Helen Vorhees Brach.

1991

February 2: Tom Burns and Harlow Arlie are arrested in Gainesville, Florida, for killing a horse named Streetwise.

1994

April 9: After a whirlwind romance, Dr. Annette Hoffman, a plastic surgeon with a practice on Chicago's ritzy Gold Coast, marries Bailey.

April 22: Hoffman has her marriage to Bailey annulled.

July 27: U.S. attorney's office announces indictments against twenty-three people for crimes involving fraud in the equestrian industry. Nineteen of those people are charged with crimes relating to the killing of horses and fraudulent filing of insurance claims on the animals. The remaining four are charged with crimes directed against people involved in financial transactions with horses. Among those four is Richard Bailey, who is accused of being tied to Brach's disappearance.

August 1: Hoffman tells the judge she wants to remarry Bailey and asks that he be released in her custody, volunteering to put up her $1.1 million home as insurance that Bailey will not skip.

December 3: Hoffman and Bailey are remarried at Chicago's Metropolitan Correctional Facility. He is not released.

1995

March 1: Richard Bailey pleads guilty to sixteen of twenty-nine counts against him, specifically denying all charges dealing with Helen Brach.

June 6: Judge Shadur determines that Bailey conspired to kill Helen Brach and solicited her murder. He sentences him to life in prison but postpones a final decision after Bailey's lawyer objects that Shadur is using wrong guidelines.

June 15: Judge Shadur sentences Bailey to thirty years in prison. Since there is no parole in the federal system, Bailey will not be eligible for release for twenty-five and a half years.

September 13: Kenneth Hansen is convicted in a Cook County court of three charges of murder in connection with the 1955 deaths of Robert Peterson and the Schuessler brothers, John and Anton. He has appealed.

September 21: A jury composed of one man and eleven women convicts George Lindemann, Jr., and Marion Hulick on three counts of wire fraud each in connection with the December 1990 death of Lindemann's $250,000 horse, Charisma. Lindemann has appealed.

October 20: Cook County Criminal Court Judge Michael Toomin sentences Kenneth Hansen to from two hundred to three hundred years in prison for the murders of three young boys in 1955. He will be eligible for parole after nine years.

1996

February 29: A year and a half after the first indictments were announced as a result of the Miller investigation, a federal grand jury in Chicago indicted eight more people in connection with alleged crimes in the equestrian industry. It brought to thirty-six the total number of people charged by state and federal prosecutors since the investigation began in December 1989.

Appendix B

Significant Horse Murders Admitted by Tom Burns

HORSE	DATE	PLACE	METHOD	OWNER	INSURANCE
Henry the Hawk	1/82	Ocala, FL	Electrocution	James Druck	$150,000
Condino[1]	3/87	Tampa, FL	"	Unidentified	$200,000
Rub the Lamp[2]	6/89	Oregon, IL	"	Nancy Marder Banefield	$50,000
Belgium Waffle[3]	7/89	Wadsworth, IL	"	Tammie Bylenga Glaspie	$40,000
Rainman[4]	8/89	St. Louis, MO	"	Allen Levinson	$50,000
Emili's Choice[5]	8/89	Mundelein, IL	"	Unidentified	$45,000
Roseau Platiere	8/89	Sugarbush, VT	"	Paul Valliere	$75,000
Gondola[6]	1/90	Naperville, IL	"	Donna Biebrach	$20,000
Empire[7]	7/90	Naperville, IL	"	Unidentified	$68,000
Charisma[8]	12/90	Greenwich, CT	"	George Lindemann, Jr.	$250,000
Streetwise[9]	2/91	Gainesville, FL	Crowbar to leg	Donna Brown	$25,000

[1] The murders of Condino, Rub the Lamp, Roseau Platiere, and Charisma all were allegedly set up by Barney Ward.

[2] Burns was assisted by Scott Thompson.

[3] The middleman in this killing was James Hutson.

[4] The murder was arranged by trainer Michael Hunter without the knowledge of its owner.

[5] The murder was set up by Donna Hunter, wife of Michael Hunter.

[6] The owner is awaiting trial on charges that she arranged the killing.

[7] The owner was unaware the horse was being killed; the execution was planned by Jerry Farmer (the horse's former owner), trainer Johnnie Youngblood, and Steve Williamson.

[8] Marion Hulick also was involved.

[9] Also playing a role in Streetwise's death was groom Harlow Arlie.

Appendix C

DISPOSITION OF THE CASES
Federal Court

NAME	CHARGE	PLEA	SENTENCE
Barney Ward	Racketeering, mail and wire fraud, obstruction of justice, conspiracy (11 counts)	Guilty to one count	*
George Lindemann, Jr.	Wire fraud (3 counts)	Not guilty (convicted 9/21/95)	33 months; $500,000 fine $250,000 restitution
Marion Hulick	Wire fraud (3 counts)	Not guilty (convicted 9/21/95)	16 months; $2,000 fine; 300 hours of community service
Robert Lee Brown	Racketeering, mail and wire fraud, defrauding six women	Guilty to one count	14 months; $2,000 restitution; 300 hours of community service
Richard Bailey	13 counts involving Helen Brach	Not guilty	30 years
Richard Bailey	16 counts not involving Helen Brach	Guilty	30 years
Phil Sudakoff	Mail fraud	Guilty	1 year home confinement
Donna Brown	Wire fraud	Guilty	3 months; 2 years supervised release; $5,000 fine
Nancy Marder Banefield	Conspiracy to commit mail fraud	Guilty	*
Scott Thompson	Conspiracy to commit mail fraud	Guilty	*
Jerry Farmer	Racketeering, obstructing the IRS	Guilty	10 years; $10,000 fine
Johnnie Youngblood	Mail fraud	Guilty	8 months
Steve Williamson	Mail fraud	Guilty	2 months; $68,000 restitution
Paul Valliere	Conspiracy to commit wire and mail fraud	Guilty	4 years probation

Name	Charge	Verdict	Sentence
Dr. Dana Tripp	Conspiracy to defraud, failure to file tax returns, concealing a felony	Guilty	4 months of home confinement
Dr. Ross Hugi	Wire fraud	Guilty	6 months; $4,000 fine; $18,000 restitution
Herbert Kroninger	Mail fraud	Guilty	8 months home confinement
Tom Burns (aka Tim Ray)	Conspiracy to commit wire and mail fraud	Guilty	*
Ronald Mueller	Lying to a federal officer	Guilty	*
Michael Hunter	Mail fraud	Guilty	8 months; $5,000 restitution
Donna Hunter	Mail fraud	Guilty	4 months of community confinement; 3 years probation; $45,000 restitution; $5,000 fine
Allen Levinson	Mail fraud	Guilty	1 year; $20,000 restitution
Tammie Bylenga Glaspie	Mail fraud	Guilty	*
James Hutson	Mail fraud	Guilty	3 months; 3 months of home confinement; 3 years probation; $4,900 fine; $4,900 restitution

Charges Filed in State Courts as a Result of the Federal Probe

Name	Charge	Verdict	Sentence
Kenneth Hansen	Murder of Robert Peterson and the Schuessler brothers, John and Anton	Not guilty (convicted 9/13/95)	200–300 years; eligible for parole after 9 years
Daniel Jayne	Arson	Not guilty	Awaiting trial
John Garvey	Arson	Not guilty	Awaiting trial
Robert Cheska	Arson	Not guilty (convicted 1/31/96)	*
James Heinsohn	Arson	Guilty	*

*Not sentenced at the time this was written.